T0369473

Born Atheist

Born Atheist

Copyright © 2010 by Tim Covell

All rights reserved. No part of this book may be used or reproduced by any means, graphic, electronic, or mechanical, including photocopying, recording, taping or by any information storage retrieval system without the written permission of the publisher except in the case of brief quotations embodied in critical articles and reviews.

iUniverse books may be ordered through booksellers or by contacting:

iUniverse
1663 Liberty Drive
Bloomington, IN 47403
www.iuniverse.com
1-800-Authors (1-800-288-4677)

Because of the dynamic nature of the Internet, any Web addresses or links contained in this book may have changed since publication and may no longer be valid. The views expressed in this work are solely those of the author and do not necessarily reflect the views of the publisher, and the publisher hereby disclaims any responsibility for them.

ISBN: 978-1-4502-6753-3 (sc)
ISBN: 978-1-4502-6752-6 (ebook)

Printed in the United States of America

iUniverse rev. date: 10/29/2010

BORN ATHEIST

Tim Covell

All rights reserved © 2010

All Biblical quotes are from the New International Version, unless otherwise noted. Scripture taken from the HOLY BIBLE, NEW INTERNATIONAL VERSION®. Copyright © 1973, 1978, 1984 Biblica. Used by permission of Zondervan. All rights reserved.

The "NIV" and "New International Version" trademarks are registered in the United States Patent and Trademark Office by Biblica. Use of either trademark requires the permission of Biblica.

*With fond memories of my mother,
whose independence, intelligence and frustration
become clearer with each passing year.*

TABLE OF CONTENTS

Preface.

Like everyone, I was born atheist. Like many atheists,[1] I was raised without religion. Although my parents sent me to Sunday School, they never asked me to believe. Until I started reading about atheism, I could not understand why five out of six of my siblings are atheists. But rating myself on a scale of religious emphasis in the home showed the answer--there was no religious emphasis in my childhood home. My parents did not attend church. Neither god nor religion was mentioned in our home. There was a Bible[2] around somewhere, but it was not considered a reference book, even less a spiritual guide.

At around 11 years of age, I challenged my mother's requirement that I attend Sunday School. I presented usual childhood issues like "if god created the universe, what created god," and I told her I did not believe in god. My mother's answer surprised me, she said, "we are not asking you to believe, we only want you to attend to learn background that may be useful later in your life." Her answer satisfied my young mind and I attended Sunday School for another year or two, but I never believed.

As I grew up, I assumed everyone was atheist. I knew religion existed, but it was not something that I, my family, or my friends cared about. When I was in college, peers occasionally commented, "you are the first atheist I have met." I thought it was odd for them to say this, but I did not think much more about it.

As a young man, my view of religion was mildly positive. I knew that religious people had some beliefs different from mine, but I thought, all and all, their thoughts and values were harmless. Additionally, I observed that religions often had charitable functions–running hospitals, providing shelter to the homeless, raising

1

funds for victims of flood and famine. I think that was where my mildly favorable impression came from.

I also theorized that religion provided an external value system for people whose internal value system failed. I knew that alcoholics, drug addicts and criminals attested that they turned their lives around when they "found" religion.

Not so many years ago, I bought a used car with a Jesus fish on it, a fish-shaped chrome emblem of the Christian faith. I left the fish there as a joke--I thought it would be funny if others saw me as Christian. I did not find the fish offensive.

I lived through the 1970's when "Born Again" bumper stickers appeared on cars. I was a complete outside observer when I saw the replies, for example a Star of David sticker with the text "born right the first time." Religion was simply unimportant to me.

But bumper stickers lead to a change in my thinking. Sometime during the George W. Bush administration I was sitting in traffic behind an SUV plastered with bumper stickers. I have always thought of myself as a "live and let live" person. As long as another person's conduct or beliefs do not interfere with my life, I have little concern. I generally do not think that I have answers that will make another person's life better and I like to associate with people who follow the same philosophy.

But the driver of the SUV ahead of me thought differently. He wanted to require prayer in schools, outlaw abortion, teach creationism instead of science, and deport immigrants. Not only did the driver advise me of his opinions, he seemed to be willing to use violence to back them up. His stickers warned that "gun control means using both hands," and that his car was protected by a .357 Magnum. Reading these stickers, it dawned on me that the driver did not share my value of "live and let live," in fact, the driver wanted to force me to live like him!

Around the same time, the world experienced an eye-opener, religious extremists crashing airplanes into the Pentagon and the World

Trade Center. Although the media downplayed it at the time, religion played a key role in the attacks.

The aftermath of 9/11 surprised me. Within 18 months, the United States attacked Iraq, a county with no link to 9/11. The same SUVs that displayed Jesus fish and W stickers began sporting pro-war ribbons. People who protested the war were harassed and arrested. It seemed the "religious right" was taking over the country.

American religionists supported Bush with faith-like fervor as the U.S. Government suspended the Constitution and spied on its citizens, suspended the rule of law to imprison terrorist suspects without charge and ignored treaties to institute illegal policies of arrest and torture. American religionists consistently provided the strongest support for these actions. It seemed that Muslims and Christians were engaging in a holy war and that truth, law and the U.S. Constitution were the first victims. The media followed the government line, neither questioning the changes nor examining the role religion played.

More and more I saw religion imposing on my life. Using their ancient texts as guidance, the religious right sought a federal Constitutional Amendment to ban gay marriage starting in 2003. States put gay marriage bans on the ballot almost every year. The city next to mine started teaching creationism in the schools. Religious violence continued. Worldwide, religious terrorists attacked over and over again. And still the media ignored the role of religion in the killings.

My youth was filled with the fear of conflict between a nuclear armed East–the Soviet Union, and a nuclear armed West, led by the United States. After the Berlin Wall fell, political conflict de-escalated and I thought, "finally, there is an opportunity for peace in my time." But horrifically, peace was not to be. The new area of conflict is religion, not politics. Now the fear is that a nuclear armed India, Pakistan, Israel, Iran or U.S. might rely on religious lies to unleash weapons of mass destruction. Instead of building a safer world based on our commonalities, we are building a more violent world based on ancient myths. The more I looked, the more I saw religion as a negative force, a force behind much of the wrong in the world.

3

I have spent most of my free time for the past four years reading about religion. The more I learn about religion, the more absurd its role in modern life appears.

In researching religion, I found many good resources. Reading the authors critics label "new atheists," presumably because they have the backbone to denounce religion, several points made sense to me:

1. Religion gets more respect than it deserves;
2. The good that religion can accomplish is easily duplicated without religious baggage;
3. Religious moderates, as benign as they might seem, support the structure that empowers religious radicals;
4. Religion is a lie; and,
5. In a world where religious radicals are willing to use guns, explosives, planes and nuclear weapons based on their religious myths, religion is an especially dangerous lie.

Although the books I read made good points, the approach of many authors struck me as overly intellectual and inaccessible. I read about things like "Occam's razor." And although I tried to understand, other than repeating the odd name, I cannot tell you what Occam's razor is or why it might be important to me. When I see 30 pages of dense text without a break, my eyes glaze over. So, I have written a book for regular people--people like me. This is a short book, with short chapters. I try to avoid big words and intellectual discussions.

I am writing this book to support existing or emerging atheists, to encourage agnostics to get off the fence and make a choice, and to encourage everyone on the religiosity scale described in Chapter 4 to move one step to the left. I feel obligated to act. I do not understand why so few people are willing to speak the truth when religionists are killing for their myths.

Atheism is an immature movement. Although it is a potentially powerful force, I am distressed by its weakness. Ted Haggard's National Association of Evangelicals claimed 30 million members, while the largest American atheist group has 14,000. Compared to religion, atheism is disorganized, leaderless and powerless. Despite being right, atheism is neither taught nor promoted, it just sits there waiting to be found. Prejudice against atheists abounds. Americans boast of respecting freedom of religion but they do not see that concept as including freedom *from* religion. I hope to do what I can to change this.

I acknowledge up-front that I am not a professional journalist. I am not a professor of philosophy or biology. I do not write for a living. I do not have a research staff, a professional editor or a proofreader. I am a regular guy, raised without religion, who has a particular concern about religion. I have spent several years reading and thinking about religion, and I have something to say.

SECTION I.

Atheists: Who are those guys?

Chapter 1. Born atheist.

All thinking men are atheists.[3] Earnest Hemingway

Everyone is born atheist. Religion is learned. As a learned behavior, peoples' religion can be accurately predicted by the religion of their parents and the place where they live. Therefore it is no surprise that 77% of Americans are Christian, 97% of Saudis are Muslim, 95% of Thais are Buddhist, 80% of Indians are Hindu and 85% of Swedes have no religion.

Religionists do not want to admit that everyone is born atheist. The statement infuriates them. Religionists want to deny the facts. They call this faith--persisting in believing something despite contrary facts. They act as if faith is a good thing. But it does not change the fact that everyone is born atheist, religion is learned. Perhaps religionists fear that if they admit religion is learned, people will realize that it can be unlearned.

Atheists have no belief in god. Some atheists never learned religion. Others have unlearned religion. Literally, atheism means "without deities." In this book, I use it slightly more broadly to mean "without religion."

Religion is generally characterized by 1.) believing in a supernatural god or gods, 2.) believing in life after death; and, 3.) following a "holy" book or "scripture" that is allegedly attributable to their god or gods.

Religion is man-made. Religion is not a divinely inspired truth, it is a product of family and society. If you were born in Saudi Arabia, you would most likely be Muslim. If you were born in Thailand, you would most likely be Buddhist. There is no one great religious truth. Today, there are many religions and over the history of man, there have been many more.[4] If you follow a religion it is almost always the result of the time, place and family into which you were born.

Each religion claims to know the one true path. But they cannot all be right. To accept one religion means denying the others. For example, a Christian finds the religious assertions of a Muslim silly or even dangerous. The Christian has no belief in the Muslim god. The Christian has no belief in the Muslim scriptures. The Christian is an atheist when it comes to Islam. Each religious person is effectively an atheist in the remainder of the world's religions. This book asks the religious person, why not add one more?

The atheist has nothing to prove.

As an atheist, I have no belief in god--not in the Jewish god, not in the Christian god, not in the Muslim god and not in the Hindu gods. When comparing myself to a religionist, I like to picture each of us holding an old mayonnaise jar. Perhaps when you were a child you poked a few holes in the lid of a mayonnaise jar and collected insects for observation. But in this instance, instead of putting insects in the jar, picture it full of religious beliefs.

The religionist's jar contains all of the beliefs of his religion. For example, a Catholic's jar would include heaven and hell, a bearded man in the sky and his human son, virgin birth, walking on water, people rising from the dead, saints, miracles and the Pope as the infallible spokesperson for god.

My jar is empty.

Often religionists feel atheists should prove there is no god. Perhaps because they have been in power for so long, they think they can set the terms of the debate. But atheists have no belief in god. My jar is empty. I have nothing to prove. All of the shouting in the world will not change this fact. It is the religionist who has a jar full of beliefs. And the religionist lacks facts to support his beliefs. So he labels them faith. Religion requires faith because it has no facts.

Chapter 2. Religion is powerful.

Religion is the world's most powerful institution.[5]

In fact, very little is known in social science about the economic operation of religious institutions. The entire subject has been largely cloaked in secrecy by the religious groups themselves and avoided by polite journalists and researchers.[6] Authors John Heinerman and Anson Shupe

[T]he inability to believe in God and to live by faith is the greatest of evils.[7] Catholic Cardinal Murphy-O'Connor

Religionists act as if they are a vulnerable minority under attack by atheists. But look where the power lies. Have you heard of an atheist city, with its own police force and army? There is none. But certainly you have heard of the Vatican City, a city-state in Italy ruled by the Pope, complete with police, soldiers and a $356 million annual budget.[8] Every American President since Eisenhower has met with the sitting Pope.[9] But politicians' obsequiousness is not limited to Catholics. Most recent American Presidents have met with the Dalai Lama, a Buddhist monk believed to be an earthly incarnation of a Bodhisattva.[10] During the 2008 American presidential campaign, each candidate appeared at preacher Rick Warren's church.[11] Each candidate professed his Christianity and the winner, Barack Obama, invited Warren to deliver a religious invocation at his inauguration.[12]

Money is a measure of power. As the second quote at the start of this chapter notes, there is very little research about the amount of money religious institutions collect and control. In the U.S., religions are exempt from reporting to the Internal Revenue Service. Rick

Warren's church discloses that it has an annual budget of $30 million and 400 employees.[13] The Charity Navigator Website reports that in 2007 Americans donated an estimated $300 billion to charity, with the largest portion going to the 350,000 American churches.[14] "Giving USA" estimates that Americans donated more than $106 billion to religious groups in 2008,[15] about $400 per religious person in the United States. The total worth of these organizations, which have been around for years, is unknown. No government agency collects the information, the media does not inquire, and the churches do not reveal it. But with an annual income of $100+ billion and years to gather assets, the figure would be astonishing.

The power of religion is not limited to money, religionists also have manpower. Just take a look around your neighborhood. A "google maps" search shows there are 12 churches within one mile of my home. Each has an impressive building and most have several full-time employees. If you live in a small town, you will likely find the house of worship sitting in the most impressive building in town and located on the nicest piece of land. If each of the 350,000 churches in the United States has just three employees, there are more than a million Americans working full-time on religious practices. When you add the number of religious volunteers, and estimate the number of religious adherents who are willing to act on directives from their church, the numbers are even more staggering. Think of how many people you see with crosses around their necks, religious tattoos on their bodies, fishes on their cars, or talismans dangling from their rearview mirrors. Each demonstrates at least enough dedication to his religion to advertise it to the world. At least 245 million Americans describe themselves as religious,[16] only about 2.15 million call themselves atheists.[17]

The number of people employed by religion today is impressive, but not new. For thousands of years religion has dominated society. It is little wonder that religionists are expert at indoctrinating children into their system. Religion applies its rituals days after birth, and stays in its members' lives through childhood, adolescence, marriage and death.

Religion controls more than money and manpower. There are about 1,600 religious television and radio stations in the US, accessed by 141 million Americans monthly.[18] Each major American religion runs countless religious schools. Catholics alone run 7,500 schools with an enrollment of 2.3 million students.[19] The U.S. has about 900 religiously affiliated universities.[20] Numerous divinity schools and seminaries teach religionists how to promote their cause to the general population. The commercial media, which earns its living pleasing the general population, never steps too far from the religious agenda.

Although history is full of conflicts between religions, religionists in the United States seem to be building an alliance–an alliance against atheists. For example, while running for president, Mitt Romney, a Mormon (see Chapter 8 for more about Mormonism), sought to align himself with long established religions and against what he called the "religion of secularism," when he said:

> [I]n recent years, the notion of the separation of church and state has been taken by some well beyond its original meaning. They seek to remove from the public domain any acknowledgment of God. Religion is seen as merely a private affair with no place in public life. It is as if they are intent on establishing a new religion in America--the religion of secularism. They are wrong. ...We are a nation 'Under God' and in God, we do indeed trust.

> [God] should remain on our currency, in our pledge, in the teaching of our history, and during the holiday season, nativity scenes and menorahs should be welcome in our public places. Our greatness would not long endure without judges who respect the foundation of faith upon which our constitution rests. I will take care to separate the affairs of government from any

religion, but I will not separate us from "the God who gave us liberty."

Nor would I separate us from our religious heritage. Perhaps the most important question to ask a person of faith who seeks a political office, is this: does he share these American values: the equality of human kind, the obligation to serve one another, and a steadfast commitment to liberty?

They are not unique to any one denomination. They belong to the great moral inheritance we hold in common. They are the firm ground on which Americans of different faiths meet and stand as a nation, united.[21]

The religious alliance has succeeded to a great degree. Although 65% of Americans believe that more than one faith can lead to eternal life,[22] an amazing 57% think that belief in a god is necessary for a person to be moral.[23] Religionists have done a great job creating prejudice against atheists. A now famous Gallup poll reports that in choosing an otherwise well-qualified presidential candidate:

> 94% of Americans would vote for a Black,
> 92% would vote for a Jew,
> 88% would vote for a female,
> 72% would vote for a Mormon,
> 55% would vote for a homosexual, but only
> 45% would vote for an atheist.[24]

A 2006 study shows Americans ranked atheists at the absolute bottom of a list of minorities including Muslims, gays, Hispanics, Jews, immigrants and racial minorities. Just a few years after the religiously motivated 9/11 attacks, Americans ranked Muslims more highly than atheists! The report noted that while Americans have become much more accepting of other racial and religious minorities over the past 40 years, attitudes toward atheists have hardly changed.[25]

American politicians have learned this well. While there are 535 members of Congress, only one, California Democratic Representative Peter Stark, is willing to acknowledge that although he attends a Unitarian Church, he does not believe in a supreme being.[26] In fact, the constitutions of nine states contain provisions similar to this one from Arkansas, "No person who denies the being of a God shall hold any office in the civil departments of this State, nor be competent to testify as a witness in any court."[27]

Religionists have asserted their political power in Congress. Religionists succeeded in putting "in god we trust" on the one cent coin in 1864. They prevailed in adopting "in god we trust" as the national motto of the United States in 1956, and starting in 1957 the phrase began appearing on paper money. It completed its spread to all paper money by 1966.[28]

Similarly, in the 1950's a Catholic men's group called the Knights of Columbus endeavored to add the phrase "under god" to the Pledge of Allegiance. They gained the support of President Dwight Eisenhower who heard a sermon that said, "Apart from the mention of the phrase 'the United States of America,' . . . [the Pledge of Allegiance] could be the pledge of any republic. In fact, I could hear little Muscovites repeat a similar pledge to their hammer-and-sickle flag in Moscow." The sponsor of the resolution said, "An atheistic American . . . is a contradiction in terms."[29] Congress passed a joint resolution changing the Pledge and Eisenhower signed it stating, "From this day forward, the millions of our schoolchildren will daily proclaim in every city and town, every village and rural schoolhouse, the dedication of our nation and our people to the Almighty."[30]

Religionists recently became upset when the new $612 million Capitol Visitor's Center did not include the motto "in god we trust" in its architecture. By a vote of 410 to 8, the House of Representatives approved making a costly change to put the words on the building.[31]

Politicians follow the lead of their religious supporters and freely disparage atheists. When a reporter for American Atheists asked Vice President (and presidential candidate) George Herbert Walker Bush, "Surely you recognize the equal citizenship and patriotism of Americans who are atheists?" Bush replied, "No, I don't know that atheists should be considered as citizens, nor should they be considered patriots. This is one nation under God." When the American Atheists organization wrote to every member of Congress asking that the newly elected President Bush be censured for his statement, not one member of Congress replied.[32]

Politicians return the favor to religionists for their support. In 2008, "born again Christian" President George W. Bush departed and Barack Obama came in with the motto, "change we can believe in." But in fact, Obama has both increased funding to religious organizations through his "faith-based initiatives" and invoked Jesus more in his speeches than former President George W. Bush.[33]

Roman philosopher Seneca the Younger said, "Religion is regarded by the common people as true, by the wise as false, and by rulers as useful." Politicians are acutely aware of the power of religion and cater to the wishes of religionists to stay in power.

The power of religion extends beyond money, manpower, political power and media control. Religion has woven itself into the fabric of our society. Religion permeates our lives. Many of our names come from the Torah or Bible. Think of how many people you know named David, Mark, John, Mary, Sarah or Deborah. Each time you call their names you make a biblical reference. Circumcision, a Jewish, Muslim and partially Christian rite is still practiced widely in the United States. We use phrases like "thank god," and "bless you," with careless regularity. Our legal system is based on the religious concepts of choice and free will. Religion pervades our thoughts and language in ways it is impossible to measure. Religion's tentacles spread through our art, music, laws and government. Religionists like to pretend they are under attack by secular America, but the religionists roost in a place of power and are firmly in control.

14

Religion is the world's most powerful institution. It has money, manpower, media, politicians on a leash and devoted adherents who will go so far as to kill on religious orders. I emphasize this for two reasons. First, religion is firmly entrenched in a position of power. It is able to set the terms of the debate between religionists and atheists. Second, one must wonder why religion is so afraid of a small, disorganized and despised minority like atheists? Religionists act very much as if they are aware that atheists are right. The next chapter examines who acts like they are right by looking at how each group treats its members who quit.

Chapter 3. Who acts like they are right?

A faith that cannot survive collision with the truth is not worth many regrets.[34] Arthur Clarke

A useful perspective on the difference between atheism and religion is found by looking at how each group treats its members who quit. Religionists act like a crime syndicate when members quit. Religionists have a special term for those who quit--apostates. "Apostate" is not a term people apply to themselves, it is a term insiders use to label outsiders. The reaction ranges from shunning the apostate, to murder.

Religious scriptures provide stiff penalties for quitting. They are a carryover from a time when religion and government freely mixed. Some theocracies maintain the strict penalties to this day.

The Muslim approach to apostasy remains truest to its scriptures. The Koran says, "They wish that you reject Faith, as they have rejected Faith, and thus that you all become equal[,] like one another. So take not . . . protectors or friends from them, till they emigrate in the Way of Allah. . . . **But if they turn back from Islam, take hold of them and kill them** wherever you find them."[35]

The Website Jihad Watch, quoting a paper by scholar Ibn Warraq,[36] notes that only two countries, Sudan and Mauritania, specifically criminalize apostasy:

> [In Sudan,] . . . [w]hoever is guilty of apostasy is invited to repent over a period to be determined by the tribunal. If he persists in his apostasy and was not recently converted to Islam, he will be put to death. [In Mauritania,] . . . all Muslims guilty of apostasy, either

16

spoken or by overt action will be asked to repent during a period of three days. If he does not repent during this period, he is condemned to death as an apostate, and his belongings confiscated by the State Treasury. This applies equally to women.[37]

The absence of mention of apostasy in the penal codes of some Islamic countries in no way implies that a Muslim is free to leave his religion.[38] For example, despite the promise of "freedom of religion" in Afghanistan's Constitution, in 2006 an Afghan man who left Islam faced the death penalty. After pressure from the occupying forces of the U.S., Germany, Italy and Canada, he was released and granted asylum in Italy.[39] Americans almost faced the specter of a country they occupied and financed executing a man who converted to Christianity.

Countries like Saudi Arabia, Iran, and Afghanistan punish apostates, but under a religious code, not a criminal code.[40] Informal enforcement of religious rules against apostasy is perhaps the greatest danger. Even in the United States, Muslim apostates fear for their lives.[41] As Ibn Warraq puts it, the spread of Islam has been through jihad, "a divine institution, enjoined specially for the purpose of advancing Islam[, where] Muslims must strive, fight, and kill in the name of God."[42]

If followers of the Judeo-Christian creeds think their scriptures are more tolerant than the Koran, they are wrong. The Old Testament of the Bible, which applies to both Jews and Christians, provides:

If your very own brother, or your son or daughter, or the wife you love, or your closest friend secretly entices you, saying, "Let us go and worship other gods" (gods that neither you nor your fathers have known, gods of the peoples around you, whether near or far, from one end of the land to the other), do not yield to him or listen to him. Show him no pity. Do not spare him or shield him. **You must certainly put him to death.**

17

Your hand must be the first in putting him to death, and then the hands of all the people. Stone him to death, because he tried to turn you away from the LORD your God, who brought you out of Egypt, out of the land of slavery.[43]

Even in the New Testament, the number one Christian hero, Jesus Christ, is recorded saying, "But those enemies of mine who did not want me to be king over them--**bring them here and kill them in front of me.**"[44]

The Bible seems to acknowledge the existence of atheists, although not very politely. A passage used to justify discrimination against atheists reads, "The fool says in his heart, 'There is no God.' They are corrupt, their deeds are vile; there is no one who does good."[45]

Jews and Christians seem to have abandoned the apostate death penalties in their scriptures, but that does not mean they are kind and understanding to apostates. Altemeyer and Hunsberger studied students who converted from religion to atheism and vice versa. Only the students who departed religion reported significant bad reactions. The majority of apostates studied felt their apostasy had cost them a "great deal," particularly in their relationship with their parents, but also with other relatives.[46] In contrast, atheists who became believers were "hard pressed to find ways in which they had suffered from their turn to religion."[47] In fact, most of them could not think of any cost at all.[48]

There is no atheist scripture specifying death for those who leave atheism. There are no atheist scriptures whatsoever. Departing atheism and adopting religion might result in a raised eyebrow from an atheist friend, but there is no systematic ostracism, no banishment from the community and certainly no death penalty. Atheists hold no strong animosity toward religionists. We decline to give religion unearned respect, but we wish to help to open the religionists' eyes to a truth they refuse to see, and that requires contact. In my experience, when I speak to religionists about atheism they often want to cover their ears and run away, not the other way around.

18

Religionists condemn atheists as evil.[49] Religionists claim atheists are neither patriots nor citizens. Religionists even isolate or kill their members who choose an atheist viewpoint. Atheists respond by inviting religionists to engage in rational dialogue. Atheists take little or no action when an atheist adopts religion. Who acts like they are right? Not religionists who ostracize or kill members who leave their fold and act threatened, frightened, and in no way like people who posses a great truth. Rather atheists, who do not punish members for leaving, are the ones who act like they are right. So who are these atheists? The next chapter provides some answers.

Chapter 4. Who are those guys?

Who are those guys? Screenplay, *Butch Cassidy and the Sundance Kid*

"Agnostic" is but "Atheist" writ respectable and "Atheist" is only "Agnostic" writ aggressive.[50] Edward Aveling

Let us start by looking at a few statistics about American atheists. First, they are more likely to be guys, by a ratio of 70% male to 30% female.[51] Second, they tend to be younger, 37% of atheists are under age 30 and 73% are under 50.[52] Although atheists in the general population are younger, those who join atheist organizations tend to be older.[53] Perhaps older people have more time, perhaps years of bearing with religious falsehoods spur them to action, or perhaps young people who are working their way up the career ladder are nervous about being identified as atheists.

The reason that the percentage of male atheists is larger than the percentage of males in the general population (70% of atheists are male, while 48% of the general population is male)[54] is open to speculation. A similar trend is found among those with no religious affiliation, 59% of "nones" are male and 41% are female.[55] It is possible that women are more inclined to be religious because of some physical or cultural difference. It is also possible that prejudice against atheists and the somewhat negative and confrontational nature of atheism in America today makes men more likely to say they are atheists.

The racial group with the highest proportion of atheists is Asians, followed by Whites. Blacks have the lowest proportion, followed by Latinos.[56] Oddly, 33% of the people responding they had no religion in the 2008 American Religious Identification Survey

(ARIS 2008) study claim Irish ancestry, even though they comprise 10% of the U.S. population.[57]

Atheists tend to have more education and higher income than the general population.[58] Atheists are less likely than the general population to be married, and more likely to live with a partner.[59] However, if married, atheists are less likely than the religious population to divorce.[60] Gays and lesbians are more likely to be atheists than the heterosexual population.[61]

The states with the largest number of nonreligious people are in the East and the West. The most religious states are located in the Southeast, commonly called the "Bible belt." Mississippi, Alabama, South Carolina, Tennessee, Louisiana, Arkansas and Georgia are the most religious states.[62] Vermont, New Hampshire, Maine, Massachusetts, Alaska, Washington and Oregon are the least religious states.

Contrary to the saying there are no atheists in foxholes, nonbelievers comprise 21% of the active duty American military.[63] However, atheists are only .08% of the federal prison population.[64]

Scientists seem to be the group with the largest number of atheists. A 1996 study of U.S. scientists found only 7% expressed belief in a personal god, while 72.2% reported disbelief and 20.8% reported doubt or agnosticism. The 1996 study updated one from 1914 that found a 58% rate of disbelief or doubt in the existence of god among all scientists and a 70% rate of disbelief or doubt among top tier scientists.[65] Disbelief in the scientific community has a long history.

In summary of the statistical profile so far, if you find yourself a young, male, Asian, gay, scientist from the East or West coast, you will most likely be dealing with an atheist.

Looking at some of the political and social characteristics of atheists, only 13% would like to see abortion be illegal and only 14% disapprove of gays and lesbians,[66] making atheists appear more liberal than the general population. Fifty percent of atheists label their political ideology "liberal," while only 14% call themselves "conservative."[67] One study showed the greatest personality distinction between atheists

21

and religionists is that atheists are more open to new experiences and that atheists are a bit less agreeable than religionists.[68] Not surprisingly, nonreligious people are more likely to have a nonreligious spouse and a nonreligious peer group.[69]

Keeping in mind that the sole definitive factor of atheism is having no belief in religion, generalizations can still be made. Hunsberger and Altemeyer note that atheists typically score low on a right-wing authoritarianism scale and predict atheists will have the traits listed in Figure 1.[70] As I read the list, it seems a pretty fair description of the atheists I know.

Many atheists cite polls showing the number of people in the United States with "no religion" has increased to 16% of the U.S. population.[71] Such numbers are impressive, but ignore the core statistic that self-identified atheists are only .7 to 1.6% of the population.[72] Though low, these figures still show there are more atheists in the U.S. than Muslims, and that the number of atheists is roughly equal to the number of Jews or Mormons.[73] And if the question is asked differently, "do you believe in god," from 3% to 10% of respondents say "no," depending on which survey you choose.[74]

Part of the problem may be the negative view of atheism, polls show the general public rates atheists below Muslims in approval.[75] Some nonbelievers may wish to avoid the negative connotations of "atheist." Another part may be the lack of a clear atheist identity. When I was a teen, I was unsure of the difference between an atheist and an agnostic and I applied both terms to myself indiscriminately. I knew I did not believe in a god or scripture, I was just not sure what to call myself. Later chapters contain thoughts about improving the public's perception of atheists.

Atheists are likely to:

1. Condemn unfair and illegal abuses of power by government authorities.
2. Distrust leaders who are untrustworthy.
3. Defend constitutional guarantees of liberty, such as the Bill of Rights.
4. Punish the crime when sentencing criminals; administer justice fairly, regardless of who the criminal is.
5. Hold authorities who commit crimes and people who attack minorities responsible for their acts.
6. Not rely on physical punishment as a way to correct behavior.
7. Resist government pressure to help persecute target groups.
8. Be understanding of those who have made mistakes and suffered.
9. Have well-integrated, non-compartmentalized minds.
10. Avoid using double standards in their judgments.
11. Not be hypocrites.
12. Be unprejudiced toward racial, ethnic, nationalistic, and linguistic minorities.
13. Accept homosexuals as people like anyone else and condemn "gay-bashing."
14. Support feminism.
15. Be less conforming to the opinions of others, and not be a yea-sayer, nor believe strongly in group cohesiveness and "group loyalty."
16. Be aware of themselves. Realize their personal failings and be open to feedback about such failings.
17. Not trust someone merely because he tells them what they want to hear.
18. Not feel the world is a dangerous place nor be self-righteous.
19. Be non-dogmatic and non-zealous.
20. Support "liberal" or "left-wing" political parties and movements.

Figure 1. Predicted characteristics of atheists.

The religiousness continuum.

Instead of picturing exclusive blocks of religiousness, it helps me to picture the various categories of belief on a continuum. If you will imagine a line, with one end being complete atheism and the other end being radical fundamentalist religionism, you can place all the other groups along the line (see Figure 2). The scale on this continuum runs from 0 to 100, representing the cumulative percentage of the U.S. population.

On the left side of the chart are the self-identified atheists. Following them are the "nones," who, when added with atheists and agnostics, form about 16% of the U.S. population. Instead of labeling themselves atheists or agnostics, "nones" simply say they have no religion. "Nones" are the largest group of nonreligious people. Some "nones" believe in god, while others do not. On either side of the "nones," I put the agnostics. "Agnostic" comes from the Greek word "gnosis," to know. Agnostic means without knowledge, or without the ability to know. Thomas Huxley invented the term in 1869 to represent his position that it is impossible to know if god does or does not exist. I have split the agnostic group to fit like slices of bread on either side of the nones. Agnostics who lean toward atheism are on the left side of the graph next to the atheists, agnostics who lean toward religion are on the right, next to the deists.

Another 12% of the chart is covered by what ARIS 2008 calls "deists."[76] Like the founding fathers, deists reject the idea of a "personal god." They do not believe there is a bearded man in the sky who answers their prayers. They do not believe in the scriptures. I think of them as people who say, "god is nature and nature is god." Perhaps, similar to their agnostic brothers, they feel it is easier to acknowledge the possibility of there being a god, even to call themselves Christian, and then be let alone to get on with their lives.

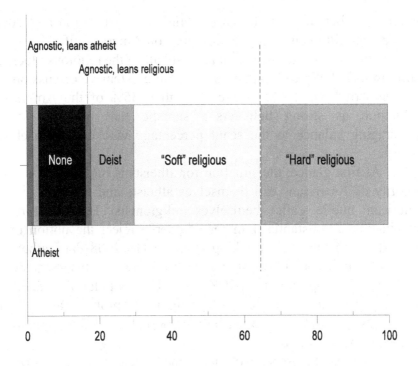

Figure 2. Religiousness on a continuum, with the scale representing the cumulative percentage of the U.S. population.

If you add together the atheists, agnostics, nones and deists, almost one in three Americans has no belief in a personal god, no belief in the infallibility of the scriptures and is likely to make decisions based on facts instead of ancient traditions. Suddenly the religious block no longer looks like an inapproachable monolith.

The remaining 70% of the graph[77] is dedicated to those who say they believe in god. But not all people believe equally. A number of religious people reject the scriptures as the word of god and favor the general philosophy of their religion. For example, only 31% of the American people think the Bible is the word of god,[78] only about 42% of religious Americans report attending church over the last seven days,

25

36% do not belong to a church or religious organization and 70% believe that religion is losing its influence on American life.[79]

I think it is safe to say that at least half of the religious block is "soft" in its belief (see Chapter 23 for a more extensive discussion of the depth of belief). That leaves less than 35% of the American population as strong believers–a statistic that provides some encouraging balance to the scant percentage who call themselves atheists.

At first glance, the situation for atheists is bleak. Only a tiny minority of Americans call themselves atheists and the bulk of the American public calls themselves religionists. But on further examination a substantial number of people reject the notion of a bearded man in the sky. Looking at the ARIS 2008 data, atheists, agnostics and deists, plus those who do not know or refuse to answer, combined make up more than 30% of the U.S. population. Added to this significant number are the "soft" religionists, probably about 35% of the U.S. population, leaving only 35% or less of the population feeling strongly about religion.

Looking at these statistics takes me back to why I have written this book. First, I want to support the strong few who are willing to swim against the current and declare themselves atheists. Second, I want to encourage the agnostics and deists to closely examine their beliefs, I would like them to stop agreeing with the religionists just because it is easier and instead to acknowledge the truth, and move toward atheism.

Third, I cannot believe that 70% of Americans, or even 35% of Americans, truly believe the religious doctrine they claim to follow. Perhaps like Daniel Dennett says, they believe in belief, that is they think it would be good to believe so they say they do.[80] Or, perhaps as I see it, they go to church to get along, to get business, to please their parents or please their spouse or because they always have. But they do not really believe. They are like the crowd in the story of *The Emperor's New Clothes* (see Chapter 24). They know the emperor is naked, but the whispers have not spread and they do not yet feel comfortable acknowledging that religion is a lie. I hope to reach a few of them and to encourage them to say what they know in their hearts is true. With small steps the tide of atheism will rise and the influence of religion will decline.

The next chapter continues the look at atheists. It examines some of the labels atheists apply to themselves, some of the groups they join, and some of the symbols they have adopted.

Chapter 5. Names and symbols.

We live in a day when there is a great war going on in the society in which we live. There are many battlefronts and aspects to the war, but the primary war in our day is between Christianity and secular humanism.[81] Abounding Joy Christian Website

[W]ords have power to mould men's thinking, to canalize their feeling, to direct their willing and acting. Conduct and character are largely determined by the nature of the words we currently use to discuss ourselves and the world around us.[82] Aldous Huxley

Religionists like to use sharp-edged terms to describe atheists-- terms like "secular humanists."[83] There is nothing inherently wrong with the term secular humanist. "Secular" simply means nonreligious and "humanism" is a philosophy that emphasizes ethics and personal responsibility for the good of humanity without the need for god.[84] There is even a "Council for Secular Humanism," that publishes the popular *Free Inquiry* magazine.[85]

But alternatively, the term "atheist" comes with a lot of baggage. Atheists are one of the most despised minorities in America. It is little wonder that the majority of people without religion avoid the term and cluster in a majority known as "nones." Only about 10% of nonreligious people call themselves atheists.[86]

Because religionists have been negative about atheists for so long, atheists have sought alternative terms to describe themselves, including: brights, freethinkers, godless, heathens, heretics, humanists, infidels, irreligious, materialists, naturalists, nonbelievers, non-theists, nones, pagans, rationalists, secularists, skeptics, unbelievers and more.

This chapter looks briefly at some of these terms, but I will be up front, the term I prefer and the term I believe we should gather under, is atheist.

Brights.

Paul Geisert[87] coined the term "brights" in 2002 as a positive term for people with a naturalistic world view and a commitment to fairness.[88] "Brights" is intended to be positive and empowering in a manner similar to the adoption of the term "gay," instead of the sharp-edged and clinical term "homosexual."

I have two concerns about the term "brights." The first is that "brights" are unknown except among those who have been reading about atheism or trolling the Internet for atheist information. If you go to the local shopping mall and announce that you are a "bright," the majority will think you are conceited and only a few will perceive you to be atheist. The second concern is that it sounds elitist, as though only smart people can be atheists and that theists are dim. I remember reading an Internet discussion of whether janitors could be atheists. I was appalled. Of course there are many atheist janitors, I was an atheist janitor at one point in my life. Atheism is not dictated by education, intelligence or high-status employment. Atheists are everywhere. Taking an elitist approach will result in atheism being limited to mostly white, college-educated males. I believe we need a more broadly recognized and inclusive term.

Freethinkers.

"Freethinker" has a long and honorable history. A freethinker is one who forms opinions on the basis of reason, independently of authority, especially one who doubts or denies religious dogma.[89] Freethought was born in Europe in the 1700's and flourished in Germany. A number of German freethinkers immigrated to the U.S. in the 1800's and established freethought communities here, including Comfort, Texas.[90] The oldest continually published atheist magazine is *The Freethinker*, started in Britain in 1881. Putting the lie to the claim that "new atheists"[91] are the first to challenge religion, the introductory issue said, "*The Freethinker* is an anti-christian organ, and must therefore be chiefly aggressive. It will wage relentless war against superstition in general, and against christian superstition in particular. It will do its best to employ the resources of science, scholarship, philosophy and ethics . . . [and] any weapons of ridicule or sarcasm that may be borrowed from the armory of common sense."[92]

I am fond of the term freethinker. However, "freethinker" describes a process of open-minded thought, rather than the status of rejecting religion. Further, some argue that religionists can be freethinkers and conversely, that not all atheists are freethinkers.[93] Additionally, applying the shopping mall test, if you went to a shopping mall and declared you were a freethinker, the majority of the people might think you were open-minded, but most would not conclude that you reject religion.

Godless.

"Godless" is a clear and powerful term. It is a virtual synonym for atheist. But it comes with a lot of baggage, even more baggage than "atheist." During the cold war, "godless" was repeatedly linked with "communist," and the "godless communists" were vilified. Additionally, "godless" is used by religionists as a synonym for "wicked or immoral." In fact, *Godless* is the title of a book by arch-conservative Ann Coulter in which she argues that liberalism is a religion.[94]

"Godless" passes the shopping mall test–the majority of the population would understand what you mean when you tell them you are godless, although it might not apply to non-theistic religions, like Buddhism. Another problem is that "godless" has the dreaded word "god" in it. Atheism has the same meaning, but the Greek origin of "atheist" softens the impact and makes it sound a little more scientific. But absent these factors, only personal preference leads me to choose "atheist" over "godless" to describe myself.

30

Irreligious, nonbelievers, non-theists and unbelievers.

The terms "irreligious, nonbelieiver, non-theist and unbeliever" are similar to "godless," in that they are quick, clean and easily understood. Each passes the shopping mall test. The hyphenated words are a little bit tricky to write, and to my ears, they lack a nice ring. The biggest problem is that none of these terms has been widely adopted by atheists to describe themselves. "Atheist" has a broader history and better identification by the general public as term describing a person with no belief in religion.

Nones.

Recent surveys recognize the rapid growth of the number of people with no religion and call them "nones."[95] The term has also gained usage in some atheist circles. Unfortunately, when spoken, "none" sounds exactly like "nun," sometimes leaving even atheist insiders wondering why the speaker is talking about a religious woman in a funny outfit. "None" is handicapped because it requires a whole lot of additional words to get the point across. In a shopping mall, the speaker would first have to explain he is not calling himself a religious woman and then add another sentence to explain "none" refers to an absence of religious belief. A quickly understood single term is preferable to the easily misunderstood "none."

Heathens, heretics, infidels and pagans.

Religionists use the terms "heathens, heretics, infidels and pagans" to demonize outsiders. Further, these terms do not designate a rejection of all religion, but rather rejection of a specific religion. Heathens, heretics, infidels and pagans might well follow a polytheistic religion–just not Judaism, Christianity or Islam. Also, these terms would not result in broad recognition if used to the general public in a shopping mall. These may be fun terms to get the attention of certain religionists, but they are not a multipurpose tool to describe a movement based on a lack of belief in religion.

31

Materialists, naturalists, rationalists and skeptics.

Multiple meanings and no immediate link to the rejection of religion are shortcomings of the labels "materialist, naturalist, rationalist and skeptic." For example, if I announce I am a naturalist, more people would think I like visiting nudist colonies than understand that I reject religion. None of these terms conveys specifically the rejection of religion and none passes the shopping mall test.

Secularists.

"Secularist" refers to someone who rejects or excludes religion. It is a fairly good synonym for atheist. I have three main objections to the term. The first is that religionists really like to use it. This may be a little silly, but I do not want religionists to choose the term that describes me. The second is that "secular" is a hard, angular sounding term. Perhaps that is why religionists like using it so much–it sounds unpleasant. Or maybe religionists like it because "secular" sounds a bit like "sexual," a term they are accustomed to using in demonizing "homo*sexuals*," and a term they think polite company wants to avoid. The third objection is that for a substantial portion of the population, the rejection of religion does not pop into mind when they hear the term "secular." The average college-educated person understands, but I would guess that 50% of the people in the shopping mall would not understand that it means a rejection of religion. Atheists need a broad coalition and a name understood by the great majority of the general public.

Humanists.

The American Humanist Association describes humanism as "a progressive philosophy of life that, without supernaturalism, affirms our ability and responsibility to lead ethical lives of personal fulfillment that aspire to the greater good of humanity."[96] Humanists seem like nice people and I have little disagreement with their goals. But I see two problems with humanism. First, humanism does not exclude religion. There are a number of humanists who are also religionists. Second,

32

humanists seem to be working awfully hard to prove that they can be good without god (see Chapter 7). I do not disagree with humanism, but it adds an unneeded factor, like saying you must be liberal to be atheist. I am both, but the categories are not necessarily intertwined, there are plenty of right-wing conservatives who are also atheists. There is no need to add an extra requirement to our common bond–the absence of religious belief. Humanists say you must be both ethical and not supernatural. I am both, but once again, the categories do not need to be intertwined. Ethical conduct and morality appear to be as important an element of the humanist agenda as the rejection of supernaturalism. To me, humanism is "atheism plus," atheism plus ethics structured in response to a challenge from religionists. In fact, humanism was originally called a new religion[97] and retains some of the structure of religion. Most humanists may be atheists, but humanism is more than atheism.

Atheists.

"Atheist" is the term I support. First, it is the most common term to describe a person with no belief in religion. When you say, "I am an atheist" in the shopping mall, almost everyone knows what you are talking about. Second, it is a term that has been around for hundreds of years, so it has a lot of history behind it.[98] Third, using the term honors the proud atheists who came before us, people who accepted the label "atheist" and worked hard to educate a mostly hostile population about the merits of atheism. Fourth, the term "atheist" does not intertwine itself with other issues like ethics. And finally, fifth, atheism does not imitate or duplicate religion, it is the absence of religious belief and nothing more. However, the first reason is the strongest reason, "atheist" is the most widely recognized term to describe a lack of belief in religion.

In a rare study of the terms organizational atheists choose to describe themselves, Luke Galen found that when they were allowed to choose *multiple* terms to describe themselves, 77% included the term atheist, 63% humanist and 29% agnostic. However, when only allowed *one term* to describe themselves, 57% choose atheist, 24% humanist and 10% agnostic. Galen additionally found that the term atheist is used more commonly by younger people.[99] So there is support that atheist is the preferred term among the godless, and is becoming increasingly preferred among our younger members who represent the future.

It is true that the term "atheist" was originally used as an insult (people were accused of being atheists, they never labeled themselves as such). But instead of minting a new term like "brights," we can take an already recognized one and make it positive, much like "homosexuals" did with the term "gay." It is also true that "atheist" is negative–it defines a person by what he is not (more about this in Chapter 6). But I find it the best term to describe myself. It does not carry the additional burdens of fairness or ethics desired by the humanists and brights. It is quickly understood by the general population to describe a person with no belief in religion, and it is a term that has stood the test of time. For these reasons, I prefer to be called an atheist. So to adopt a marching chant of others seeking equality, "Say it loud, atheist and proud."

Atheist organizations.

Atheists have little in common other than their lack of belief in religion. Additionally, atheism, as a mass movement, is a relatively recent phenomenon. As such, there are few national organizations with broad membership. The American Humanist Association, which claims to be America's largest and oldest, has 15,000 members.[100] The Freedom From Religion Foundation which claims to be America's largest atheist organization, has around 14,000 members.[101] American Atheists, one of the oldest national atheist groups still operating in the U.S. has about 3,000 members.[102] The Secular Coalition for America has attempted to become an atheist umbrella group, but as of this writing, it has just ten member groups.[103] The Atheist Alliance International serves a similar purpose with an international scope and has about 56 member groups.[104] The Secular Student Alliance is doing better than its elders with about 186 U.S. member groups.[105]

Atheists have not yet developed a strong national voice. Atheist organizations look pitiful when compared to religionists. For example the National Association of Evangelicals claims a membership of 30 million people.[106] Although there are national atheist organizations, no single organization has succeeded in uniting the atheists' voices. At this point in time atheists remain a relatively powerless and generally despised minority.

Symbols.

Atheists have no single, unifying symbol by which to identify themselves. Christians use the cross and now almost as frequently, the Jesus fish. Jews have the Star of David. Muslims have the crescent moon and star. Atheists are still searching. Perhaps the difficulty selecting a symbol is understandable, what do you use to represent a non-belief?

American Atheists.

One of the oldest symbols is from American Atheists. The organization was founded in 1963 by Madalyn Murray O'Hair[107] and adopted an "atomic whirl" with an A inside as shown in Figure 3. Surprisingly, the open whirl is supposed to represent the "A" for atheism, while the printed "A" inside comes from the first letter of the country in which the organization is located,[108] in this case, "America." The design of the atomic whirl seems stuck in the 1960's, and as the copyrighted symbol of a group of just 3,000 members, it has not traveled very far. A symbol with broader recognition is more desirable.

Figure 3. American Atheist symbol.

Empty Symbolism.

Perhaps focusing on the non-belief of atheists, several people have suggested symbols of a lack of belief. One suggestion is a mathematical "null set" symbol, something like this: { } or this: ⊘. Variations on this theme include more artistic empty circles. Figure 4 contains a variation on the empty circle theme with the circle constructed of the words "AGNOSTIC, HUMANIST, RATIONALIST, FREETHINKER, SECULAR, INFIDEL, NONBELIEVER, ATHEIST, HERETIC, and GODLESS" suggested by Adrian Barnett.[109]

Figure 4. Circle of terms.

The circle is an interesting symbol. I saw a lot of circles appearing on cars and was impressed by the number of atheists, until I learned that the State of Oregon is using "O" for itself, as is the popular sunglass company Oakley. Unfortunately, few of the O's I saw were atheist symbols. The empty circle has limited recognition and too much competition.

The rise of the "A."

Because "atheist" starts with the letter "A" in many languages, some have suggested the letter "A" as an atheist symbol. Atheist author Richard Dawkins has promoted the scarlet letter A in Figure 5. Dawkins claims no copyright to the symbol which has aided its spread, particularly on the Internet.[110]

Figure 5. Dawkins' scarlet A.

The Atheist Alliance International had a competition and selected a stylized "A" as their symbol as well,[111] as shown in Figure 6. There are a number of variations on the "A" design, including ones that look like a symbol for the *Star Trek* television and movie shows. Besides invoking unpleasant memories of

Figure 6. Atheist Alliance International A.

reading *The Scarlet Letter* in school, recognition of the "A" symbol is limited to mostly organizational atheists. A more effective symbol would be one recognized by both insiders and outsiders.

Fishy Business.

The Christian fish symbol, which I call the "Jesus fish," is one of the most recognized religious symbols in America. The "Darwin fish" adopts the outline of the Jesus fish, but adds legs and the word "Darwin" in the middle. Now in the public domain, it was the subject of a lawsuit between creators Al Shekel and John Edwards, who used it on atheist materials in the early 1980's, and Chris Gilman who began making silver car ornaments with a similar design in 1990.[112]

Figure 7. Atheist fish.

Variations on the Darwin fish include one with the word "evolve" in the center (thereby avoiding deifying Darwin) and a tool in its hand, another with the word "science" at its center, as well as a fish made only of bones. The best of the species, from my point of view, is a fish with legs and the word "atheist" in the middle, as shown in Figure 7. This clarifies that the user not only supports evolution (which many religionists also support) but also that the user rejects religion.

Figure 8. Fish eating dinosaur. (Figure 8 appears courtesy of evolvefish.com, which sells this image online.)

Religionists responded to the Darwin fish with a compound symbol of a Jesus fish labeled "truth" eating a Darwin fish. Ring of Fire Enterprises created a symbol of a dinosaur eating a Jesus fish in response (Figure 8) as well as developing a Darwin fish copulating with a Jesus fish. Part of the humor of the dinosaur is that religious fundamentalists have a hard time objecting to the symbol since many do not believe in dinosaurs. The Darwin fish is currently well recognized, but does not apply exclusively to atheists. Replacing the word "Darwin" with "atheist" makes it a strong atheist symbol.

Humanists.

Humanists worldwide have adopted the "happy humanist" symbol, first designed in 1965.[113] It is a stylized person standing with arms up-stretched (Figure 9). It has gained fairly good recognition among humanists and atheists, but is not widely recognized outside of those groups.

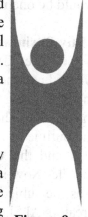

Figure 9. The happy humanist.

The flying spaghetti monster.

The Church of the Flying Spaghetti Monster was introduced in a 2005 letter by Bobby Henderson to the Kansas School Board suggesting that "pastafarianism" be taught along with creationism. After all, there is as much evidence supporting the flying spaghetti monster as there is for god.[114]

The flying spaghetti monster spoof spread quickly, mostly among younger people, who display the flying spaghetti monster symbol on their cars or clothes.

Figure 10. The flying spaghetti monster.

The flying spaghetti monster is a fun way to counter religion; however, the church of the flying spaghetti monster is an in-group joke. Religionists and the majority of the population are unaware of the meaning of the googly eyes and noodly appendages of the creature (Figure 10). It gets a laugh from those "in the know" but misses the mark when it comes to educating the uninitiated as to the merits of non-religion.

A rock solid symbol.

All of the symbols here are two-dimensional representations for use on cars and clothes. Since this is my book and I can say what I like, I suggest a stone cairn as a three-dimensional representation of atheism (Figure 11). Cairns are stacks of rocks used to show a trail or simply built in celebration. Cairns have been used to show the way for tens of thousands of years (well before "people of the book" admit the world was created). The top two stones of the cairn form a figurative "A," and cairns can be created anywhere to let

Figure 11. A simple stone cairn.

others know an atheist has passed before. Rocks are everywhere (just like atheists). You can put a cairn in front of your house, on the trail when hiking, and even in front of the neighborhood church!

But enough of my attempt at originality. I believe the most easily recognized symbol of atheism is simply the full word "ATHEIST." It may not be very artistic, but it gets the message across to the largest number of people in the easiest manner (Figure 12). A

ATHEIST

Figure 12. A plain atheist symbol.

slightly more interesting choice is the atheist variation of the Darwin fish shown in Figure 7. It creates a bit of humor, is visually interesting and clearly communicates that the person displaying the symbol is without religion. Between the two, I favor slightly the atheist fish.

Chapter 6. Atheism is neither a religion nor the opposite of religion (or, why atheists should not wear their hats on their elbows).

They seek to remove from the public domain any acknowledgment of God. Religion is seen as merely a private affair with no place in public life. It is as if they are intent on establishing a new religion in America--the religion of secularism.[115] American Presidential Candidate Mitt Romney

Atheism is the religion whose belief about God is that there is no God. . . . it must be subject to the same legal restrictions imposed by governments on all other religions. In particular, in the United States, the teaching of Atheism must be prohibited wherever the teaching of Christianity is prohibited.[116] The Reverend Bill McGinnis

Atheism is defined by religion, but it is not the opposite of religion. Neither is atheism a form of religion. Everyone is born atheist, just as everyone is born human. Some humans learn religion, some do not, and some learn religion and later reject it.

It is kind of like humans and hats. All humans are born without hats, just as all humans are born without religion. Some humans have hats put on their heads pretty soon after birth, but they are not born that way. Humor me and let me call newborns "a-hatist" (that is without hats, just like "a-theist" is without religion). If hats were never invented, there would be no need for the term "a-hatist," but a-hatism would still exist.

Similarly, atheism is defined by religion. Atheism is a lack of belief in religion. If men had never invented religion, there would be no need for the term "atheist," but atheism would still exist.

Neither is atheism a religion. Religionists want to call atheism a religion.[117] They seize on language in a 1961 U.S. Supreme Court case that labeled secular humanism a religion.[118] The language is located in a footnote and is what lawyers call *dicta*–incidental words that are thrown into the case but have no bearing on the decision and do not serve as binding legal precedent. Religionists call us secular humanists more frequently than they call us atheists. There is a reason for this.

If religionists succeed in categorizing atheism as a religion, they can claim victory. Atheism would just be another supernatural theory, no better or worse than their own. They could call evolution a religion and demand that their bearded man myths get equal billing.[119] But they are wrong. Religion is a belief in the supernatural. Atheism is the absence of that belief. Think back to Chapter 1 where I described the mayonnaise jars of religionists and atheists. A Christian religionist's jar is full of supernatural beliefs like: the world was created in six days, woman was created from man's rib, a virgin gave birth to a child, dead people can come back to life, and so on. The atheist's mayonnaise jar is empty. No matter how much the religionists try, they cannot transmute the lack of supernatural belief into a supernatural belief. That is, unless we let them.

It is easy to imitate the religious model and allow religionists to set the agenda. Satanists are a good example. They take Christianity and flip it on its head. Satanists worship Lucifer instead of Yahweh. They have black masses instead of white. It seems that some people get a rebellious thrill by claiming to be Satanists, but they are misdirecting their frustration with Christianity by being its opposite. They let the religionists set their agenda and act in a manner as equally silly as the religionists they are rebelling against.

The Church of the Flying Spaghetti Monster is a spoof of Christianity. It provides a bit of comic relief in the debates over religion and creationism. Tongue in cheek, the Church announces, "Some claim that the church is purely a thought experiment, satire, illustrating that Intelligent Design is not science, but rather a pseudoscience manufactured by Christians to push creationism into public schools.

41

These people are mistaken."[120] Admittedly, I laugh at the irreverent references. But all fun aside, the Church of the Flying Spaghetti Monster is a limited joke that conforms to the religious model.

On the serious side of things, the Church of Reality gives little more than a wink before announcing it is "winning souls for Darwin" and then plugging common sense concepts into the religious model.[121] Although spoof remains evident, it is a more serious attempt to fit atheism into a religious model. They have even obtained tax-free status for their organization from the Internal Revenue Service.[122]

The American Humanist model is a very serious attempt to mold atheism into a religion. Humanists are so intent on answering the religionist posed question "can you be good without god," that they create an alternative church. In fact, their first Humanist Manifesto repeatedly labeled humanism a religion.[123] Their recent billboard campaign advertises, "Millions are good without god."[124] Humanists have allowed religionists set their agenda. Humanists seem like nice people but I believe they have gone down the wrong path.

Everyone has a right to express their beliefs but I believe that these "churches" fall into the trap set by religionists to make atheism another religion. It is like "a-hatists" proclaiming:

> Hat-ists are wrong
> to wear their hats on their heads,
> so we will wear hats
> on our elbows instead.

Atheism is the absence of religion, it is not the opposite of religion and it is not a new religion. To behave otherwise allows the religionists to set our agenda.

Even an organization with the hopeful title "Freedom From Religion Foundation (FFRF)" falls into the same trap. Their co-leader is a former preacher who went from traveling around the country singing Christian songs and preaching Christianity to traveling around the country singing atheist songs and preaching atheism.[125] They even

42

print atheist recipes in their church bulletin–um, I mean freethought paper. An FFRF billboard campaign adopts a religious stained glass motif and proclaims, "Praise Darwin!"[126] Perhaps I am missing the sophisticated humor of juxtapositioning religious imagery with atheism in the campaign, but it looks to me like they are elevating Darwin to the position of saint or deity. I believe Darwin was a brave and bright scientist. But I think that making him a saint is allowing the religionists to set the agenda. Atheism is the absence of religion. If we make atheism the opposite of religion, it is like (going back to the a-hatism example) wearing a hat on our elbow instead of wearing no hat. And if we wear our hats on our elbows, we are letting religionists dictate the rules.

A personal example is my recent decision to grow my hair long. Styles are changing, it reminds me of my youth when I first grew long hair, and it is a final opportunity to wear long hair before it turns white. These are my rationalizations. But I also decided to grow my hair long about the time I learned a Bible passage[127] dictates that men should wear their hair short. If I am growing my hair simply to be the opposite of what the Bible dictates, I am letting the religionists set the agenda. It is like I am wearing a hat on my elbow. I believe I am growing my hair for the reasons I first stated, but I must admit the possibility exists it is simply to oppose religion.

Religionists have a mayonnaise jar full of myths. Atheists have an empty jar. Where religionists promote myths, atheists look to facts. If religionists can convince us to comply with their model, to fill our mayonnaise jar with replacement myths, then they have a battle of myth versus myth, something they want. Then, for example, religionists can say that in the conflict between teaching religion versus science in the classroom (creationism v. evolution); that no myth can have priority over another myth and that the law gives them equal opportunity. One reason religionists label their enemy "secular humanists" is because the humanist belief structure fits better into the myth versus myth battle than that of atheists. Religionists have a much harder time creating the battle with atheists who point out that their mayonnaise jar is empty.

When it comes to facts, the religionists' position is indefensible. Look at creationism. There are no facts to support that the world was created in six days, no evidence that the world was created less than 10,000 years ago, and nothing indicates that the species are fixed in their current form. But, bargaining from their position of power, if the religionists can keep atheists chasing after a red herring like "can you be good without god," then the religionists can maintain their dominance–they never need to face the facts. Atheists reject religious myths. We must also reject the religionists' agenda of making the debate myth versus myth instead of myth versus reality. Atheism is not a religion. There should be no atheist churches. We do not put our empty mayonnaise jars on altars. That is the difference between atheists and religionists.

When religion goes away there will be no need for the term "atheist." But the status will still exist. Humans can exist without religion, but religion cannot exist without humans. Religion is a byproduct of human behavior but atheism is not a product at all, it is the absence of religion.

Atheism and negativity.

In emphasizing that we should not allow religionists to set our agenda, I do not mean to deny that there is an oppositional aspect to atheism. Atheism is defined by religion, it is not the opposite of religion, but there is an element of opposition to religion contained within atheism. In fact, I believe a negative factor is a key element of atheism. When pressed, "nones" admit, "I have no religion." Atheists, on the other hand, are proud to announce they have no religion. They advertise it. When you ask an atheist about religion, he happily responds, "can I tell you more?" Atheists are willing to speak out to some degree against religion, that is what distinguishes them from "nones."

Returning to the religiousness scale from Chapter 4, but changing the scale from the percentage of the population to a numerical rating of religiousness, the scale appropriately extends from negative

44

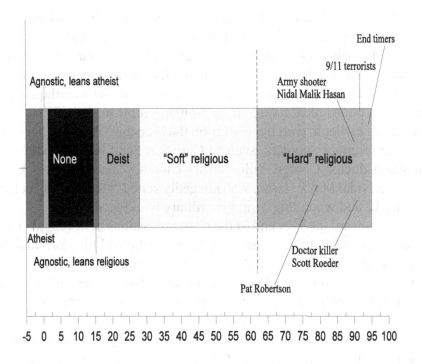

Figure 13. Religiosity with the scale representing
the strength of religious belief.

numbers to positive numbers. That is, "nones" would sit around zero on the scale. Religious zealots would be near 100, and atheists would fall below zero into the negative numbers as shown in Figure 13.

Religionists could argue that the negative scale should go to –100. However, I see no evidence that atheists are as extreme as religionists. For example, I am one of the most vocal atheists I know. However, my atheist activism goes no further than talking to religionists, being open about my atheism, putting bumper stickers on my car and writing this book. To me, it seems reasonable to call my anti-religionism a –5. Some religionists, on the other hand, kill for their religion. The 9/11 terrorists come quickly to mind. These radical acts earn a higher number--close to 100, on my religiosity scale.

To help make sense of the chart, I mentally put a few stories from the news on the scale. To the right falls Pat Robertson, the former presidential candidate and preacher who said the 2010 earthquake in Haiti was punishment for a pact the Haitian people made with the devil 200 years earlier to gain freedom from the French.[128] A bit further right fall the religious shooters, such as Christian Scott Roeder, who shot abortion doctor George Tiller at his church,[129] and Muslim Army shooter, Nidal Malik Hasan, who allegedly yelled "god is great" before killing 12 and wounding 31 at his military workplace.[130]

Toward the very end of the chart are zealous believers who use improvised weapons of mass destruction, like the 9/11 hijackers and the Detroit underwear bomber. At the very far right are the "end timers" who may seek to use nuclear weapons, especially in the Middle East, because they believe it will accelerate the appearance or return of their messiah.

I use the religiosity scale as a tool to give a graphic depiction of the range of religious behavior. First, I use it to acknowledge that atheism has a negative, antireligious element. It is not the sole element of atheism, but it is a factor. Second, I use it for encouragement. Facing the statistic that 80% of Americans believe in god, is disheartening. But the scale helps me to see that they do not all believe equally. The religious block is not a solid monolith, but a gradation of belief. The scale helps me to see that a large number of people are closer to atheism than at first appears. This helps me to target my message and encourages me to continue my efforts.

Chapter 7. Who gave them the moral high ground?

Religion is an insult to human dignity. With or without it you would have good people doing good things and evil people doing evil things. But for good people to do evil things, that takes religion. Steven Weinberg, Nobel Prize Winning Physicist[131]

People who reject the idea of a God--who think that we're just accidental protoplasm--have always been with us. What bothers me is . . . if there is no eternal standard of right and wrong, then all that matters is power. And atheism leads to brutality. All the horrific crimes of the last century were committed by atheists--Stalin and Hitler[132] and Mao and so forth--because it flows very naturally from an idea that there is no judgment and there is nothing other than the brief time we spend on this Earth. Indiana Governor Mitch Daniels[133]

One of the most common defenses of religion (and assaults on atheism) is the presumption that religion makes people good. The persistence of this myth demonstrates the power of religionists to set the agenda. I reject completely the notion that religion makes people good. Further, atheists should feel no obligation to prove that they are good without religion. The question "can you be good without god," should be as offensive and out of place as the question, "can a slave be good without his master?"

Religionists have been setting the agenda for so long, that their goodness premise is accepted without question. For example, laws on the books in some states prohibit atheists from testifying in court. The Arkansas Constitution provides, "No person who denies the being of a God shall hold any office in the civil departments of this State, nor be competent to testify as a witness in any court."[134] Incredibly, such provisions were not judicially overridden nationwide until a 1961 U.S. Supreme Court decision[135] and as recently as 2009 attempts to change the Arkansas Constitution to allow atheists to have equal rights failed.[136] Atheists are still prohibited from testifying against Muslims in many Muslim countries.[137] But, however deeply rooted in history and vehemently defended by the powerful majority the goodness myth may be, it is false.

For example, the scriptures religionists use to support their claims of superiority are reprehensible. American religionists who oppose equal rights for gays and lesbians often cite the biblical story of Sodom and Gomorrah. After reading that tale, it shocks me that the 31% of Americans who believe the Bible is the literal word of god, and the additional 47% who believe the Bible is the inspired word of god (a total of 78% of Americans)[138] can find an iota of moral guidance in the story.

In that story, two men visit Lot. Unknown to him, they are "angels." A crowd gathers around Lot's house and demands that Lot send the men outside to be raped. Lot, being a "moral" man, refuses, but instead offers his two daughters, probably about 14-years-old, to be raped instead. The "angels" do not object to this substitution, but the crowd does.

The "angels" then blind the crowd and give Lot and his family a chance to escape. But the Lot family's prospective sons-in-law are left behind. For some bizarre reason, the "angels" instruct Lot and his family not to look behind them. Lot's wife does, maybe thinking about what happened to her daughters' fiances. She is turned inexplicably into a pillar of salt. Lot then moves into a cave with his daughters. The daughters get Lot drunk and have sex with him, thereby getting pregnant.

In case you think I am making this up, here is the Bible story:

Sodom and Gomorrah Destroyed

The two angels arrived at Sodom in the evening, and Lot was sitting in the gateway of the city. When he saw them, he got up to meet them and bowed down with his face to the ground. "My lords," he said, "please turn aside to your servant's house. You can wash your feet and spend the night and then go on your way early in the morning."

"No," they answered, "we will spend the night in the square."

But he insisted so strongly that they did go with him and entered his house. He prepared a meal for them, baking bread without yeast, and they ate. Before they had gone to bed, all the men from every part of the city of Sodom--both young and old--surrounded the house. They called to Lot, "Where are the men who came to you tonight? Bring them out to us so that we can have sex with them."

Lot went outside to meet them and shut the door behind him and said, "No, my friends. Don't do this wicked thing. Look, I have two daughters who have never slept with a man. Let me bring them out to you, and you can do what you like with them. But don't do anything to these men, for they have come under the protection of my roof."

"Get out of our way," they replied. And they said, "This fellow came here as an alien, and now he wants to play the judge! We'll treat you worse than them." They kept bringing pressure on Lot and moved forward to break down the door.

But the men inside reached out and pulled Lot back into the house and shut the door. Then they struck the men who were at the door of the house, young and old, with blindness so that they could not find the door.

The two men said to Lot, "Do you have anyone else here--sons-in-law, sons or daughters, or anyone else in the city who belongs to you? Get them out of here, because we are going to destroy this place. The outcry to the LORD against its people is so great that he has sent us to destroy it."

So Lot went out and spoke to his sons-in-law, who were pledged to marry his daughters. He said, "Hurry and get out of this place, because the LORD is about to destroy the city!" But his sons-in-law thought he was joking.

With the coming of dawn, the angels urged Lot, saying, "Hurry! Take your wife and your two daughters who are here, or you will be swept away when the city is punished."

When he hesitated, the men grasped his hand and the hands of his wife and of his two daughters and led them safely out of the city, for the LORD was merciful to them. As soon as they had brought them out, one of them said, "Flee for your lives! Don't look back, and don't stop anywhere in the plain! Flee to the mountains or you will be swept away!"

* * *

By the time Lot reached Zoar, the sun had risen over the land. Then the LORD rained down burning sulfur on Sodom and Gomorrah—from the LORD out of the heavens. Thus he overthrew those cities and the entire plain, including all those living in the cities—and also the vegetation in the land. But Lot's wife looked back, and she became a pillar of salt.

* * *

Lot and His Daughters

Lot and his two daughters left Zoar and settled in the mountains, for he was afraid to stay in Zoar. He and his two daughters lived in a cave. One day the older daughter said to the younger, "Our father is old, and there is no man around here to lie with us, as is the custom all over the earth. Let's get our father to drink wine and then lie with him and preserve our family line through our father."

That night they got their father to drink wine, and the older daughter went in and lay with him. He was not aware of it when she lay down or when she got up.

The next day the older daughter said to the younger, "Last night I lay with my father. Let's get him to drink wine again tonight, and you go in and lie with him so we can preserve our family line through our father." So

they got their father to drink wine that night also, and
the younger daughter went and lay with him. Again he
was not aware of it when she lay down or when she got
up.

So both of Lot's daughters became pregnant by their
father. The older daughter had a son, and she named
him Moab; he is the father of the Moabites of today.
The younger daughter also had a son, and she named
him Ben-Ammi; he is the father of the Ammonites of
today.[139]

How a book that promotes this bizarre story can be held as a moral
guide is grotesque, and how this specific story can be used to condemn
gays and lesbians defies imagination. The religionists' claim that this
sacred text makes them "moral" is incredible. What is the "moral"
lesson of offering innocent children to be raped in the name of
hospitality to strangers? The story would have much more authority if
Lot had announced that no one in his house would be raped. What
lesson does this story teach about the value of women and children?
Apparently they have less value than male strangers. What kind of a
deity kills all inhabitants of a city, including animals and children?
Were newborn children sinners too? Why would the deity destroy the
vegetation if he was angry with the humans? Christians' claim that this
text makes them moral or justifies their discrimination against gays and
lesbians is appalling.

Horror stories like Sodom and Gomorrah are not isolated in the
Bible. Another story involves a crowd accepting the offer of a substitute
for rape. The poor woman survives the sexual assault, only to be
murdered by her boyfriend (a holy man)[140] and cut into pieces! Once
again, I am not making this up. Here is the text from the Bible:

While they were enjoying themselves, some of the
wicked men of the city surrounded the house. Pounding

on the door, they shouted to the old man who owned the house, "Bring out the man who came to your house so we can have sex with him."

The owner of the house went outside and said to them, "No, my friends, don't be so vile. Since this man is my guest, don't do this disgraceful thing. Look, here is my virgin daughter, and his concubine. I will bring them out to you now, and you can use them and do to them whatever you wish. But to this man, don't do such a disgraceful thing."

But the men would not listen to him. So the man took his concubine and sent her outside to them, and they raped her and abused her throughout the night, and at dawn they let her go. At daybreak the woman went back to the house where her master was staying, fell down at the door and lay there until daylight.

When her master got up in the morning and opened the door of the house and stepped out to continue on his way, there lay his concubine, fallen in the doorway of the house, with her hands on the threshold. He said to her, "Get up; let's go." But there was no answer. Then the man put her on his donkey and set out for home.

When he reached home, he took a knife and cut up his concubine, limb by limb, into twelve parts and sent them into all the areas of Israel.[141]

The apparent "moral" lesson of this story appears to be, if you force your girlfriend to get raped in your stead, you should murder her. Once again, that a book containing these brutal tales can be called a moral guide is beyond belief.

Expected to sin.

Looking beyond the absurdities of the Bible, there is no logic behind Christians' claims of moral superiority. Christian doctrine expects people to act immorally–to sin. But church doctrine forgives them for their sinful conduct. For example, Catholics can confess their sins to a priest and be dispensed a magical incantation that removes the violation. The Catholic Encyclopedia reads, "Penance is a sacrament of the New Law instituted by Christ in which forgiveness of sins committed after baptism is granted through the priest's absolution to those who with true sorrow confess their sins and promise to satisfy for the same."[142]

In fact, a Christian can live his whole life in "sin" and by speaking some magic words, achieve forgiveness. In the Jesus story, a criminal who was sentenced to death along with Jesus acknowledged his guilt. But he spoke kindly to Jesus, and Jesus told the criminal that he would join Jesus that day in paradise.[143] No muss, no fuss, just instant forgiveness. Christians are faced with being brother to notorious serial killer and cannibal Jeffrey Dahmer, who "found god" and was baptized before his murder in prison.[144] The preacher who baptized Dahmer declares him forgiven,[145] saying, "God forgives all sins, God does not consider one sin greater than the other."[146]

So, Christians are expected to sin and can get forgiveness by saying magical words. But an even bigger flaw in their claim of moral superiority is that the god they supposedly answer to is imaginary. There is no enforcer of their moral code. There is no heaven, there is no hell, there is no man in the sky who sees what they do and punishes them.

Perhaps children believe in the sky god's power for a while, but a little scientific experimentation with his "powers" quickly proves the myth false. A cute story is of a child who experiments "taking the lord's name in vain," violating one of the infamous Christian ten commandments,[147] but suffering no supernatural consequences. Sickening stories of adults who know there is no moral enforcer are found in countless newspaper accounts of "holy" people who abuse children.[148] The acts are different, but the result is the same, the religionist quickly establishes there is no bearded man in the sky enforcing the rules.

Contrast that to the position of an atheist like me. I carry my moral code in my head. I do not expect myself to violate the code and I do not forgive myself for violations. My conduct will be unaffected if the bearded man myth is incontrovertibly refuted, or if the myth continues unabated. In chart form, a comparison of the morality of an atheist and a Christian creates a "morality matrix" that looks like this:

	Christian	Atheist
Expected to sin	Yes	No
Forgiven for sins	Yes	No
Enforcement of Code	No, there is no god	Yes, enforced by self

Morality in action.

All the talk in the world can be refuted by a few facts. A 2005 study published in the Journal of Religion and Society looked at the religiosity and various measures of moral health of first world nations. It concluded:

> In general, higher rates of belief in and worship of a creator correlate with higher rates of homicide, juvenile and early adult mortality, STD infection rates, teen pregnancy, and abortion in the prosperous democracies. The most theistic prosperous democracy, the U.S., is exceptional, but not in the manner Franklin predicted. The United States is almost always the most dysfunctional of the developed democracies, sometimes

spectacularly so, and almost always scores poorly. The view of the U.S. as a "shining city on the hill" to the rest of the world is falsified when it comes to basic measures of societal health. . . . No democracy is known to have combined strong religiosity and popular denial of evolution with high rates of societal health. Higher rates of non-theism and acceptance of human evolution usually correlate with lower rates of dysfunction, and the least theistic nations are usually the least dysfunctional. None of the strongly secularized, pro-evolution democracies is experiencing high levels of measurable dysfunction.[149]

Another way of looking at it, a 2009 report rated the world's happiest countries as Denmark, Finland and the Netherlands.[150] The same countries are among the least religious and have the lowest crime rates in the world.

Divorce.

The pro-religionist Barna Research Group conducted a survey in 1999 and found that Christians have a higher divorce rate than atheists. The survey showed the following results:

Religion	% divorced
Jews	30%
Born-again Christians	27%
Other Christians	24%
Atheists, agnostics	21%

George Barna commented, "While it may be alarming to discover that born again Christians are more likely than others to experience a divorce, that pattern has been in place for quite some time. . . . [T]he research also raises questions regarding the effectiveness of how churches minister to families. The ultimate responsibility for a marriage belongs to the husband and wife, but the high incidence of divorce within the Christian community challenges the idea that churches provide truly practical and life-changing support for marriages."[151] The 1999 Barna survey is no longer available on the group's Website, but Ontario-based Religious Tolerance.org provides a summary of the results on theirs.[152] Barna was roundly criticized by the Christian community for his 1999 survey. So he did another one in 2008.

Barna, a pastor, and his business serve the Christian community.[153] If anyone had a horse in the race, it was Mr. Barna. Nonetheless, his second study found no statistically significant difference in the divorce rate of the general population and born again Christians. Atheists would have had the lowest divorce rate, however, Barna created a small Christian subgroup he labeled "Evangelical Christians" for whom he reported a divorce rate of 26%, the lowest in the 2008 survey, but still way above the 21% rate for atheists found in the 1999 survey.[154]

Crime.

Although Christians would likely argue that divorce rates are related to "morality" or being good, atheists likely would not. Morals and ethics are amorphous concepts difficult to measure.[155] However, crime rates are not. Crime rates measure both a "moral" violation as well as a violation of the social contract called law. The following chart looks at the rates[156] of crime in the three most religious and least religious states:[157]

State	% who say religion important	Violent Crime	Murder	Forcible Rape	Robbery	Burglary
Mississippi	85%	284.9	8.1	30.3	102.6	885.6
Alabama	82%	452.8	7.6	34.7	157.6	1081.3
South Carolina	80%	729.7	6.8	36.6	147.3	1026.1
National Average	**65%**	**454.5**	**5.4**	**29.3**	**145.3**	**730.8**
Vermont	42%	135.9	2.7	20.4	14.3	557.2
New Hampshire	46%	157.2	1.0	29.7	31.8	325.7
Maine	48%	117.5	2.4	28.5	25.3	495.4

There is no overlap, the crime rate is higher--often significantly higher--in each category in the most religious states.

Prison.

A telling statistic is that in January 2010, only .08% of the federal inmate population was atheist.[158] Using the Pew 2008 statistic of 1.6% of the U.S. population being atheist,[159] this means the federal prisons have 1/20th the expected number of atheists. Now of course, this alone does not mean atheists are more law abiding than religionists. It could mean that atheists do not get caught as much, or it could mean that atheists think parole boards like religionists, so they say they are religious. But, nonetheless, the fact stands that atheists appear in federal prison at 1/20th of the rate one would expect from their presence in the general population. This statistic must really irritate religionists like Indiana Governor Mitch Daniels, quoted at the start of this chapter, whose assertion that atheists are evil should be supported by a disproportionate number of atheists in prison.

Godless communists.

Religionists frequently say, "Stalin, Mao, and godless communists" to justify their position you need god to be good. The quick reply is "Hitler, Hirohito, Franco, Ahmadinejad," all despised religionists. A more thoughtful reply is to quote Nobel Laureate Steven Weinberg, "Religion is an insult to human dignity. With or without it you would have good people doing good things and evil people doing evil things. But for good people to do evil things, that takes religion."[160] But an even deeper answer involves the shared psychological profile of religious and totalitarian followers. The same "right-wing authoritarian follower" psychological profile of the ultra-religious applies equally to the party loyalists in communist countries. That is right, the communist party loyalists the religionists attack exhibit the same traits as the religionists themselves. The distinction is that religionists follow a religious authority while communists follow a political authority. The crowd yelling "godless communist" is ironically vilifying the segment of the population most like them.

A question that should not be answered.

Asking whether people can be good without religion is as crazy as asking if a slave can be good without his master. Both questions are offensive and reflect a mind-set that has been in place for too long and questioned too little. If anything, atheists are more "moral" than religionists. Entertaining the question "can a person be good without religion" is letting religionists set the agenda. It is time that we stop dancing to their tune.

SECTION II.

Problems with religion, small and large.

Chapter 8. Mormonism: religion is the strangest fiction.

And the angel said unto me, behold, these shall dwindle in unbelief. And it came to pass that I beheld that after they had dwindled in unbelief, they became a dark, and loathsome, and a filthy people, full of idleness and all manner of abominations.[161] The Book of Mormon

We are called the State Legislature [of Utah], but when the time comes, we shall be called the Kingdom of God. Our government is going to pieces, and it will be like water that is split upon the ground that cannot be gathered. For the time will come when we will give laws to the nations of the earth. Joseph Smith organized this government before, in Nauvoo, and he said if we did our duty, we shall prevail over all our enemies.[162] Second Mormon President Brigham Young

    To me, all religions are equal–equally wrong. The tenets of one are no more or less ridiculous than those of another. But I have elected to look at Mormonism before the "people of the book" (Jews, Christians and Muslims), for a specific reason. I am hoping to influence you, the reader. First, Mormons compose only about 1.7% of the population,[163] therefore, chances are slim that you are a Mormon. Second, Mormonism was created recently, around 1830, so the historical record of the creator and its early tenets are not yet lost. Finally, Mormonism has many unusual features that the average reader will likely find easy to reject.

    I am presenting Mormonism first in hopes that you will critically analyze the tenets of this religion, and once in the habit of doing so, apply the same critical skills to more popular religions, including your own, if you have one.

61

As a preliminary matter, "Mormon" is a nickname, disfavored by many followers of "The Church of Jesus Christ of Latter-day Saints."[164] In fact, many of them refer to themselves as "Saints," and to nonbelievers as "Gentiles" (since Mormons think they are grafted onto the tribes of Israel). However, the term "Mormon" is in the title of their scripture, the Book of Mormon, first published by founder Joseph Smith in 1830. In fact, the original edition refers to Joseph Smith as the "author and proprietor."[165] And "Mormon" is the name by which they are best known, so I will use that term here.

Joseph Smith was born in 1805 and grew up in the area of Palmyra, New York–a town located between Rochester and Syracuse, about 95 miles east of Buffalo. He alleged that in 1820, when he was 14 years old, he was visited by a spirit, in some versions of the story, god and Jesus; who told him not to attend any of the many churches or revivals that were popular at that time. There is no record of him telling this story until 1832.[166] The story has gone through a number of versions through the years.

Smith spent his early years as a "money digger," a con man who charged a fee to "help" people find buried treasure. He used a "seer stone" he had found digging a well to lead him to the buried treasure, which would supernaturally slip away before the diggers could retrieve it.

Smith was first charged with a crime in 1826 for being a "disorderly person and an imposter," in conjunction with his search for a lost silver mine. In court, he acknowledged that he used a stone to find buried treasures. Although he was convicted of a misdemeanor,[167] the court allowed Smith to leave town with no further punishment.[168]

Around the same time, Smith began telling his friends that he knew of a "golden book," buried in the ground that would help him to find other buried treasure. In many of the early stories, Smith used his seer stone to find the golden plates on which the Book of Mormon was purportedly written. But later a story emerged of a "second vision." In that vision, which supposedly occurred in 1823, Smith said an angel named Moroni (or Nephi) visited him and told him god wanted him to translate a book of golden plates that contained the pure doctrines of Christianity. Smith related that as he heard this, he could see where the plates were buried, conveniently only about a mile from his home. He said he visited the place yearly, and in 1827 an angel allowed Smith to retrieve the golden plates.[169]

No one but Smith reported seeing the plates, and when he was done translating them, he said he put them in a cave filled with treasure. The plates were written in "Reformed Egyptian." Smith sent a paper copy, labeled "Caractors" (characters), to a professor of Greek and Latin at Colombia College in hopes of having his claim verified. The professor was not impressed, labeling the inscription a meaningless batch of crooked characters including "Greek and Hebrew letters, crosses, and flourishes, Roman letters inverted or placed sideways."[170] Nonetheless, Smith said the professor pronounced the characters authentic, something the professor refuted by saying, "the whole story of my having pronouncd [sic] the Mormonite inscription to be 'reformed Egyptian Hieroglyphics' is *perfectly false* . . . [T]he paper contained anything else but 'Egyptian Hieroglyphics.'"[171]

The golden plates, allegedly measuring six inches by eight inches, and six inches thick,[172] must have included a lot of text, because Smith spent more than a year creating a 588-page[173] story. Key to the story was that the tribes of Israel had migrated to North America between 2,200 BCE[174] and 421 CE. They created a complex and thriving society with massive cities, but conflict erupted and eventually the tribes became the modern day Native Americans. The tribes allegedly used numerous metal instruments, including iron, steel, brass, copper, silver and gold, as well as having swords, coins, wheels, elephants, asses, oxen, cows, horses, and clothes of silk and linen.[175] One of the punishments for a group god disfavored was dark skin, which was "loathsome" and unattractive to the favored, light-skinned group that was "white, and exceedingly fair and delightsome."[176] Smith's book also included language copied exactly from the 1611 King James Bible, a book written a thousand years after the alleged creation of the golden plates. One commentator noted that Smith, who was not too familiar with Elizabethan English, "continually slipped out of this King James pattern and repeatedly confused the norms as well."[177]

Modern English was also a weakness for Smith. Sentences in his 1830 Book of Mormon include:[178]

[T]hey did not fight against God no more.
[I] have not sought gold nor silver, nor no manner of riches of you.
[A]nd also of Adam and Eve, which was our first parents.
[B]oth Alma and Helam was buried in the water.
[T]hey was angry with me.

An interesting twist is that Smith wrote 116 pages, which his scribe, Mr. Harris then took home to show Mrs. Harris. Mrs. Harris, angry that her husband was being duped, hid or burned the pages.[179] Smith, apparently afraid the missing pages would later be used to show he was not translating but was rather creating the book, refused to "retranslate" the missing pages, saying in the preface to the Book of Mormon that satan had changed the words once they left his possession and that god told him not to retranslate the lost section, but to simply summarize it.[180]

Stylistically, the Book of Mormon was poorly written. Anyone who wishes to question Mormonism needs only pick up the Book of Mormon and read it to conclude it is patently ridiculous. But do not take my word for it, judge for yourself. Here is how it starts:

I, NEPHI, having been born of goodly parents, therefore
I was taught somewhat in all the learning of my father;
and having seen many afflictions in the course of my
days--nevertheless, having been highly favored of the
Lord in all my days; yea, having had a great knowledge
of the goodness and the mysteries of God, therefore I
make a record of my proceedings in my days; yea, I
make a record in the language of my father, which

consists of the learning of the Jews and the language of the Egyptians. And I know that the record which I make, to be true; and I make it with mine own hand; and I make it according to my knowledge.

For it came to pass, in the commencement of the first year of the reign of Zedekiah, king of Judah, (my father Lehi having dwelt at Jerusalem in all his days;) and in that same year there came many prophets, prophesying unto the people, that they must repent, or the great city Jerusalem must be destroyed. Wherefore it came to pass, that my father Lehi, as he went forth, prayed unto the Lord, yea, even with all his heart, in behalf of his people.

And it came to pass, as he prayed unto the Lord, there came a pillar of fire and dwelt upon a rock before him; and he saw and heard much; and because of the things which he saw and heard, he did quake and tremble exceedingly.

And it came to pass that he returned to his own house at Jerusalem; and he cast himself upon his bed, being overcome with the spirit and the things which he had seen; and being thus overcome with the spirit, he was carried away in a vision, even that he saw the Heavens open; and he thought he saw God sitting upon his throne, surrounded with numberless concourses of angels in the attitude of singing and praising their God.[181]

The term, "it came to pass" appears about 2,000 times in the original Book of Mormon, it has been edited to fewer in later editions.

Mark Twain called the Book of Mormon "chloroform in print" and further commented:

> The book seems to be merely a prosy detail of imaginary history, with the Old Testament for a model; followed by a tedious plagiarism of the New Testament. The author labored to give his words and phrases the quaint, old-fashioned sound and structure of our King James's translation of the Scriptures; and the result is a mongrel--half modern glibness, and half ancient simplicity and gravity. The latter is awkward and constrained; the former natural, but grotesque by the contrast. Whenever he found his speech growing too modern--which was about every sentence or two--he ladled in a few such Scriptural phrases as "exceeding sore," "and it came to pass," etc., and made things satisfactory again. "And it came to pass" was his pet. If he had left that out, his Bible would have been only a pamphlet.[182]

After publishing his book, Smith formed a church, which he and his followers moved from New York to Ohio in 1831. Smith began preaching the doctrine of "millenialism," that the United States government would fall apart, Jesus would return, and Mormons would eventually take over the world. That doctrine continues today, for example one-time presidential candidate Orrin Hatch spoke in 1999 of "the transformation of the U.S. government into a Mormon-ruled theocracy divinely ordained to 'not only direct the political affairs of the Mormon community, but eventually those of the United States and ultimately the world.'"[183] Smith also began taking multiple wives. Facing money troubles, Smith opened the "Kirtland Safety Society Anti-Bank," that issued money. One month after opening, its "currency" was worth 12.5 cents on the dollar and Smith was convicted of violating state bank laws and fined $1,000 plus costs.[184]

In 1838, Smith moved to Caldwell County Missouri and joined a thriving Mormon settlement. On the banks of the Grand River, he declared that a rock outcropping was an altar built by Adam, the first man, after he and Eve fled from the Garden of Eden, which Smith declared was located near Independence, Missouri.[185]

The Mormon's situation in Missouri deteriorated into armed conflict with non-Mormons and the state militia. Several battles occurred, and eventually troops confronted Smith and his followers. Smith surrendered and was jailed. He faced charges of murder, arson, robbery and treason. After about six months in jail, Smith bribed his jailer with $800 and a jug of whiskey and escaped. He left Missouri and moved to Illinois.[186]

In Illinois, Smith formed an army of 4,000 soldiers, about one-half the number in the entire U.S. military. He set himself up as a military leader and even initiated a run for the U.S. Presidency. He declared himself, "King over the immediate house of Israel." Smith married an additional eleven wives in 1842 and seventeen in 1843, resulting in at least 33 marriages, but perhaps as many as 48. Smith was subject to numerous arrest warrants, including one that alleged he attempted to arrange the assassination of the ex-governor of Missouri who was wounded by an un-apprehended attacker.[187]

Public sentiment built against Smith and the Mormons. Angered by critical articles in a newspaper, Smith ordered the newspaper office destroyed. Fleeing arrest, Smith escaped to Iowa, but then returned to face trial. While in jail, a mob attacked and killed Smith on June 27, 1844.[188]

After Smith's death, Brigham Young emerged as leader, and facing arrest himself, moved the Mormons to Utah. The Mormons have since grown to the richest religion, per capita, in the United States.[189] Mormons altered their dogma to prohibit polygamy around 1890 and started allowing Black people to hold office within the church in 1978.[190] Mormons have converted themselves from a despised minority to one with wide acceptance. A 2007 survey found that 27% of Americans had an unfavorable view of Mormons, compared to 53%

who had an unfavorable view of atheists.[191] Considering how far-out the Mormon doctrine is, it is surprising there are more self-declared Mormons in the United States than atheists.[192]

Looking critically at Mormon doctrine, choosing a convicted criminal like Joseph Smith as a prophet seems inconsistent with the actions of an all-knowing god. Additionally, Smith was a bad choice as a translator, as his English skills were limited and he needed to use other people as scribes. An outsider looking at this religion will likely conclude that Smith was not succeeding as a treasure hunter and decided to try a new con--religion.

The Mormon scriptures suffer from the same flaw as all religious scriptures, they were written by men and are fixed in time. When Smith wrote the Book of Mormon, the fields of anthropology and archeology were limited and DNA was undiscovered. Popular books of his time theorized that Native Americans were the descendants of tribes that migrated from Israel and the tales in the Book of Mormon could not be scientifically debunked. Slavery was still legal in the Southern States and prejudice against dark-skinned people prevailed. Smith wrote a book that reflected his time.

Smith embellished the stories about the "tribes of Israel" in America with great detail. He said they had animals such as elephants, donkeys, cows and horses. They wore clothes of silk and linen. They used metals including iron, copper, brass, steel, gold and silver. They had great battles where two million warriors were killed at a time. They had coins made of silver and gold with values assigned to each. They had barley, figs, grapes and wheat. These stories may have been accepted in 1830, but in modern times, archeology and anthropology have demonstrated there were no donkeys or cows in America before the Europeans came, steel and most metals are absent from American archeological digs, no massive grave sites where two million warriors (plus their plural wives and children) died have been found, and no ancient metal coins have been located. Neither has evidence been found that Adam and Eve lived near Independence Missouri, nor that Adam built an altar on the Grand River in Missouri. In addition, there is no explanation of why the tribes of Israel would write their story in "Reformed Egyptian."

Additionally, DNA testing demonstrates that Native Americans did not come from Israel 1,500 to 4,400 years ago. In fact they came from Asia thousands of years earlier.[193] The highly reputable Smithsonian Institute in Washington, D.C. was regularly plagued by Mormon-sourced rumors it used the Book of Mormon as a research document. The Smithsonian issued this statement in 1988:

Statement Regarding the Book of Mormon

1. The Smithsonian Institution has never used the Book of Mormon in any way as a scientific guide. Smithsonian archeologists see no direct connection between the archeology of the New World and the subject matter of the book.

2. The physical type of the American Indian is basically Mongoloid, being most closely related to that of the peoples of eastern, central, and northeastern Asia. Archeological evidence indicates that the ancestors of the present Indians came into the New World--probably over a land bridge known to have existed in the Bering Strait region during the last Ice Age--in a continuing series of small migrations beginning from about 25,000 to 30,000 years ago.

3. Present evidence indicates that the first people to reach this continent from the East were the Norsemen who briefly visited the northeastern part of North America around A.D. 1000 and then settled in Greenland. There is nothing to show that they reached Mexico or Central America.

4. One of the main lines of evidence supporting the scientific finding that contacts with Old World civilizations, if indeed they occurred at all, were of very little significance for the development of American Indian civilizations, is the fact that none of the principal Old World domesticated food plants or animals (except the dog) occurred in the New World in pre-Columbian times. American Indians had no wheat, barley, oats, millet, rice, cattle, pigs, chickens, horses, donkeys, camels before 1492. (Camels and horses were in the Americas, along with the bison, mammoth, and mastodon, but all these animals became extinct around 10,000 B.C. at the time when the early big game hunters spread across the Americas.)

5. Iron, steel, glass, and silk were not used in the New World before 1492 (except for occasional use of unsmelted meteoric iron). Native copper was worked in various locations in pre-Columbian times, but true metallurgy was limited to southern Mexico and the Andean region, where its occurrence in late prehistoric times involved gold, silver, copper, and their alloys, but not iron.

6. There is a possibility that the spread of cultural traits across the Pacific to Mesoamerica and the northwestern coast of South America began several hundred years before the Christian era. However, any such inter-hemispheric contacts appear to have been the results of accidental voyages originating in eastern and southern Asia. It is by no means certain that even such contacts occurred; certainly there were no contacts with the ancient Egyptians, Hebrews, or other peoples of Western Asia and the Near East.

7. No reputable Egyptologist or other specialist on Old World archeology, and no expert on New World prehistory, has discovered or confirmed any relationship between archeological remains in Mexico and archeological remains in Egypt.

8. Reports of findings of ancient Egyptian, Hebrew, and other Old World writings in the New World in pre-Columbian contexts have frequently appeared in newspapers, magazines, and sensational books. None of these claims has stood up to examination by reputable scholars. No inscriptions using Old World forms of writing have been shown to have occurred in any part of the Americas before 1492 except for a few Norse rune stones which have been found in Greenland.[194]

The story of the "Kinderhook plates" provides a final insight about Mormonism. In 1843, two farmers buried some bell-shaped metal plates with characters on them and contrived to "find" them with a Mormon present. The Mormon newspaper in Nauvoo promptly concluded the plates contributed to the authenticity of the Book of Mormon and Joseph Smith's secretary recorded, "I have seen 6 brass plates which were found in Adams County. . . . President Joseph has translated a portion and says they contain the history of the person with whom they were found & he was a descendant of Ham through the loins of Pharaoh king of Egypt, and that he received his kingdom from the ruler of heaven & earth."[195] The perpetrators of the hoax later admitted it. In 1879, a participant wrote, "We read in Pratt's prophecy that 'Truth is yet to spring out of the earth.' We concluded to prove the prophecy by way of a joke. We soon made our plans and executed them. Bridge Whitton cut them out of some pieces of copper; Wiley and I made the hieroglyphics by making impressions on beeswax and filling them with acid and putting it on the plates. When they were finished we put them together with rust made of nitric acid, old iron and lead, and bound them with a piece of hoop iron, covering them completely with the rust."

However, the Mormons continued to profess the plates were real until a 1980 chemical analysis scientifically demonstrated the plates were from the 1800's, not ancient.[196] As Mormon apostate and author Charles Shook said, "Only a bogus prophet translates bogus plates."[197] Smith had also "translated" some authentic Egyptian funeral texts and claimed they were written by Abraham and supported the Mormon story. Later professional translations demonstrated Smith's translation to be fiction.[198]

Unless you were raised Mormon, you will likely say, "Mormonism is ridiculous, how could anyone believe it?" As someone raised without religion, that is exactly the way I feel about all religions. In the upcoming chapters I will discuss problems small and large with the three major monotheisms, the "people of the book," Jews, Christians and Muslims. If you were raised in any of these traditions, I challenge you to maintain the skepticism you feel toward Mormonism when you look at your religion.

Chapter 9. The people of the book.

If the People of the Book accept the true faith and keep from evil, We will pardon them their sins and admit them to the gardens of delight. If they observe the Torah and the Gospel and what is revealed to them from Allah, they shall be given abundance from above and from beneath.[199] The Koran

When I speak of religion in this book, I am generally referring to the three most influential religions in the United States: Judaism, Christianity and Islam. More than half the people in the world belong to these religions, 33% of the world population is Christian, 20% is Muslim, and .23% is Jewish.[200] Within the United States, Christians are the majority, at 78.4% of the population, Jews are 1.7% and Muslims are .6%.[201] However, Judaism and Islam have impact beyond the number of adherents; Judaism, because it is the original monotheism upon which Christianity and Islam are based; and Islam, because its predatory dogma has impacted the lives of almost every American. Looking solely at the religiously motivated 9/11 attacks and the wars the United States has mounted in response, Islam has had wider impact than the small number of adherents living in the U.S. would seem to indicate.

Most Americans are aware of the close relationship between Judaism and Christianity. The Jewish scriptures form the first half of the Christian Bible, the "Old Testament." The Jewish and Christian creation myths are identical. The stories of Adam and Eve, Abraham, Moses and Noah are the same. However, fewer are aware that Islam traces its roots to the same characters.

As the quote at the start of this chapter shows, Muslims somewhat approvingly refer to Jews and Christians as "people of the

73

book." The Muslim religion is the most recent of the three, created around 622 CE,[202] and just like Mormonism described in Chapter 8, it freely borrowed from Judaism and Christianity in its formation.

All of the "people of the book" (Jews, Christians and Muslims) believe that Adam and Eve were the first people. All three religions trace their lineage through Abraham and believe that their god reached a covenant with him. All three believe Moses was a prophet. All three believe there was a great flood and that Noah preserved life on an Ark.

All three religions arose in the same general area of the Middle East. Even the names of their god sound similar in their source languages, "Eloah" in Hebrew,[203] "Elaha" in Aramaic, and "Allah" in Arabic.[204] Jews, Christians and Muslims are all the children of Abraham. Perhaps the horrible way that Christians and Muslims have treated their parent religion makes people think they are unrelated. But this is not unheard of, certainly in life you have come across a child who was horrible to his parent.

Other similarities abound. Jews, Muslims and Christians believe in one, superior god, who excludes all others. They are collectively known as the three "great" monotheisms. They all believe the bearded man in the sky communicates with them and they all think they exclusively worship the correct bearded man. Similarly, each group believes communication with the bearded man is a two-way affair. "Proper" belief and conduct in each religion will lead to "salvation" and everlasting life.

Each has in the past blended the roles of church and state. Each religious group wants political leaders who belong to the same religion as the voters. Each has used military power to enforce or expand its authority.

They maintain similar rituals. Although Jews and Muslims despise one another, they mark their male children as separate with ritual circumcision. Circumcision is also practiced by a large number of American Christians.

Each group has prohibited food groups. Muslims are prohibited from eating pork, Jews avoid shellfish, and Catholics do not eat red meat on Fridays. Each group has previously allowed polygamy (and many Muslims still do) and animal sacrifice.

Each group has engaged in horrible hostility to people who hold other beliefs. Further, followers of each religion believe their religion entitles them to act outside of the law for religious purposes. For example, they feel religiously entitled to enter other countries to assassinate perceived enemies (Jews), to kill abortion providers (Christians), and to shoot and bomb businesses such as a hotel in Mumbai or the World Trade Center in New York (Muslims, more on this in Chapter 21).

Each group worships in a special house, labeled synagogue, church or mosque; and each has a seven-day worship cycle with a special day of worship: Friday (Muslims) Saturday (Jews) or Sunday (Christians). Similarly, they have special people, usually men, who interpret the scriptures for them: "rabbis" for Jews, "imams" for Muslims, and "priests, pastors or ministers" for Christians. Each religion considers Jerusalem a holy site. Each group believes in resurrection of the bodies of believers and destruction of the physical world. They all believe in heaven and the existence of angels and demons.

All three worship essentially the same god, they just disagree on the details of whether that god sent a messiah. Jews believe the messiah has not yet come, Christians believe he has, and Muslims believe that although Mohammed was a prophet, the messiah is yet to come. Regarding Jesus specifically, Muslims believe Jesus was a prophet, sent by Allah and they even buy into the tale of the virgin birth.[205] Jews believe Jesus was a man.

And horribly, each believes in the "end times," a time when their bearded man's male representative will come to earth to reward the believers and punish the nonbelievers. All three believe the "end times" will be announced by a trumpet, their prophet will appear, life on earth will be destroyed, and the believers will be rewarded in heaven or paradise. A great danger of religion is that believers will act, including using nuclear weapons, to accelerate the arrival of these "end times."

Finally, the "people of the book" not surprisingly rely on a holy book, a scripture they allege was at least inspired (if not dictated) by their god. The next chapter introduces a phrase I will use throughout this book, "the scriptures, written by men and fixed in time."

Chapter 10. The scriptures–written by men and fixed in time.

There's no surer way to make an atheist than to get someone to actually read scripture.[206] PZ Myers

The Christian's Bible is a drug-store. Its contents remain the same; but the medical practice changes. . . . During many ages there were witches. The Bible said so. The Bible commanded that they should not be allowed to live. Therefore the Church . . . gathered up its halters, thumbscrews, and firebrands, and set about its holy work in earnest. She worked hard at it night and day during nine centuries and imprisoned, tortured, hanged and burned whole hordes and armies of witches, and washed the Christian world clean with their foul blood. Then it was discovered that there was no such thing as witches, and never had been. One does not know whether to laugh or to cry. . . . There are no witches. The witch-text remains; only the practice has changed. Hell-fire is gone, but the text remains. Infant damnation is gone, but the text remains. More than two hundred death penalties are gone from the law books, but the texts that authorized them remain. Is it not well worthy of note that of all the multitude of texts through which man has driven his annihilating pen he has never once made the mistake of obliterating a good and useful one?[207] Mark Twain

Changes in my lifetime.

Although I have lived only a short time, the world has changed enormously. When I was born, a dark-skinned man would have drunk at a "coloreds only" water fountain in some states, now a dark-skinned man, Barack Obama, is the President of the United States.

During my lifetime, laws limiting access to birth control were overturned and birth control changed from a crime to a right. Similarly, homosexuality has gone from being a crime and a disease, to a valid alternative lifestyle, with gays and lesbians having the right to marry in five states and the District of Colombia.

The role of women has changed in my lifetime. I remember it was odd to see women driving trucks or working in certain jobs. Now women are entering leadership roles in all areas of life.

Doctors have gone from promoting cigarettes to condemning them. An old ad used to read:

> According to a recent nationwide survey, more doctors smoke Camels than any other cigarette! Family physicians, surgeons, diagnosticians, nose and throat specialists, doctors in every branch of medicine, a total of 113,597 doctors, were asked the question: 'What cigarette do you smoke?' And more of them named Camel as their smoke than any other cigarette! Three independent research groups found this to be a fact. You see, doctors too smoke for pleasure. That full Camel flavor is just as appealing to a doctor's taste as to yours, that marvelous Camel mildness means just as much to his throat as to yours.[208]

Carbon-dating methods now allow scientists to estimate with great accuracy the age of man-made artifacts. Genetic testing has proved the innocence of hundreds of people wrongfully convicted of crimes, and shown links between the tribes of man.

Telephones have gone from being rotary dialed boxes to mobile devices. Computers have shrunk from room-sized to pocket sized. The Internet has developed into a significant source of information and socialization.

When we look back at movies from 50 years ago, they seem quaint and antiquated. Many of the morals, values and ideas of 50 years ago are out of place today.

78

The same factor is multiplied when the time period is not fifty years, but thousands of years. The Torah, Bible and Koran are products of their times. Each was written by men and is fixed in time. The scriptures reflect the knowledge and values of their authors, and when they are used for modern guidance they act sort of like a time machine, inappropriately dragging outdated knowledge and values into the modern world.

The scriptures, written by men and fixed in time.

The scriptures that define the "people of the book" were written by men and remain fixed in time. For example, if two thousand years ago, the Bible recorded facts not then known, there might be reason for inquiry into whether it contains some otherworldly knowledge. But in fact, two thousand years ago people believed the sun rotated around the earth and the men who wrote the Bible recorded the belief of their time.[209] Other stories demonstrate that the Bible's authors thought the earth is flat like a pancake.[210] When the scriptures were written, there were no airplanes, no spaceships and no meteorologists. Flying was the stuff of legend, reserved for characters like Mohammed and his winged horse.[211] Clouds looked fairly solid from the ground and the bearded man lived somewhere above them. The Bible says a tall ladder could reach heaven,[212] and god "sits enthroned above the circle[213] of the earth, and its people are like grasshoppers. He stretches out the heavens like a canopy, and spreads them out like a tent to live in."[214] Just as one would expect from a book written by men, the earth was perceived as the center of the universe with the sun circling it. God lived in the sky above the earth. Very few Americans act as if the earth is the center of the universe or that god lives above the clouds, yet almost three quarters of them follow a book written by men who thought that way.

Similarly, in accordance with the knowledge and values of men at the time it was written, the Bible endorses slavery. The Bible says:

> Your male and female slaves are to come from the
> nations around you; from them you may buy slaves.

You may also buy some of the temporary residents living among you and members of their clans born in your country, and they will become your property. You can will them to your children as inherited property and can make them slaves for life, but you must not rule over your fellow Israelites ruthlessly.[215]

* * *

If a man sells his daughter as a servant, she is not to go free as menservants do. If she does not please the master who has selected her for himself, he must let her be redeemed. He has no right to sell her to foreigners, because he has broken faith with her. If he selects her for his son, he must grant her the rights of a daughter. If he marries another woman, he must not deprive the first one of her food, clothing and marital rights. If he does not provide her with these three things, she is to go free, without any payment of money.[216]

* * *

If a man beats his male or female slave with a rod and the slave dies as a direct result, he must be punished, but he is not to be punished if the slave gets up after a day or two, since the slave is his property.[217]

The biblical endorsement of slavery is not only found in the Old Testament. It continues in the New Testament:

All who are under the yoke of slavery should consider their masters worthy of full respect, so that God's name and our teaching may not be slandered. Those who have believing masters are not to show less respect for them because they are brothers. Instead, they are to serve them even better, because those who benefit from their service are believers, and dear to them. These are the things you are to teach and urge on them.[218]

Perhaps progressive when written, the Bible verses about slavery are abhorrent today. The Koran similarly endorses slavery.[219] Slavery is now universally condemned. Religionists would like to ignore the endorsement of slavery in their scriptures, however, it remains there, a product of the men who wrote the book and the beliefs of their times.

The Bible also endorses human and animal sacrifice. Many people are familiar with the story of Abraham and his son, found in Genesis 22:1-18. In that story, god supposedly told Abraham to, "take your son, your only son, Isaac, whom you love, and go to the region of Moriah. Sacrifice him there as a burnt offering on one of the mountains I will tell you about."[220] At the last minute, the story goes, god let Abraham off the hook and let him burn a ram instead of his son.

But not all human sacrifice stories in the Bible end up with cooked animals. In the story of Jephthah, in a trade for a victory in battle, the "hero" agrees to sacrifice the first thing that comes out of his house on his return. In this case, it is his only child, whom he grants a reprieve of two months before making the human sacrifice:

Then the Spirit of the LORD came upon Jephthah. He crossed Gilead and Manasseh, passed through Mizpah of Gilead, and from there he advanced against the Ammonites. And Jephthah made a vow to the LORD: "If you give the Ammonites into my hands, whatever comes out of the door of my house to meet me when I return in triumph from the Ammonites will be the LORD's, and I will sacrifice it as a burnt offering."

Then Jephthah went over to fight the Ammonites, and the LORD gave them into his hands. He devastated twenty towns from Aroer to the vicinity of Minnith, as far as Abel Keramim. Thus Israel subdued Ammon.

When Jephthah returned to his home in Mizpah, who should come out to meet him but his daughter, dancing to the sound of tambourines! She was an only child. Except for her he had neither son nor daughter. When he saw her, he tore his clothes and cried, "Oh! My daughter! You have made me miserable and wretched, because I have made a vow to the LORD that I cannot break."

"My father," she replied, "you have given your word to the LORD. Do to me just as you promised, now that the LORD has avenged you of your enemies, the Ammonites. But grant me this one request," she said, "Give me two months to roam the hills and weep with my friends, because I will never marry."

"You may go," he said. And he let her go for two months. She and the girls went into the hills and wept because she would never marry. After the two months, she returned to her father and he did to her as he had vowed.[221]

This story exhibits the fact both that the Bible was written by men and that it is fixed in time. Human and animal sacrifice are not accepted in modern culture, neither is treating girls as little better than animals to be sacrificed in the name of god. But religionists are stuck with these inflexible tales.

Another example is that when the Bible stories were made up, genetics was an unknown science. So the authors had little trouble having all human life originating with a single human, Adam, less than ten thousand years ago.[222] Further, the story tellers had no problem wiping out all humans on earth other than Noah, his three sons and their spouses, again limiting the gene pool around four thousand years ago.[223] Little did the authors know that the stories would be disproved by genetics.

The Noah story raises some fun issues. In that story, god, being angry, had no problem killing all life, including children and animals. But he apparently liked fish, since they would have been spared in a flood. In addition, Noah took no plants on the boat, so what happened to the trees? In fact, the oldest dendrochronology (tree ring dating) now goes back 12,000 years–long before Noah's supposed flood, and long before the Bible admits to the earth's creation.[224] The animals Noah supposedly brought on his boat included "every creature that moves along the ground . . . and every bird . . . [and] everything with wings"[225] The authors of the story were unfamiliar with the vast array of life in the world, such as creatures in distant places like Australia and the Americas. How did the kangaroo and slow-moving koala get from Australia to the Middle East? Speaking of slow-moving animals, how did the sloth cross the ocean from South America? How did Noah collect and house god's favorite creature (since he made so many of them) the beetle, of which there are more than 350,000 species?[226] What provisions were made for the millions of species of microbes–unknown by the men of that time?

All fun aside, the holy books were written by men and reflect the knowledge and values of their time. The Torah, Bible and Koran act as a kind of time machine. They drag forward knowledge and values that belong in the past. Provisions about slavery and animal sacrifice are selectively ignored, but scriptural sexism, homophobia and tribalism are alive and well. It is crazy to allow books written years ago and limited by the knowledge of men of that time, to have so much power over life today.

Chapter 11. Small miracles.

I tell you the truth, if you have faith as small as a mustard seed, you can say to this mountain, 'move from here to there' and it will move. Nothing will be impossible for you.[227] Jesus

If we are to suppose a miracle to be something so entirely out of the course of what is called nature, that she must go out of that course to accomplish it, and we see an account given of such miracle by the person who said he saw it, it raises a question in the mind very easily decided, which is, is it more probable that nature should go out of her course, or that a man should tell a lie? We have never seen, in our time, nature go out of her course; but we have good reason to believe that millions of lies have been told in the same time; it is therefore, at least millions to one, that the reporter of a miracle tells a lie.[228] Thomas Paine

Crutches only are hung on the walls of the miraculous grottoes [of Lourdes]; never a wooden leg.[229] Dr. Maurice de Fleury

Religious mythology is filled with stories of miracles. A miracle is a fictitious event or fictitious explanation for a real event offered as evidence of the existence of a supernatural power. Religionists insist that belief in miracles is a necessary element of faith.[230] One author explains that Jesus' birth, life and resurrection are all "miracles," therefore, "Christianity without miracle is not Christianity. No one who thinks, 'miracles do not happen' can be a Christian."[231] A reported 79% of Americans believe in miracles, and 47% believe strongly.[232]

Reports of modern miracles are rare, since they are subject to skeptical and scientific scrutiny. In the modern day, a teen who claims

84

to see Jesus' mother and does not capture a photo on her cell phone will not be believed. Similarly, bleeding statutes can be chemically analyzed to establish the substance is not blood, and if it is blood, who it belongs to. However, the men who wrote books like the Bible were not subject to such examination. But even with unfettered ability to create the most fantastic stories, they were limited by their knowledge and time.

A good example of this is demons. The Bible reflects the man-held beliefs of its time that epilepsy and mental illness were caused by demons. Even the more recent books have Jesus endorsing this belief. Here is a Bible story of Jesus performing a "miracle" by exorcizing an epilepsy-causing demon:

> When they came to the other disciples, they saw a large crowd around them and the teachers of the law arguing with them. As soon as all the people saw Jesus, they were overwhelmed with wonder and ran to greet him. "What are you arguing with them about?" he asked.
>
> A man in the crowd answered, "Teacher, I brought you my son, who is possessed by a spirit that has robbed him of speech. Whenever it seizes him, it throws him to the ground. He foams at the mouth, gnashes his teeth and becomes rigid. I asked your disciples to drive out the spirit, but they could not."
>
> "O unbelieving generation," Jesus replied, "how long shall I stay with you? How long shall I put up with you? Bring the boy to me." So they brought him. When the spirit saw Jesus, it immediately threw the boy into a convulsion. He fell to the ground and rolled around, foaming at the mouth.
>
> Jesus asked the boy's father, "How long has he been like this?"

"From childhood," he answered. "It has often thrown him into fire or water to kill him. But if you can do anything, take pity on us and help us."

"If you can?" said Jesus. "Everything is possible for him who believes." Immediately the boy's father exclaimed, "I do believe; help me overcome my unbelief!"

When Jesus saw that a crowd was running to the scene, he rebuked the evil spirit. "You deaf and mute spirit," he said, "I command you, come out of him and never enter him again." The spirit shrieked, convulsed him violently and came out. The boy looked so much like a corpse that many said, "He's dead." But Jesus took him by the hand and lifted him to his feet, and he stood up.

After Jesus had gone indoors, his disciples asked him privately, "Why couldn't we drive it out?" He replied, "This kind can come out only by prayer."[233]

For most modern people, epilepsy is a neurological disorder, not the result of demon possession. The passing of a seizure is part of the disorder, not a miracle. Yet the text of the Bible shows first that it was written by men and exhibits the knowledge of the time and second that the so-called miracle was nothing of the kind.

Despite being unfettered by reality, the men who wrote the Bible invented miracles that seem paltry when compared with any recent blockbuster movie. Other than casting out demons, miracles attributed to Jesus include changing water to wine. The changing water into wine was a real attention getter in the Bible. The story ends with the sentence, "This, the first of his miraculous signs, Jesus performed in Cana of Galilee. He thus revealed his glory, and his disciples put their faith in him."[234] Perhaps by ancient standards, creating a bottomless jug of wine was a great miracle, but by modern standards it shows a lack of imagination.

The "water into wine" miracle was not the only culinary trick Jesus allegedly performed, he miraculously served an all-you-can-eat buffet to 5,000 people with two fish and five loaves of bread.[235] Other alleged miracles had a little more zing, like healing people with various diseases, walking on water and raising the dead. I kind of like the coin in a fish's mouth "miracle":

> After Jesus and his disciples arrived in Capernaum, the collectors of the two-drachma tax came to Peter and asked, "Doesn't your teacher pay the temple tax?"
>
> "Yes, he does," he replied. When Peter came into the house, Jesus was the first to speak. "What do you think, Simon?" he asked. "From whom do the kings of the earth collect duty and taxes--from their own sons or from others?"
>
> "From others," Peter answered. "Then the sons are exempt," Jesus said to him. "But so that we may not offend them, go to the lake and throw out your line. Take the first fish you catch; open its mouth and you will find a four-drachma coin. Take it and give it to them for my tax and yours."

Frankly, the coin in the fish story would not make it into a blockbuster Hollywood movie, but in a simpler time when the Bible was written, it was impressive enough to be counted as one of Jesus' "miracles."

When I was a child, a plot of the popular *Superman* television show (the original one) involved Superman flying around the earth to reverse its rotation and turn back time so he could save his girlfriend's life. Regardless of the scientific basis of this TV plot, I found it a heck of a lot more impressive than walking on water or feeding a crowd.

87

Since the time men made up the Bible, the best miracles they could dream have been eclipsed by a simple television show from the 1950's. The Bible, written by men and fixed in time, contains only small miracles that fail to inspire the modern imagination.

Never a wooden leg.

Biblical miracle stories were limited only by the imaginations of the men who created them. Modern miracle stories have many more constraints. In the age of televised news, cell phones that take movies and modern scientific tests, stories seem to be limited to seeing the image of Jesus on a tortilla, or a statue that appears to cry or bleed. Even the Catholic Church is toning down the miracles required to declare a person a "saint." The Pope has accepted a story that a locket with Mother Theresa's photo was placed on a woman's abdomen in Calcutta in 1998 and cured her of cancer. This "miracle" has put Mother Theresa on the fast track to sainthood. However, the Health Minister for Calcutta and the "cured" woman's husband[236] say there was nothing unusual about the disappearance of the tumor after prolonged medical treatment. Perhaps the real miracle is that the 30-year-old illiterate patient, who speaks only her tribal dialect, was able to produce a statement about the "miracle" in written English including the requisite Catholic references to classify the remission a miracle.[237]

The strongest refutation to the claims of miracles however is found in a truism written more than a hundred years ago about the supposedly miraculous curative properties of the water at Lourdes, France. At that site in 1858, a 14-year-old girl claimed to see Jesus' mother.[238] Since then, a huge industry has developed selling cures to afflicted believers. Like many shrines, the believers leave behind their walking aids, but "crutches only are hung on the walls of the miraculous grottoes; never a wooden leg."[239]

The same point is made today in a more high tech manner at the Website, "Why Won't God Heal Amputees?"[240] The "miracles" religionists promote are cheap and tawdry. If prayer makes an amputated limb grow back, atheists will pay attention. Until then miracles are silly myths to help believers keep faith in their silly gods.

"Miracles" are considered evidence of a supernatural power. Yet the "miracles" of the scriptures–like the coin in a fish's mouth, are the products of the limited imaginations of the men of that time. "Modern miracles" are either so limited in scope as to be laughable, like the image of Jesus on a tortilla,[241] or fail under scientific scrutiny. Small miracles are a large failure for religionists who wish to use them to show the existence of a supernatural power.

Chapter 12. Jesus rising.

The great miracle of the New Testament can be seen as a combination of the Death and Resurrection of Jesus. If one is able to believe this, then all other miracles of the Gospels and Acts are easily believed.... The resurrection, more than any other miracle of the New Testament, is the foundation on which . . . Christian faith and hope rest.[242] Dr. C. Matthew McMahon

Christ's resurrection is the central event of Christianity, a fundamental truth that must be reaffirmed with vigor at all times, as to deny it in different ways, as has been attempted and continues to be attempted, or to transform it into a merely spiritual event is to make our faith vain. If Christ has not been raised, then our preaching is in vain and your faith is in vain.[243] Pope Benedict XVI

    The Jesus coming-back-from-the-dead story is probably the most important miracle myth for Christians. You might think they would have their story straight, especially since they had years to rehearse it before writing the Bible. But if you think so, you are wrong. Take this multiple choice test about the Jesus rising story:

1. What time of day was an empty tomb found?
      A.   While it was still dark (John 20:1)
      B.   Very early in the morning (Luke 24:1)
      C.   At dawn (Matthew 28:1)
      D.   After sunrise (Mark 16:2)
      E.   All of the above

2. Who first went to Jesus' tomb?

    A.   Mary Magdalene (John 20:1)

    B.   Mary Magdalene and the other Mary (Matthew 28:1)

    C.   Mary Magdalene, Mary the mother of James and Salome (Mark 16:1)

    D.   Mary Magdalene, Mary the mother of James, Joanna and the others with them (Luke 24:10)

    E.   All of the above

3. Did the woman or women meet anyone at the tomb?

    A.   Yes, a young man dressed in white was already sitting in the tomb (Mark 16:5)

    B.   Yes, two men in clothes that gleamed like lightening were not there initially but quickly appeared (Luke 24:4)

    C.   Yes, an angel who rolled away a stone from the tomb entrance and some guards who were standing there (Matthew 28:2-4)

    D.   Not at first, but later that day two angels appeared inside the tomb and talked to Mary Magdalene (John 20:12)

    E.   All of the above

4. To whom did Jesus speak first?

    A.   Two disciples (Luke 24:13)

    B.   Mary Magdalene and the other Mary (Matthew 28:9)

    C.   To Mary Magdalene alone (Mark 16:9)

    D.   In the presence of two angels, to Mary Magdalene, who first thought Jesus was a gardener (John 20:14-15)

    E.   All of the above

5. How long did Jesus hang around before heading up to heaven?
    A.   Only one day (Mark 16:19, Luke 24:51)
    B.   An unspecified period of time, but at least long enough for his disciples to get to Galilee (probably several days walk)(Matthew 28:16)
    C.   More than a week (John 20:26, 21:1-25)
    D.   Forty days (Acts 1:3)
    E.   All of the above

My guess is that you answered "all of the above" to each. That means either you are a cynic, a Bible scholar, or you figured the citations next to each answer means that I read the Bible passages and reported the answers accurately. The correct answer is "all of the above."

It is difficult to believe that almost one-third of Americans[244] think the Bible is the inerrant word of god when the story tellers cannot even keep their most important story straight. If the "testimony" of the Bible were presented in court, the case would be dismissed for lack of reliable evidence. Religion requires faith because it lacks facts. The great mystery is why so many people let these poorly constructed ancient myths dictate their modern behavior.

Chapter 13. No good dogs go to heaven.

If there are no dogs in Heaven, then when I die I want to go where they went.[245] Will Rogers

The poor dog, in life the firmest friend,
The first to welcome, foremost to defend,
Whose honest heart is still the master's own,
Who labours, fights, lives, breathes for him alone,
Unhonour'd falls, unnoticed all his worth,
Denied in heaven the soul he held on earth,
While man, vain insect hopes to be forgiven,
And claims himself a sole exclusive heaven.[246] Lord Byron

Atheists have no problem with what happens after a pet dies. The pet ceases to be, just as the atheist will cease to be. I have a dog that I love irrationally. He will likely die first and I will cremate him. I will likely die later, and if my instructions are followed, I will be cremated. What happens to the ashes is unimportant, we will both cease to be. This makes the time we spend together more loving and poignant.

But religionists have a problem. Their scriptures are written by men and fixed in time. The role of pets has evolved enormously over the past 1,500 years. Five hundred years ago, a dog might have made a tasty snack in lean times. A farmer from 200 years ago would likely be appalled at the privileges we give our animals. Fifty years ago, dog parks were virtually nonexistent, now they are found in almost every community in the United States. Today, owners (or guardians) spend substantial amounts of time and money to assure the quality of life of their pets.

When the scriptures were written, men claimed complete dominance over animals. The Muslim tradition is the most direct, dogs are forbidden. Although the Koran does not specifically mention dogs, the Hadiths have multiple prohibitions.[247] Basically, Muslims cannot or will not own dogs. In Ohio, a Muslim taxi driver refused to serve a blind woman who used a guide dog because the dog was "impure" according to his religious beliefs.[248] I have been amazed at the reaction of Muslims whom I encounter walking my very friendly dog. They march away with a look of horror. What a shame that their man-made myth prevents them from appreciating the companionship so many of us cherish.

The Jewish and Christian scriptures contain no direct prohibitions against pet ownership, but written as they were thousands of years ago, they did not anticipate the love modern people feel for their pets. The Bible claims to give men complete dominance over all the creatures of the earth, including our pets. The Bible does say there will be no sea in heaven, so if your pet is a fish, it is explicitly excluded.[249] And further, the Bible provides that only those who believe in Jesus and say magic words will get into heaven,[250] something pets would have a hard time doing. Catholics, in particular, seem to have fixed on the idea that pets do not have souls, and therefore cannot pass through the imaginary pearly gates. In an article posted on the Website of the Catholic Global Network, Richard Geraghty, Ph.D. says:

> Now when any living thing dies, its soul is separated from its body. In the case of plants and animals the soul goes out of existence. But in the case of man, the soul remains in existence because it is a spiritual or immaterial thing.
>
> * * *
>
> In the light of this essential difference between human beings and animals, it would seem that we would not

94

see the souls of our pets in heaven for the simple reason that they do not have immortal souls and are not responsible for their actions. They do not have the intelligence which allows them to choose either God's will or their own will. There is, then, an incomparable distance, say, between the soul of the sorriest human being who ever lived and the most noble brute animal that ever walked the earth.[251]

Religionists, well, Christians and Jews at least, are scrambling to find ways to include their believers' pets in heaven. But the reality exists that the books written thousands of years ago make no accommodation for pets in that mythical heaven.

The Will Rogers quote that opens this brief chapter works fine for atheists. When we die, we cease to be, the same as our pets. Religionists are stuck with their ancient scriptures that exclude pets, or with dishonest readings of their texts to try to conform to modern sensibilities.

Chapter 14. Religion, health and the environment.

WARNING: Quitting Religion Now Greatly Reduces Serious Risks to Your Health. Modified cigarette warning label

God blessed them and said to them, "Be fruitful and increase in number; fill the earth and subdue it. Rule over the fish of the sea and the birds of the air and over every living creature that moves on the ground." Then God said, "I give you every seed-bearing plant on the face of the whole earth and every tree that has fruit with seed in it. They will be yours for food. And to all the beasts of the earth and all the birds of the air and all the creatures that move on the ground-- everything that has the breath of life in it--I give every green plant for food. "[252] The Bible

So will it be with the resurrection of the dead. The body that is sown is perishable, it is raised imperishable; it is sown in dishonor, it is raised in glory; it is sown in weakness, it is raised in power; it is sown a natural body, it is raised a spiritual body. If there is a natural body, there is also a spiritual body.[253] The Bible

Religionists believe that their god has given them dominion over the world. Further, they believe that upon death they will be given both a new place to live and a new body. These beliefs affect the way religionists treat their current homes and bodies. Many think they are entitled to defile their bodies and the environment because they believe they will get new ones when they die.

Environment.

Religionists are not shy about trying to contradict science with myth. Creationism is one example. Dealing with environmental issues a more dangerous example. Consider Congressman John Shimkus of Illinois, who testified before the U.S. House Subcommittee on Energy and the Environment about carbon dioxide in the atmosphere in 2009 and quoted the Bible, saying, "The earth will end only when God declares it is time to be over. Man will not destroy this earth, this earth will not be destroyed by a flood . . . I do believe God's word is infallible, unchanging, perfect."[254] Similarly, Congresswoman Michele Bachmann, a possible future presidential candidate, speaking about god and energy policy, said, "Man is here not to serve Earth. The Earth is here for our benefit to serve us and it's a beautiful union and picture that God has given us with the Earth."[255]

Looking at anecdotal evidence, the vehicle I see most often displaying a Jesus fish is a large, four wheel drive SUV. Christians seem to feel entitled to drive large vehicles. Research supports this. A survey showed only 34% of white evangelical Protestants believe global warming is caused by human activity, and 31% of the same group thought there was no evidence of global warming.[256] Similarly, The Barna Group found that while 69% of atheists and agnostics are concerned about global warming, only 33% of evangelicals feel global warming is a major challenge.[257]

An article by James Sherk of the Evangel Society deals specifically with the link between religious belief, global warming and SUVs. Mr. Sherk says, "If . . . human CO2 emissions do not contribute to global warming, then the question 'What Would Jesus Drive?' becomes an utter absurdity, since then gas guzzling would . . . harm no one, and carpooling does nothing to help the earth or one's fellow man. . . . [S]cientists have uncovered little reliable evidence to support the popular hype that surrounds global warming. As a result, Christians have no reason to fear contributing to global warming, and may drive any vehicle with a clear conscience."[258] Mr. Sherk's analysis is short-sighted. Even if there were no such thing as global warming, the SUV takes more resources to build, consumes more of a finite resource, oil, and produces more pollution than an ordinary car.

The evangelical vehicle of choice is the SUV. The choice demonstrates their sense of entitlement and superiority. It is almost as if they are announcing "we are the chosen and we can do as we please, we are going to heaven and you are going to hell along with the garbage we produce along the way." Religionists, who believe that the environment they despoil will be replaced by one pristine and new, are living a dangerous myth.

Religious scriptures written by men thousands of years ago cannot evolve to include modern scientific knowledge. People who maintain their scriptures are the "infallible, unchanging and perfect" word of god are more inclined to harm the environment. This myth affects both religionists' treatment of the world and religionists' treatment of their bodies.

Health.

How does the promise of a new body at death affect the way religionists treat their current bodies? I know I have only one body and one life, so I try to take care of it the best I can. I know a religionist who is so grossly obese that her life is threatened, yet she takes no steps to change her condition. Could it be that her belief she will get a new body is leading her to neglect the only body she will truly ever have?

The most religious state in the U.S., Mississippi, is also the most obese.[259] Similarly, the second most religious state, Alabama is the second most obese.[260] In fact, nine out of ten of the most religious states are also the most obese: Mississippi, Alabama, South Carolina, Tennessee, Louisiana, Arkansas, North Carolina, Oklahoma and Kentucky all fall within the top ten in the religiousness and obesity ratings (see the obesity/religiosity correlation chart on the following page). The least religious states rank lower in obesity.[261] There is a startlingly clear relationship between religiosity and obesity. Whether there is a causal relationship warrants further examination, but obesity and religiosity are linked.

State	Religion Ranking	% who say religion important	Obesity Ranking	% Obese/ Overweight
Mississippi	1	85%	1	70.2%
Alabama	2	82%	2	68.1%
S. Carolina	3	80%	9	65.7%
Tennessee	4	79%	3	68.9%
Louisiana	5	78%	5	67.6%
Arkansas	6	78%	8	66.5%
N. Carolina	8	76%	10	65.3%
Oklahoma	9	75%	6	67.4%
Kentucky	10	74%	7	66.9%

A tragic answer to the question of how religion can affect health care is found in the regular newspaper reports of the way religionists subject innocent children to harmful beliefs about god and health. *Newsweek* reported about the following tragedy in Oregon:

> Carl and Raylene Worthington told investigators they first noticed the bump on their daughter's neck when Ava was 3 months old. A doctor later said it was a benign cyst battling an infection in the child's blood; it continued to grow as she grew older. By the time little Ava reached 15 months, the bump measured three by four inches--the size of Clackamas County Deputy District Attorney Greg Horner's wallet, he told a jury in the Portland, Ore., suburb of Oregon City last week. By

Feb. 29, 2008, Horner said, this "cystic hygroma," a congenital lymphatic lesion, was pressing up against the girl's windpipe, according to a ruling from the county's medical examiner. She was slowly choking to death.

Carl and Raylene called in the devoted parishioners of their Oregon City place of worship, the Followers of Christ, to seek God's help. They anointed Ava with oil. They fed her diluted wine. They extracted phlegm from her throat with the kind of suction bulb used to baste a Thanksgiving turkey. They laid their hands upon the toddler and prayed she would get better. What the Worthingtons did not do is call an ambulance.

The first physician ever to examine Ava was the Clackamas County coroner, who performed her autopsy. "Almost up until the end, if they had gotten her adequate medical treatment, they would have been able to help her," Horner said during his opening statement.[262]

In the end, the jury cleared the faith healing parents of manslaughter, allowing the mother to go free and convicting the father of a misdemeanor charge of criminal mistreatment.[263]

Horrifically, this is not the end of the story for the faith healing family in Oregon. Four months later, Raylene Worthington's 16-year-old brother, a member of the same church, died of a treatable urinary tract infection. His parents went to trial for treating him with prayer instead of medicine. This time the jury came back with a conviction of both parents for negligent homicide.[264]

Oregon is an easier place to prosecute these cases because in 1999 the state eliminated a criminal law that provided an exemption from prosecution for faith healing.[265] In Wisconsin, the legal situation is different. Wisconsin, like 30 other states,[266] limits prosecution of parents who treat illness with prayer instead of medicine.

In Wisconsin, 11-year-old Madeline Kara Neumann died of otherwise treatable juvenile diabetes. Her parents, followers of an online group called Unleavened Bread Ministries, treated her with prayer instead of medicine.[267] Despite a Wisconsin law that provides, "A person is not guilty of an offense . . . solely because he or she provides a child with treatment by spiritual means through prayer alone for healing in accordance with the religious method of healing . . . in lieu of medical or surgical treatment," prosecutors charged the parents with reckless homicide.[268] In this case, both parents were convicted in separate trials.[269] The parents were sentenced to staggered 10 year terms of probation and staggered 30 day jail sentences so they could continue to care for their three surviving children whose medical welfare would be monitored by the court.[270]

The 30 states with laws protecting parents who treat children with prayer instead of medicine ignore the fact that a broad study found prayer has no positive effect on the health of heart patients. The $2.4 million study was funded in large part by the pro-religion Templeton Foundation. Patients at six hospitals who received coronary artery bypass graft surgery were randomly assigned to three groups of about 600 each. Two groups were told they might or might not receive intercessory prayer, one of the two groups received the prayer, the other did not. The third group was told it would receive intercessory prayer and did. The group that did not receive prayer did the best, with 51% of the patients experiencing complications. Those who received prayer, but were not sure they did, came in second, with 52% experiencing complications. Those with the most complications, 59%, were patients who received prayer and knew it. The study concluded, "Intercessory prayer itself had no effect on complication-free recovery from [bypass surgery], but certainty of receiving intercessory prayer was associated with a higher incidence of complications."[271] The study offered no explanation for why the group that knew it was being prayed for did worse, other than it might be a result of chance. One coauthor of the study thought the group with knowledge of the prayers may have thought they were worse off than they were, and therefore got sicker.[272] That is a pro-religious view. But there is an alternate explanation that has not been explored. If people thought they were sicker, they would probably take better care of themselves and have a better result. However, if they thought god was taking care of things, they may have been more lax in their care and had a worse result. All of the commentators looked for ways that religion could make patients healthier. None of the commentators allowed for the possibility (suggested by this study) that religious belief made the patients sicker.

Oddly, religious belief acts like a two-sided knife blade when it comes to health. In some cases religionists deny children health care that would keep them alive and in other cases they keep alive adults who would prefer to die. Think about the national furor over the Florida woman named Terri Schiavo. Ms. Schiavo unfortunately collapsed in her home in 1990 and ended up in a persistent vegetative state. A Florida court found that Ms. Schiavo was in a persistent vegetative state and she had made consistent and reliable statements that she would not want to be kept alive that way.[273] As her court appointed guardian, her husband directed that her feeding tube be removed and she be allowed to die naturally. Ms. Schiavo's Catholic parents objected to this order and began a tortured journey through the state and federal legal systems.

In more than 20 hearings, the courts upheld Mr. Schiavo's decision, but the parents, backed by the religious right, continued to appeal. The Schiavo matter was adopted by the religious right and the "right to life" movement as an essential defense of their religious beliefs. When all state appeals were exhausted, the Florida Legislature gave Governor Jeb Bush authority to force Ms. Schiavo to remain on a feeding tube. When that law was held unconstitutional, the U.S. Congress acted in just three days to adopt a special law transferring jurisdiction of the matter from state court to federal court. The bill was supported by then Senator Barack Obama. President George W. Bush flew from Texas to Washington to sign the bill into law.

Unfortunately for the religionists that wished to force Ms. Schiavo to live against her wishes, the federal courts upheld Mr. Schiavo's decision and allowed her to die. An autopsy showed that Ms. Schiavo had extensive brain damage and the claims that she had brain function, including shouting, "I want [to live]," as her parents' attorney alleged, were false.[274] Reckless quantities of time, money and emotion were wasted trying to impose a religious value of life on a woman who wanted to die naturally. It is not enough that religionists invent a bearded man in the sky, claim to know his will and govern their lives by scriptures written by men and fixed in time. No, to validate their myths they try to force others to live like them. Religionists use power–like the guardianship over innocent children, and political power like passing special laws to keep Terry Schiavo alive against her will to justify and perpetuate their myths. Religion is dangerous.

Religious lies–forcing children to die when they cannot yet make the choice to live, and forcing adults to live with artificial life support when they would want to die naturally, are harmful examples of how religion negatively impacts us all. Religion is not harmless, it is bad for your health and bad for the environment.

Chapter 15. Women.

A man ought not to cover his head, since he is the image and glory of God; but the woman is the glory of man. For man did not come from woman, but woman from man; neither was man created for woman, but woman for man.[275] The Bible

And say to the believing women that they cast down their looks and guard their private parts and do not display their ornaments except what appears thereof, and let them wear their head-coverings over their bosoms, and not display their ornaments except to their husbands or their fathers . . . and let them not strike their feet so that what they hide of their ornaments may be known.[276] The Koran

The role of women in modern society is still evolving. In 1920, the United States amended the Constitution giving women the right to vote. In 1964, Title VII of the Civil Rights Act prohibited employment discrimination on the basis of sex as well as race. In 1965 a Supreme Court decision legalized birth control for married couples in all states and seven years later the right was extended to unmarried couples.[277] In 1972 Congress adopted Title IX which prohibits sex discrimination in education, including athletics, resulting in a surge in women's sports. The first female U.S. Supreme Court Justice was appointed in 1981. Hilary Clinton was a leading presidential candidate in 2008.[278] Although women have not yet achieved full equality, their right to do so is now generally accepted.

Religion, with its scriptures written by men and fixed in time, lags far behind the social changes in the role of women. The most shocking examples of inequality come from Muslim countries. In America's ally, Saudi Arabia, Islam is the official religion and women

104

suffer. Women are effectively treated as minors and need the permission of a male relative to access the limited rights available.[279] Men are allowed to have multiple spouses, women are not. Women are not allowed to drive or vote. Restrictive costumes are required for women who go out in public. Women are limited in their access to public places, their opportunity for education or employment, and their ability to travel. Violence against women and spousal abuse is common.[280]

In other Muslim countries, women are virtual slaves. Burqas are required, education is denied, child marriage accepted, and honor killings conducted. A 2008 movie, *The Stoning of Soraya M.*, shows the horror that some Muslim women face. Based on a true story, it tells of an Iranian woman whose husband wants to marry a 14-year-old and no longer wants to support her. So the husband falsely accuses his wife of adultery and villagers dutifully bury her waist deep in dirt and stone her to death. Her father, husband and two sons participate in the stoning.[281] It is hard to see the religious fundamentalism described in that movie being much more advanced than the Stone Age.

With Stone Age logic, leading Iranian cleric Hojatoleslam Kazim Sadeghi[282] recently claimed, "Many women who do not dress modestly lead young men astray, corrupt their chastity, and spread adultery in society, which increases earthquakes."[283] The statement would be laughable if he were not a high-ranking Muslim leader in a 98% Muslim country with more than 67 million inhabitants.[284]

In the brutal world of the primitive past, men succeeded in dominating women through force, but in the modern world of tools, technology and information, women can stand shoulder to shoulder with men. It is crazy to allow a primitive ethic and ancient texts to dictate sex roles in the modern world. Yet religion drags ancient roles and superstitions forward and applies them today.

Look at any photo of the streets in Muslim countries. They are crowded with men, women are absent. One must wonder, where are the women and do they want to be there? The photo is even more troubling when it comes from Iraq or Afghanistan where U.S. tax dollars prop up the government. American taxpayers are paying for regimes that subjugate women. The religiously justified dominance of Muslim men over women troubles most any Western person who observes it, even Western religionists. There is little disagreement among Americans that Muslim woman lack equality. However, there is little recognition that the dominant religion in America contains similar ancient myths. The Bible is full of quotes relegating women to second-class status.

Although some religious sects accord women respect on par with that of general American society, you do not need to look very far to find a group that does not. The Catholic Church claims about 25% of Americans (more than 58 million people) as members.[285] But the Catholic church resolutely refuses to allow women to take leadership roles. Only men can become priests and they are referred to as "Father." Catholic doctrine also denies members the right to birth control. Birth control was key to allowing sexually active heterosexual women to time their families or choose not have a family at all. Birth control has been called a primary cause of the "sexual revolution" of last century and similarly is a major factor in women stepping successfully into the workplace and achieving closer parity with men.

The Bible has many negative statements about women, for example:

> A woman should learn in quietness and full submission.
> I do not permit a woman to teach or to have authority
> over a man; she must be silent. For Adam was formed
> first, then Eve. And Adam was not the one deceived; it
> was the woman who was deceived and became a
> sinner.[286]

* * *

> To the woman he said, "I will greatly increase your
> pains in childbearing; with pain you will give birth to

106

children. Your desire will be for your husband, and he will rule over you."[287]

* * *

Wives, submit to your husbands as to the Lord. For the husband is the head of the wife as Christ is the head of the church, his body, of which he is the Savior. Now as the church submits to Christ, so also wives should submit to their husbands in everything.[288]

It is not just Muslims and Christians who are unfair to women. Traditional Judaism sees women who are menstruating as impure and forbids contact with their spouses for seven days thereafter. The same text is part of the Old Testament of the Christian Bible:

When a woman has her regular flow of blood, the impurity of her monthly period will last seven days, and anyone who touches her will be unclean till evening.

Anything she lies on during her period will be unclean, and anything she sits on will be unclean. Whoever touches her bed must wash his clothes and bathe with water, and he will be unclean till evening. Whoever touches anything she sits on must wash his clothes and bathe with water, and he will be unclean till evening. Whether it is the bed or anything she was sitting on, when anyone touches it, he will be unclean till evening.

If a man lies with her and her monthly flow touches him, he will be unclean for seven days; any bed he lies on will be unclean.

When a woman has a discharge of blood for many days at a time other than her monthly period or has a discharge that continues beyond her period, she will be unclean as long as she has the discharge, just as in the days of her period. Any bed she lies on while her discharge continues will be unclean, as is her bed during her monthly period, and anything she sits on will be unclean, as during her period. Whoever touches them will be unclean; he must wash his clothes and bathe with water, and he will be unclean till evening.

When she is cleansed from her discharge, she must count off seven days, and after that she will be ceremonially clean. On the eighth day she must take two doves or two young pigeons and bring them to the priest at the entrance to the Tent of Meeting. The priest is to sacrifice one for a sin offering and the other for a burnt offering. In this way he will make atonement for her before the LORD for the uncleanness of her discharge.[289]

The rules about menstruating women are further evidence that the scriptures are written by men and fixed in time. Even most of the religionists who believe the scriptures are the "inerrant word of god" disregard these requirements. However, some traditionalists still follow the strictures. An Israeli-based women's health guide instructs:

A woman enters the ritual status of *niddah* when she experiences uterine bleeding not due to injury. . . . Jewish law forbids all physical contact (not only intercourse) between a husband and wife while she is *niddah*. Certain other behaviors are forbidden as well-- for example: passing objects to each other, sitting on the same surface, sleeping in the same bed, eating from the same plate, and seeing each other undressed.[290]

The men who wrote the scriptures had limited understanding of menstruation and responded superstitiously. For even some to allow these superstitions to hold sway in modern times simply because they are in the religionists' books of myths is unjustifiable.

As with so many other issues, religionists are not satisfied with keeping their superstitions to themselves. They use their position of power to apply their rules to everyone. An example of this is the defeat of the proposed Equal Rights Amendment to the U.S. Constitution.

The Equal Rights Amendment, which finally passed through both houses of Congress in 1972, provided forthrightly, "Equality of rights under the law shall not be denied or abridged by the United States or by any state on account of sex."[291] Initially, the Amendment had broad public support. The Amendment needed 38 States to ratify it to become part of the Constitution. The original deadline of seven years was extended to ten, but the time passed with only 35 States ratifying the Amendment.[292] The States which did not ratify the amendment cluster around the "Bible belt" of the South, with the addition of the heavily Mormon[293] western states of Utah, Arizona and Nevada.[294]

A leading opponent of the Equal Rights Amendment was religionist Phyllis Schlafly, whose Eagle Forum notes, "We support the sanctity of human life as a gift from our Creator, as proclaimed in the Declaration of Independence" and then boasts, "Eagle Forum successfully led the ten-year battle to defeat the misnamed Equal Rights Amendment with its hidden agenda of tax-funded abortions and same-sex marriages."[295] The Mormon Church was key to defeating the Equal Rights Amendment in Utah, as well as supporting anti-Amendment activities in Florida, Nevada, North and South Carolina, Missouri, Illinois and Arizona.[296] Christian groups like the "Concerned Women of America" also worked hard to defeat the Amendment.[297] Conservative Catholics joined the opposition because of their fear the Amendment would encourage abortion.[298] Jumping aboard, Pat

Robertson, Former Republican presidential candidate and founder and then President of the Christian Coalition, said unbelievably, "The feminist agenda is not about equal rights for women. It is about a socialist, anti-family political movement that encourages women to leave their husbands, kill their children, practice witchcraft, destroy capitalism and become lesbians."[299] Robertson's statement would qualify as comedy if he were not at the time President of the 2.5 million strong Christian Coalition,[300] founder and Chairman of the Christian Broadcasting Network,[301] and then as now, host[302] of TV's "The 700 Club," which is viewable in 95% of the television markets in the United States,[303] and seen by as many as 200 million people a year worldwide.[304] With statistics like these in mind, Robertson's statements are terrifying.

Just as with the defeat of gay marriage in California in 2008, a coalition of conservative Christians and Mormons used time, money and manpower to change a generally positive public opinion into a negative one. Equal Rights Amendment opponents claimed it would force women into military combat, require recognition of gay marriage and even result in the sexes having to share the same bathroom.[305] The conservative religious coalition succeeded and the Amendment died.

Looking at the most and least religious states, their relationship to the Equal Rights Amendment is predictable: the eight most religious did not ratify the Equal Rights Amendment, while the eight least religious did.

State	Religion Ranking	Ratification of the Equal Rights Amendment
Mississippi	1	No
Alabama	2	No
South Carolina	3	No
Tennessee	4	No[306]
Louisiana	5	No
Arkansas	6	No
Georgia	7	No
North Carolina	8	No
Vermont	50	Yes
New Hampshire	49	Yes
Maine	48	Yes
Massachusetts	47	Yes
Alaska	46	Yes
Washington	46	Yes
Oregon	45	Yes
Rhode Island	44	Yes

The driving force behind the death of the Equal Rights Amendment was religion. Absent religion, what organized group had the power to change the public's support for equality? Absent religion, what basis is there for failing to recognize women as full, equal, valuable human beings?

Religionists have a problem. If they are true to their scriptures, women are not equal. If they accept that women should be equal, they are ignoring their scriptures, just like they ignore the scriptural endorsement of slavery. This may offer a wedge into religionists' beliefs. If they believe women should be equal and chuck their scriptures, where else do their scriptures fail? Are they against slavery? Are they for equal rights for gays? Do they believe in evolution? If the scriptures are wrong in so many places, we can justifiably ask why they do not dump the whole thing and become atheists.

Religious scriptures, written by men and fixed in time, have not kept pace with the changes in women's roles in modern society. Allowing ancient texts to dictate the treatment of more than one-half of the world's population is unjustifiable and wrong.[307] The subjugation of women is a major problem with religion.

Chapter 16. Sexuality.

Know ye not that the unrighteous shall not inherit the kingdom of God?
Be not deceived: neither fornicators, nor idolaters, nor adulterers, nor
effeminate, nor abusers of themselves with mankind, nor thieves, nor
covetous, nor drunkards, nor revilers, nor extortioners, shall inherit the
kingdom of God.[308] The Bible

Religion has dug its claws into human sexuality and it will not let go. Perhaps at one time religious preoccupation with sexuality was functional. When a male priest wrote, "God said unto them, Be fruitful, and multiply"[309] around 600 BCE, the world population was less than 100 million[310] and the "tribes of Israel" were a minority that could gain strength by increasing their numbers. But times changed. By 1500 CE, the world population grew to 450 million; by 1800, 813 million; by 1900, 1.5 billion; by 1950, 2.4 billion;[311] by 1980, 4.5 billion; by 1999, 6 billion, and today, there are 6.8 billion people living on earth. By 2050, the world population will be 9.4 billion[312] (see Figure 14). Unbridled reproduction has gone from helping to preserve mankind to endangering mankind's existence by overburdening our natural resources. Even once plentiful resources like water are threatened.[313] But religious scriptures, written by men and fixed in time, are unable to adapt to changing human conditions.

And even if religion's preoccupation with sexuality had a functional origin, it has morphed far beyond its original purpose. Perhaps religion has gained power by attempting to harness the human sex drive and yoke it to the church. Religionists go as far as claiming that all sexual activity is a sin, unless it is for procreation.[314] Up until the 1965 U.S. Supreme Court decision in *Griswold v. Connecticut*[315] (extended to unmarried couples by the 1972 decision in *Eisenstadt v.*

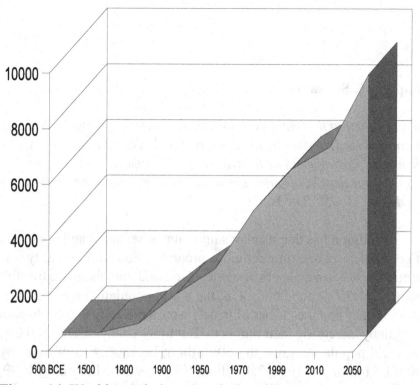

Figure 14. World population growth (in millions) since 600 BCE.

Baird[316]), religionists succeeded in denying American couples access to birth control in many states. They had forced their ancient dogma that sex is for procreation not recreation on everyone, whether religious or not.

Religionists promote their procreation-only policy not only to the exclusion of pleasure, but even at the risk of death. In sub-Saharan Africa 22 million people are infected with HIV, the virus that causes AIDS. However, the Pope, an allegedly celibate man, condemned the use of condoms, even though they have been demonstrated to limit the spread of the virus.[317] The Vatican's head of the Pontifical Council for the Family went even further, saying condoms are not effective in blocking the AIDS virus because they are full of tiny holes, and that condoms help spread AIDS through a false sense of security.[318] This application of Catholic doctrine against birth control subjects millions to the risk of death from disease–bizarrely claiming to protect life by causing death.

Religionists of the past made American children feel frightened and guilty about masturbation, and to this day some religious groups condemn this widespread and harmless act.[319] Perhaps during ancient times when children married at 14, prohibiting masturbation encouraged marital reproduction, but in the modern world marriage is discouraged until after 18, and the median marriage age in the U.S. is 27 for men and 25 for women.[320] Once again the scriptures have not kept pace with modern life.

Further, religion for some reason even attempts to make the way we were born, naked, a prohibited status. Although appalling acts of violence, both actual and dramatized, are regularly shown on television, a fraction of a second glance at Janet Jackson's nipple during the entertainment at a football game netted a $550,000 fine,[321] a penalty cheered by religionists.

In part influenced by Umar Farouk Abdulmutallab, who tried to blow up a Detroit-bound airliner with explosives hidden in his underwear, aviation officials have begun using "body scanners," which electronically strip away a person's clothes to search for explosives. A group of Islamic officials has issued a religious ruling that says going through a body scanner violates Islamic rules prohibiting nudity. They say, "It is a violation of clear Islamic teachings that men or women be seen naked by other men and women . . . The Quran has commanded the believers, both men and women, to cover their private parts."[322] Similarly, the Pope has warned that when using body scanners "the primary asset to be safeguarded and treasured is the person, in his or her integrity."[323] Jumping aboard, Orthodox Jews say the scanners violate religious law and conservative Christians have voiced modesty concerns.[324] Through some twisted logic, religionists think they are entitled to prohibit and create guilt about nakedness, humans' natural state. I think the body scanners are a waste of money because anyone who is going to blow up themselves (and their fellow passengers) will also be willing to hide the explosives in a body cavity to avoid detection. However, beyond that I have no religion to make nudity anything other than a natural state and therefore I have no objection to body scans.

Christians have gone even further than limiting sexual behavior, they attempt to make thinking about sex a sin. The Bible bizarrely quotes Jesus as saying, "You have heard that it was said, 'Do not commit adultery.' But I tell you that anyone who looks at a woman lustfully has already committed adultery with her in his heart. . . . if your right hand causes you to sin, cut it off and throw it away. It is better for you to lose one part of your body than for your whole body to go into hell."[325]

Perhaps the guilt true believers feel when their thoughts wander to sex binds them closer to their church. Atheists, in contrast, are free to think about sexuality without religious prohibition. For example, a survey found that only 15% of evangelical Christians found it morally acceptable to have sexual fantasies about another person, compared with 78% of atheists and agnostics.[326] No doubt evangelicals have fantasies, they just feel guilty about them.

A bit of twisted motivation involving youth, sexuality and religion is found in the tale of the Detroit underwear bomber. Umar Farouk Abdulmutallab, the man who tried to blow up a plane landing in Detroit in late 2009, blogged about the conflict between his sexual desires and his duty as a Muslim to lower his gaze in the presence of women. He said fasting was not helping him to overcome his desires.[327] Ironically, the same religion that denied him the pleasure of looking at women (considered a veritable sport in some countries) promised to reward him with the services of seventy-two virgins at his death.[328] Interestingly, some feel the correct translation is seventy-two white raisins,[329] not virgins, which would be quite funny if this lie did not influence lonely young men to kill themselves and others.

The Muslim religion is not as anti-sex as its brothers of the book, as long as you are a heterosexual male who does not mind

116

treating women as property. Besides the seventy-two virgins promised to martyrs, heaven is supposed to be full of food, wine and full-breasted women: "Verily, for the Muttaqûn,[330] there will be a success (Paradise); Gardens and vineyards, And young full-breasted (mature) maidens of equal age. And a full cup (of wine)."[331] Heaven is a male's paradise: "They will recline on Carpets, whose inner linings will be of rich brocade: the Fruit of the Gardens will be near (and easy of reach). . . . In them will be (Maidens), chaste, restraining their glances, whom no man or Jinn[332] before them has touched."[333] Of course, the concerns of women, who make up about one-half of the world's population, as well as the concerns of gays, are nowhere mentioned.

The problem with the "one size fits all" approach of religion to sexuality is that it leaves lots of people out of the happiness equation. For example, even accepting Iranian President Ahmadinejad's statement that there are no gay men in 98% Muslim Iran, it is highly unlikely that more than half the population (the men, that is) is satisfied with the sexual roles and relationships dictated by the Koran. At least some of the men must be looking for a full and equal partner, not a piece of property. Assuming that the women are unhappy and a portion of the men are unhappy too, who is their religion serving? Certainly not the majority. It is simply a carryover from another time that should be discarded.

In the Christian model, if you are a heterosexual, monogamous person, you might be happy. But what about the person who has no interest in sex? Conversely, what about the person who is interested in a series of partners? He is rejected by the Christian model. And woe to those that do not want a traditional heterosexual relationship. The Christian model denies happiness and equal rights to gays and lesbians, as well as to a myriad of other variations and inclinations that exist.

Without religion, people are allowed to own their sexuality. If a person has little or no interest in sex, he can go through life without coupling and be free of condemnation. Alternatively, if a person wishes to experience a wide range of partners, as owner of his own sexuality, he can do so. What consenting adults do in the privacy of their home is of little concern to me. For example, I have read that some people have a sexual preoccupation with feet. If a couple up the street shares a foot fetish, I could care less. I am much more concerned with whether they mow their lawn and paint the trim on their house, than what they do behind closed doors, and that is whether they are a gay, lesbian or heterosexual couple. Religionists, on the other hand (or foot), would likely condemn the relationship as sinful–not based on whether it affects them or not, simply based on the antiquated rules of their religion.

Religionists give ownership of their sexuality to an institution mired in the past. Atheists are free to own their sexuality. As long as sex involves consenting adults who do no harm, atheists have no reason for concern. However, when an atheist exchanges mutual promises of fidelity, he is more likely to keep them.[334] It is a personal contract, enforced by him, with no expectation of deviation. In contrast, a religionist is expected to sin. The religionist enters into a contract written by an imaginary god, enforced by an imaginary god, for which there is no consequence for violation. Consider again the "morality matrix" from Chapter 7. The matrix provides some explanation of why religionists espouse morality but act otherwise. Keeping this in mind, the next chapter looks at the real life sexual conduct of a famous religionist.

Abortion and abstinence.

Many religious groups in the United States make abortion a cornerstone of their religious and political lives. Religionists label the people who get abortions "sinners" and the abortion providers "monsters." But the religionists themselves are frequently responsible for creating the conditions that make abortion common. Think about it, young people are denied education about contraception. They are denied the tools needed to prevent pregnancy. Young people, already inclined to be sexual, are raised in a sexually charged society where, by 12th grade, 62% of American school children acknowledge engaging in sexual intercourse.[335] Until religionists provide youths with the knowledge and tools to prevent pregnancy, they should not be allowed to make political hay with the issue of abortion.

A much more enlightened approach is taken by the Olympics, where at the 2010 Winter Games in Vancouver, 100,000 condoms were provided free to the athletes during their two week stay–about 15 per participant.[336] Until condoms and accurate information about contraception, pregnancy and sexually transmitted diseases are freely available to American youths, religionists should not be allowed to claim the moral high ground on the issue of abortion. But of course, abortion is not really the issue for religionists, control is. Religionists do not want people to own their sexuality, they want sexuality to belong to the church, temple or mosque.

If ceding their sexuality to an imaginary bearded man in the sky was the sole act of religionists, I would not be concerned. However, they are trying to force others to follow the same standard. Religiously based limits on access to birth control are one example. "Abstinence only" education is another. From 1994 to 2000, the United States spent $500 million on childhood "education" programs that encouraged abstinence but did not teach about contraception and the prevention of sexually transmitted diseases.[337]

I remember seeing a billboard near a high school paid for through this program. It said, "Only abstinence prevents pregnancy." Of course it is true that abstinence prevents pregnancy, but that is not what the sign said, it said "*Only* abstinence prevents pregnancy." The first thing I thought when I read it was, "oral sex prevents pregnancy." But on second thought, I figured it could also say, "same-sex encounters prevent pregnancy." It is silly to lie to our youths. They are not ignorant. These crazy programs divert money that could be spent equipping young people to make intelligent choices in the modern world. Instead, they are provided patently silly catchphrases like "only abstinence prevents pregnancy" that cater to the powerful religionists and their unscientific myths. A fact ignored by religious mythologists is that 97% of Americans who have had sex, do so before marriage.[338] Failing to educate youths about reproduction, contraception and

119

sexually transmitted disease prevention is like putting them on the road in cars without teaching them how to drive and then blaming them when collisions inevitably occur.

A review of abstinence only programs' effectiveness in 11 states concluded, "Abstinence only programs show little evidence of sustained (long-term) impact on attitudes and intentions. Worse, they show some negative impacts on youth's willingness to use contraception, including condoms, to prevent negative sexual health outcomes related to sexual intercourse . . . none of these programs demonstrates evidence of long-term success in delaying sexual initiation among youth exposed to the programs or any evidence of success in reducing other sexual risk-taking behaviors among participants."[339] Another study confirmed that teens in abstinence only programs were just as likely to have sex as others, but were less likely to use condoms and other forms of birth control.[340] Despite years of funding abstinence only programs, the United States has the highest teen birth rate[341] and one of the highest levels of teen sexually transmitted disease infection rates in the industrialized world. As many as one in four teenage girls in the U.S. has a sexually transmitted disease.[342] The ineffective and expensive abstinence only programs serve religious fictions, not the needs and realities of the modern world. That abstinence only education is funded through 2015[343] is a tribute to the power of religion and demonstrates the harm caused by religionists forcing their myths on others.

The cruel application of ancient prohibitions against gays is discussed more in Chapter 18. The way religionists apply their rules to sexual minorities is also hypocritical. Gay sex and adultery are subject to the same penalty in the Bible: death.[344] Yet religionists work hard to deny rights to gays while they welcome the 20-50% of their members[345] who have been divorced[346] and the more than 21% of married men who have had extramarital affairs.[347]

Absent religion, what reason is there to be guilty about sexuality? Religionists promote dysfunctional beliefs about sex, create guilt about sex, and behave no differently when it comes to sex, they just make themselves feel bad about it. Religion's attempt to own and control its adherents' sexuality is a significant problem. This problem is compounded when religionists use political power to force their myths about sexuality on others.

Chapter 17. Faith in action: the ballad of Ted Haggard.

[W]e don't have to debate what we think about homosexual activity. It's written in the Bible.[348] Ted Haggard

Thou shalt not lie with mankind, as with womankind: it is abomination.[349] The Bible

Born in 1956, Ted Haggard became one of the most influential evangelical Christians in America. A 2005 Time Magazine article named him one of the 25 most influential evangelicals noting that Haggard led the 30 million strong "National Association of Evangelicals" and spoke weekly with the George W. Bush White House. High on Haggard's agenda was opposition to gay marriage.[350]

Married, Haggard fathered five children and led a 14,000 member church in Colorado Springs, Colorado. Housed in an $18 million building, Harper's Magazine called Haggard's New Life Church, "the most powerful megachurch in America."[351] In 2006, he earned an annual salary of $338,000 and lived in a house worth more than $700,000.[352] In addition, he collected royalties from 12 books and earned fees for speaking and public appearances.

In 2006, Haggard and his church supported "Amendment 43" to the Colorado Constitution.[353] It provided, "Only a union of one man and one woman shall be valid or recognized as a marriage in this state."[354] Although Colorado law already defined marriage as being between a man and a woman, Haggard and other gay rights opponents sought to enshrine the prohibition in the state constitution.

Six days before the election on the anti-gay amendment, a 49-year-old Denver man named Mike Jones came forward and said Haggard, whom he knew as "Art" (Haggard's middle name), had over

122

a period of three years paid him for sex about once a month and also used methamphetamines (meth) in his presence. Jones provided a letter and two answering machine messages in support of his claims. Jones said, "After sitting back and contemplating this issue, the biggest reason is, being a gay man all my life, I have experienced with my friends some sadness. I had two friends that were together 50 years, when one of them would get in a hospital for an accident or something, their partner could not get in to see them. I saw a lot of sadness. I felt it was my responsibility to my fellow brothers and sisters that I had to take a stand."[355]

Haggard's immediate response was denial. He told a Denver television station, "I did not have a homosexual relationship with a man in Denver . . . I am steady with my wife. I'm faithful to my wife." Haggard also said, "I have never done drugs--ever. Not even in high school. I didn't smoke pot. I didn't do anything like that. I'm not a drug man. We're not a drinking family. I don't smoke cigarettes. I don't socially drink. We don't socially drink. We don't have wine in our house. We don't do that kind of thing." Cornered by his voicemail to Mike Jones requesting meth, Haggard told the press, "I bought it for myself but never used it. I was tempted but I never used it." Haggard claimed he bought the meth but threw it away.[356]

Although well enough versed in Bible lore to write multiple books, he must not have remembered the biblical instruction to tell the truth.[357] He must also have forgotten a quote from his own book *Primary Purpose*, "As soon as we believe that we can think, say or do secret things, there is a greater opportunity for the enemy to persuade us to violate God's Word. After all, the newspaper's best headlines are accounts of people doing things they thought would remain a secret." But there is some humor in his final New Life Church sermon, where he prayed, "Heavenly Father give us grace and mercy, help us this next week and a half as we go into national elections and Lord we pray for our country. Father we pray lies would be exposed and deception exposed."[358] Despite the revelations about Haggard's misdeeds, anti-gay Amendment 43 passed by a 57% to 43% vote.[359]

123

Soon after Mike Jones' revelations, New Life Church member Grant Haas came forward with more allegations about which Brady Boyd, Haggard's successor leading the church, said an "overwhelming pool of evidence" pointed to an "inappropriate, consensual sexual relationship" that "went on for a long period of time . . . it wasn't a one-time act."[360] Haas alleged Haggard masturbated in front of him and sent him thousands of sexually explicit text messages including Haggard talking about sexual positions, pornography, masturbation and drugs.[361] Haas estimated Haggard sent 1,000 to 2,000 messages a month and included descriptions of Haggard's sexual experiences and drug use while traveling. New Life Church agreed to pay Haas $179,000 because of his claim.[362] That is not all. A Colorado Springs bail-bondsman claims he has uncovered ten additional cases of sexual misconduct by Haggard.[363]

In 2010, as part of the promotion of her new book, Haggard's wife Gayle said her knowledge of Haggard's extramarital affairs dated back to the late 1980's when Haggard told her he had sex with a man in an adult bookstore. She further said, "Our marriage is everything I ever hoped it would be," and that her husband had cleared up his issues with homosexuality.[364]

Haggard has made a bizarre journey through the media and ended up back where he started, with a church in Colorado Springs. One day after Mike Jones' allegations, Haggard resigned from New Life Church and left the American Association of Evangelicals.[365] In exchange for severance pay, he agreed to leave Colorado Springs and to avoid media contact. Haggard moved to Phoenix where he attended the same church that helped "rehabilitate" fellow evangelical Jim Baker after he finished his prison sentence for bilking supporters of $158 million.[366] Despite his relative financial well-being, Haggard emailed devotees asking for donations to help support him.[367] Haggard went on to appear in HBO movie *The Trials of Ted Haggard*, to appear on *Larry King Live*, *Oprah*, and TV's *Divorce Court*, to fail as an insurance agent, and to return to Colorado Springs. Bit by bit, Haggard admitted almost all of the allegations against him, including using meth.[368]

In November 2009, Haggard began holding prayer meetings in his Colorado Springs basement. One hundred and ten people attended the first prayer meeting.[369] By the next meeting, the large number of attendees forced him to move the prayer meeting to his barn. Haggard also says he has been named an overseer at a church, someone who counsels and advises church leaders on moral, ethical and religious issues.[370] In May 2010, Haggard announced he was incorporating a new church for accounting purposes,[371] perhaps so that he could operate his business tax-free as he had in the past.[372] And by June 2010, Haggard said he would operate a full-blown church.[373] Gayle Haggard's book *Why I Stayed: The Choices I Made in My Darkest Hour*, is making money. Haggard's Website, TedHaggard.com, included this message in early 2010:

> [Gayle and I] are both writing, traveling, and speaking testifying to the faithfulness of the Lord Jesus, the Scriptures and the body of Christ in our lives. The dynamics that created the confusion in my life and consequently the sin that gripped my life have been resolved through counseling accompanied by Jesus' faithfulness, the supportive decisions of Gayle and my children, and patient friends. It is true, he who has been forgiven much loves much. Thank God![374]

The problem with Ted Haggard is not his gay relationships, the problem is his illegal conduct of patronizing prostitutes, buying and using illegal drugs, using his position of trust to take advantage of a congregant and violating his promises to his spouse and family. Ted Haggard is probably eligible to be named one of the top hypocrites of the decade. But I do not include his story for that reason. Instead, I include it as a sad lesson in the role of religion in his and his family's life.

Haggard is obviously a talented man. He built a successful business, amassed considerable political power, and wrote 12 books.

But think of the great unhappiness he must suffer because he refuses to be true to his nature, simply because of teachings from an ancient book, written by men and fixed in time.

If Haggard were raised differently, if he had different beliefs, or if he admitted the truth, both about himself and about religion, things could have been different. He might have become a similarly successful gay rights activist. His efforts would have been to make life better for himself and his brethren, rather than condemning his fellow gays to second class status. At least he could have helped change the nasty political climate evangelical Christians have created for gays and lesbians. And as a healthy, self-actualized gay man he could have had healthy relationships instead of using drugs, prostitution and coercion to satisfy his desires.

Take, for example, Congressman Barney Frank. He too had a scandal involving a male prostitute.[375] But instead of sweeping it under the rug, he acknowledged his errors, acknowledged his sexuality, and today he is a role model for young gays. Currently, he serves as Chair of the House Financial Services Committee. Both before and after coming out he was a strong supporter of gay and minority rights. He is openly gay and has a long term boyfriend.[376] Ted Haggard could have had a life like Frank's. Instead, he is back in Colorado Springs, building a new church.

And think about the pain for Haggard's wife and family. Gayle Haggard could have married someone who truly wanted to be with her, not a man who led a double life patronizing prostitutes and using drugs and then bringing the risks of his secret lifestyle home to her.

But instead of taking the opportunity to live an honest life, Haggard has returned to his Christian roots. Instead of trying to create a world where a boy like he was could live a happy well-adjusted life; he keeps supporting a world where gay kids are called sinners, and where gay kids are two to seven times more likely to kill themselves than their heterosexual peers.[377]

Ted Haggard presents a pitiful story, not just because of his hypocrisy, but because he is unable to accept the truth about himself and the truth about religion. Instead he continues to live a lie–both his sexuality and his religion.

Chapter 18. Gays and religion.

If a man also lie with mankind, as he lieth with a woman, both of them have committed an abomination: they shall surely be put to death; their blood shall be upon them.[378] The Bible

Society's understanding of gays[379] has changed dramatically in my lifetime. In the past 50 years, homosexual relations have gone from being illegal in every state, to being legal in all states with domestic partnerships authorized in eight states and gay marriage recognized in five states and the District of Colombia.[380] As recently as 1973, homosexuality was considered a mental illness by the American Psychiatric Association and up until 1975 by the American Psychological Association.[381] Until 1961, every state in the U.S. outlawed gay sex.[382] By 2003, it was only nine states, and after the 2003 U.S. Supreme Court decision in *Lawrence v. Texas* all laws prohibiting gay sex were overturned. In that case, writing for the majority, Justice Kennedy said gays, "are entitled to respect for their private lives. The State cannot demean their existence or control their destiny by making their private sexual conduct a crime. Their right to liberty under the Due Process Clause gives them the full right to engage in their conduct without intervention of the government. 'It is a promise of the Constitution that there is a realm of personal liberty which the government may not enter.' [Such a law] . . . furthers no legitimate state interest which can justify its intrusion into the personal and private life of the individual."[383] In a short time, gays have moved from being "outlaws" in all states to ever-increasingly becoming "in-laws."

In the past 50 years, science has not clearly established what makes people gay, but it has established that they are born that way.[384] Gay people are born that way, and it is grossly unfair to apply ancient

128

rules to deny them equality in the modern world. Without religion, there is no reason other than prejudice to deny gays equal rights, including the right to marry. As in so many other instances, religious scriptures, written by men and fixed in time, have been unable to adapt to a changing world.

Religionists have singled out gays for particularly venomous attacks. The battle cry of "god, guns and gays" helped to form a coalition of the rich and stupid, where the rich got tax breaks, pro-business judges and lax enforcement of laws and regulations while the stupid got "protection" from gay marriage and a promise that one day abortion would be outlawed. Hatred against gays has served as a strong fund-raising issue for both the religious right and the Republican party.

Why the majority of religionists hate gays is unclear. Perhaps it springs from the goal of enforcing procreation not recreation when it comes to sexuality. Or perhaps it encourages in-group dedication when a weak minority is singled out for abuse. Having a scapegoat may be useful to religionists. For example, the 9/11 attacks and Hurricane Katrina have been blamed on gays.[385] Or maybe the religionists fear same-sex attractions in themselves and prove they are heterosexual by condemning homosexuals. But perhaps it is just a reliable fund-raising technique. Whatever the reason, the negative approach to gays affects a sizable minority. Studies estimate that between 2-10% of the American population is gay.[386] Working with an intermediate figure of 5%, there are 15 million gays in the U.S., more than all the atheists, Jews and Mormons combined. That is a lot of people who are hurt by the religionists' prejudices.

The negative social environment for gays has had devastating consequences. Gay youths got to see the President of the United States call for a Constitutional Amendment banning gay rights during George W. Bush's 2004 State of the Union Speech.[387] Gay teens are two to seven times more likely to attempt suicide than the general population.[388] Facing a world of social condemnation and discrimination gays are more likely to misuse alcohol and drugs and tend to die earlier than heterosexuals.[389]

Religionists are happy to assist their gay congregants to feel bad about themselves. Conservative Christians have even started an "ex-gay" movement to encourage self loathing and denial among believing homosexuals. A Catholic group, "Courage" says, "[T]he individual dealing with same-sex attractions truly . . . [needs] to experience the freedom of interior chastity and in that freedom find the steps necessary to living a fully Christian life in communion with God and others. . . . With the endorsement of the Holy See, Courage now has more than 110 Chapters. . . . It has become a mainstream Catholic Apostolate helping thousands of men and women find peace through fellowship, prayer, and the Sacraments."[390] The Catholic Church, notably, first blamed its pedophile priest problem on Jews, before settling on blaming it on gays.[391] Regarding ex-gay programs, The American Psychological Association says, "Despite the general consensus of major medical, health, and mental health professions that both heterosexuality and homosexuality are normal expressions of human sexuality, efforts to change sexual orientation through therapy have been adopted by some political and religious organizations and aggressively promoted to the public. However, such efforts have serious potential to harm young people because they present the view that the sexual orientation of lesbian, gay, and bisexual youth is a mental illness or disorder, and they often frame the inability to change one's sexual orientation as a personal and moral failure."[392] The "ex-gay" movement is an example of pursuing religious myth to the exclusion of scientific fact, with harmful consequences.

Kill 'em.

Religious apologists try to find ways around the scriptural condemnation of gays. But the language is crystal clear. The New International Version of the Bible puts it in modern terms: "If a man lies with a man as one lies with a woman, both of them have done what is detestable. They must be put to death."[393]

It is doubtless that religionists are hypocrites in their application of biblical rules. They do not stone adulterers.[394] They do not stone children who curse their parents.[395] They do not stone disobedient children.[396] They do not stone those who work on Sunday.[397] They do not stone those who say "god damn."[398] They do not avoid clothing of blended fibers[399] and they do not avoid clipping the edges of their hair or beards.[400] But hypocrisy aside, there is no way to read around the scriptural condemnation of gay sex. The scriptures were written by men and are fixed in time. By the terms the religionists have established, the scriptures cannot now be rewritten to incorporate a modern understanding of gays. If gays are okay, the scriptures are wrong. If the scriptures are right, then gays should be killed.

Therefore it should be no surprise that killing gays is what religionists are demanding in Uganda. Three American Christian evangelists traveled to Uganda in 2009 to expose "the gay agenda--that whole hidden and dark agenda--and the threat homosexuals posed to Bible-based values and the traditional African family."[401] Among them was "ex-gay" Caleb Brundidge, whose International Healing Foundation claims to change homosexuals into heterosexuals. The Ugandans took the challenge and ran with it, introducing a bill to increase the penalty for gay sex from less than 14 years in prison to making it punishable by life imprisonment and in certain instances, death. One of the supporters is linked with President Obama's inaugural invocation reading pastor, Rick Warren. Martin Ssempa, an Ugandan pastor, traveled several times to make presentations at Warren's church and *Newsweek* described Warren as "warmly embracing" Ssempa. Warren had visited Uganda in 2008.[402] With regard to Warren's position on the anti-gay legislation, *Newsweek* said:

> Warren won't go so far as to condemn the legislation itself. A request for a broader reaction to the proposed Ugandan antihomosexual laws generated this response: "The fundamental dignity of every person, our right to be free, and the freedom to make moral choices are gifts endowed by God, our creator. However, it is not my

131

personal calling as a pastor in America to comment or interfere in the political process of other nations."[403]

Ugandan religionists, American missionary provocateurs and even Rick Warren are doing what their scriptures tell them–calling for the death of gays. They are being more honest than their religious peers who mask their prejudice with nicer sounding terms like "pro-family" or "pro-marriage."

Sadly, the approach of Jewish and Christian religionists seems mild when compared to Muslims. The Koran has multiple verses condemning homosexuality,[404] and the application of Islamic law results in harsh penalties for gays in most Muslim countries.[405]

I have often asked myself, "what came first, religion or hate?" Hate and religion enjoy a rich marriage, and that relationship is particularly clear in the area of religion and gay rights. That is not to say that hate will go away when religion goes away. Hate will remain. But religion creates an effective vessel for hate. Religionists do not need to create a "we hate gays" club, they can join a socially approved religion and mask their prejudices with phrases like, "we follow the law of god." The haters can get the support of liberal apologists who give money to the church and would not dream of discriminating against their gay friends, but whose church leaders regularly lobby and organize to deny equal rights to gays.

Religion is a vessel for hate and it is based on myths and lies. There is no compromise available between religion and gay rights. If religion is right, gays should be killed. If gays are equal human beings deserving respect and dignity, then religion is a lie. My position and the position of most atheists is clear: gays deserve equal rights and religion is a lie.

Transforming belief into law.

As with so many other issues, religionists are not satisfied with applying their rules to themselves, they use their position of power to make others comply with their beliefs. Equality for gays is probably the

132

most important civil rights issue our generation will face. In countries where religion is less important, gays are granted more rights. The ten countries that recognize gay marriage are among the least religious: Argentina,[406] Belgium, Canada, Iceland, The Netherlands, Norway, Portugal, South Africa, Spain and Sweden.[407] In contrast, countries that provide the death penalty for gay sex are among the most religious: Iran, Mauritania, Nigeria, Qatar, Saudi Arabia, Sudan, and Yemen.[408] Within the United States, the most religious people are the most likely to oppose gay marriage. Eighty-one percent of evangelicals oppose gay marriage, joined by 69% of those who attend church weekly and 67% of all Protestants, while only 25% of the religiously unaffiliated share that view.[409]

The California Supreme Court, when asked to decide if gay people in California had the right to marry, phrased the issue in terms of civil rights:

> [T]he change in this state's past treatment of gay individuals and homosexual conduct is reflected in scores of legislative, administrative, and judicial actions that have occurred over the past 30 or more years. (See, e.g., Stats. 1975, ch. 71, §§ 7, 10, pp. 133, 134 [revising statutes criminalizing consensual sodomy and oral copulation]; Governor's Exec. Order No. B-54-79 (Apr. 4, 1979) [barring sexual orientation discrimination against state employees]; *Morrison v. State Board of Education* (1969) 1 Cal.3d 214 [homosexual conduct does not in itself necessarily constitute immoral conduct or demonstrate unfitness to teach].) Thus, just as this court recognized in *Perez* that it was not constitutionally permissible to continue to treat racial or ethnic minorities as inferior (*Perez*, supra, 32 Cal.2d at pp. 720-727), and in *Sail'er Inn* that it was not constitutionally acceptable to continue to treat women as less capable than and unequal to men (*Sail'er Inn*,

supra, 5 Cal.3d at pp. 17-20 & fn. 15), we now similarly recognize that an individual's homosexual orientation is not a constitutionally legitimate basis for withholding or restricting the individual's legal rights.[410]

The California Supreme Court granted gays the right to marry in June 2008. A group called the "renewal project" started a "Protect Marriage" campaign to put discrimination against gays into the California Constitution thus overruling the California Supreme Court. Initially, public opinion supported gay marriage by as many as 17 points over opponents.[411] Frank Shubert and Jeff Flint of Schubert Flint Public Affairs said, "When we signed our firm up to manage the Yes on Proposition 8 campaign to put the traditional definition of marriage-- one man, one woman--into California's constitution . . . we had 'no chance' to win the campaign." But the religionists flexed their muscles. Protect Marriage raised almost $40 million. Anti-gay Proposition 8 was supported by an array of religions including Mormons, Catholics, evangelical groups, Focus on the Family, and President Obama's choice to give a prayer at his inauguration, Rick Warren of Saddleback Church.[412]

Although Mormons comprise only 2% of California's population, the Mormon Church played an important role in the fight against gay marriage in California.[413] Mormons gave over one-half of the total $40 million raised to fight gay marriage,[414] and perhaps as much as 71% of the total money raised.[415] In an article analyzing their win, Shubert and Flint said, "Even though the LDS[416] were the last major denomination to join the campaign, their members were immensely helpful in early fundraising, providing much-needed contributions while we were busy organizing Catholic and Evangelical fundraising efforts. Ultimately, we raised $22 million from July through September with upwards of 40 percent coming from members of the LDS Church." The Mormon Church directed members to donate both their time and money in opposition to gay marriage, and 45% of Protect Marriage's out-of-state contributions came from Utah, where 72% of the residents are Mormon.[417] Jeff Flint estimates that Mormons made up 80 to 90 percent of the early door-to-door volunteers in California.[418] Trying to deflect complaints about Mormons influencing the outcome, Shubert and Flint spread the blame to all religionists, "Members of the Mormon faith played an important part of the Yes on 8 coalition, but were only a part of our winning coalition. We had the support of virtually the entire faith community in California."[419]

For about seven months, gays in California had the right to marry. But in November 2008, the people of California passed proposition 8, amending the state constitution and mandating that, "Only marriage between a man and a woman is valid or recognized in California." The measure passed by a 52% to 48% margin, the early support for gay marriage was overcome by a powerful religionist campaign.

Gay marriage in Maine faced similar defeat and Mormons, allied with Catholics and other religionists, played a key role. The Maine legislature passed a bill allowing gay marriage, but the law never went into effect because of a 2009 ballot initiative. The Catholic Church began the petition drive to overturn the law. The Catholic Church added special collections to its religious services where it encouraged members to give money to help to defeat gay marriage.[420] Just as in California, early poll results showed voters favoring gay marriage. The anti-gay marriage group, "Stand for Marriage Maine," hired the same public relations firm that worked for the religionists in California. The Mormon-linked National Organization for Marriage provided more than one-half of the funding.[421] The gay rights opponents used similar tactics to the California group, claiming gay marriage and gay sexuality would be taught to school children. The religionists prevailed in Maine, overturning the gay marriage law by a 53% to 47% vote.[422]

Mormons have been leaders in the campaign against gay marriage for years. Mormons are adamantly against gay marriage. The Mormon Church's statement on gay marriage says, "[M]arriage is neither a matter of politics, nor is it a matter of social policy. Marriage is defined by the Lord Himself. . . . It is not an institution to be tampered with by mankind, and certainly not to be tampered with by those who are doing so simply for their own purposes. There is no such thing in the Lord's eyes as something called same-gender marriage. Homosexual behavior is and will always remain before the Lord an abominable sin."[423] Mormon involvement in this issue started with the effort to defeat gay marriage in Hawaii in the mid-1990's.[424] In Hawaii, the Mormons established the secretive pattern they have duplicated in other states. Mormons provide the money and control the group while hiding their role and allowing other religionists to be out front.[425] Utah, 72% Mormon,[426] in 1995 was first state to enact a "defense of marriage" law, which additionally provided Utah need not recognize same sex unions from other states.[427] Utah, unsurprisingly, is the lowest ranked state in the U.S. when it comes to favoring equal rights for gays.[428] The largest contributor to the anti-gay Maine group was the "National Organization for Marriage." An opponent of the group has filed a complaint claiming the "National Organization for Marriage" is a front for the Mormon Church to funnel funds into anti-gay campaigns.[429] The National Organization for Marriage provided the largest initial contributions to challenge gay marriage in Maine,[430] and $1.9 million of the total $3.8 million raised throughout the campaign.[431] The National Organization for Marriage, which refuses to identify its funding sources, is currently fighting gay rights in a number of states and on the national level.[432]

The strategy has been highly effective. Thirty states now enshrine prejudice against gays in their constitutions. For example, the Ohio Constitution provides, "Only a union between one man and one woman may be a marriage valid in or recognized by this state and its political subdivisions. This state and its political subdivisions shall not create or recognize a legal status for relationships of unmarried individuals that intends to approximate the design, qualities, significance or effect of marriage."[433] Gay rights opponents have already used the Ohio ban to challenge a city domestic partner registry,[434] and some fear the amendment could ban insurance benefits

136

for same sex partners, or the right to make medical decisions pursuant to a durable power of attorney.

Not surprisingly, the largest contributor to the Ohio Amendment was a nonprofit group called "Citizens for Community Values," which gave $1,182,1239, or 98.94% of all donations. The next largest contributor was an individual who gave $2,000. After a complaint that the "Citizens for Community Values" group would not disclose its donors, an investigation was begun but later dropped because all Republicans on the panel opposed it, and there were not enough votes to go forward.[435] The role the Mormon church played in the Ohio amendment has not been disclosed, but the pattern is familiar.

There is one bright point about Mormon involvement. Mormons, a small minority, by targeting their time, money and effort, have had an oversized impact on the gay rights debate. As one commentator put it, "Without the LDS [Mormon] church, gay marriage would remain settled law in California."[436] This is troubling on one hand, but inspiring on another. Atheists are as numerous[437] and economically powerful as Mormons. If atheists organized, we could have similar impact on important issues. In fact, the potential pool of atheists (especially if you include "nones") is larger than the Mormon population.

Religionists are not satisfied with beating up gays within their congregations. As with so many other issues, they use their position of power to force their scriptural values on others. The bumper sticker slogan, "Against gay marriage? Don't have one," does not satisfy religionists. They instead use their power to apply their rules to everyone, enshrining discrimination against gays in the constitutions of 30 states and the laws of 41 states.[438] Religionists' hateful treatment of gays is an ongoing problem.

Chapter 19. Art to die for.

Good art makes you think.[439]

This crime called blasphemy was invented by priests for the purpose of defending doctrines not able to take care of themselves.[440] Robert Ingersoll

The collision of art, free speech and religion is enlightening. Historically, in Western countries, art and free speech usually win. The situation is reversed in Muslim countries, where "blasphemy" is often a crime.[441] But the trend is shifting. Religionists' reaction to art which is legal, but offends their religious mores, often shifts into superlegal action–supernaturally authorized illegal acts (see Chapter 21). The use of religion to justify illegal activities, including murder, for often innocuous art, is one of the most shocking and unjustifiable functions of religion.

In 2004, Theo Van Gogh, a distant relative of artist Vincent Van Gogh, directed a ten-minute English language film called "Submission." "Submission" is a literal translation of the word "Islam." The screenplay was written by a Somali-born refugee who fled an arranged marriage and eventually became a member of the Dutch Parliament. The film shows four women, who while praying, describe the physical and sexual abuse they have suffered from men. The women have verses from the Koran written on their skin and are wearing transparent garments.[442]

The verses from the Koran included:

Men are the maintainers of women because Allah has made some of them to excel others and because they

138

spend out of their property; the good women are therefore obedient, guarding the unseen as Allah has guarded; and (as to) those on whose part you fear desertion, admonish them, and leave them alone in the sleeping-places and beat them; then if they obey you, do not seek a way against them; surely Allah is High, Great.[443]

They ask thee concerning women's courses. Say: They are a hurt and a pollution: So keep away from women in their courses, and do not approach them until they are clean. But when they have purified themselves, ye may approach them in any manner, time, or place ordained for you by Allah. For Allah loves those who turn to Him constantly and He loves those who keep themselves pure and clean.[444]

(As for) the fornicatress and the fornicator, flog each of them, (giving) a hundred stripes, and let not pity for them detain you in the matter of obedience to Allah, if you believe in Allah and the last day, and let a party of believers witness their chastisement.[445]

Following the airing of the film, both Van Gogh and the author of the screenplay, Hirsi Ali, were threatened with death. Ms. Ali already had police protection. Van Gogh declined police protection and told Ms. Ali, "if they kill me, remember the rule of law has to be protected against extremists."[446]

In November 2004, on a city street in broad daylight, a Dutch-Moroccan Muslim man shot Van Gogh six times, slit his throat, and then pinned a six-page letter to his body with a knife.[447] The letter declared jihad against Holland, Europe and the United States and included this statement (translated from Dutch):

Islam will be victorious through the blood of the martyrs. They will spread its light in every dark corner of this earth and it will drive evil, with the sword if necessary, back into its dark hole. This struggle which has burst forth is different than those of the past. The unbelieving fundamentalists have started it and Inshallah the true believers will end it.

There will be no mercy shown to the purveyors of injustice, only the sword will be lifted against them. No discussions, no demonstrations, no petitions; DEATH will separate the Truth from the Lies.

Verse: Be warned that the death that you are trying to prevent will surely find you, afterwards you will be taken back to the All Knowing and He will tell you what you attempted to do.[448]

The story of Danish cartoonist Kurt Westergaard has also become well known. Westergaard drew a political cartoon showing the face of a bearded man with a bomb in his turban. The bomb was a simple black circle, the kind you would see in a child's cartoon, with a lit fuse. Dutch newspaper Jyllands-Posten (Jyllands Post) ran the cartoon as part of a series of 12 in 2005. The editor commented:

I commissioned the cartoons in response to several incidents of self-censorship in Europe caused by widening fears and feelings of intimidation in dealing with issues related to Islam . . . over two weeks we witnessed a half-dozen cases of self-censorship, pitting freedom of speech against the fear of confronting issues about Islam. This was a legitimate news story to cover, and Jyllands-Posten decided to do it by adopting the well-known journalistic principle: Show, don't tell. I wrote to members of the association of Danish cartoonists asking them "to draw Muhammad as you see him."

* * *

As a former correspondent in the Soviet Union, I am sensitive about calls for censorship on the grounds of insult. This is a popular trick of totalitarian movements: Label any critique or call for debate as an insult and punish the offenders. That is what happened to human rights activists and writers such as Andrei Sakharov, Vladimir Bukovsky, Alexander Solzhenitsyn, Natan Sharansky, Boris Pasternak. The regime accused them of anti-Soviet propaganda, just as some Muslims are labeling 12 cartoons in a Danish newspaper anti-Islamic.

The lesson from the Cold War is: If you give in to totalitarian impulses once, new demands follow. The West prevailed in the Cold War because we stood by our fundamental values and did not appease totalitarian tyrants.[449]

Two Danish imams added photos of a French comedian wearing a pig nose at a pig calling contest and other materials to the cartoons and distributed them at a Muslim summit in Mecca, leading to protests across the Muslim world, including 70,000 gathered in Pakistan.[450] Ensuing riots resulted in the deaths of as many as 200 people and millions of dollars in damages.[451] The simple cartoon has resulted in at least two Muslim attempts to murder Westergaard. His house has been modified to include a "safe room" that saved him in a 2009 attack and $3.9 million has been spent protecting him.[452] Westergaard commented, "I realize that when issues of religion are involved emotions run high, and all religions have their symbols, which possess great importance … But when you live in a secularized society, it's clear that religion can't demand some sort of special status . . . I have a problem with the fact that we have people from another culture who don't accept that we use religious elements in a drawing."[453]

On an anniversary reprinting of the cartoons, the Vatican issued a joint statement with a Sunni Muslim University condemning--*not* the riots, deaths and death threats to the cartoonist, but the publication of the cartoon. It read, "Both sides vehemently denounce the reprinting of the offensive cartoon and the attack on Islam and its prophet. We call for the respect of faiths, religious holy books and religious symbols. Freedom of expression should not become a pretext to insult religions and defaming [*sic*] religious sanctities."[454]

Attempted murder of cartoonists drawing Mohammed is not a one time thing. In 2007, Swedish artist Lars Vilks, as part of an exhibition about the dog in art, drew three sketches of Mohammed's head on a dog's body. The exhibition withdrew the pictures before displaying them because of the fear of violence. Vilks then submitted them to a teacher's exhibition at an art school where he lectures. The school rejected the pictures for security concerns. Finally, several newspapers printed the pictures.

A group called "al-Qaeda in Iraq" has offered a $100,000 bounty for killing Vilks, with a 50% bonus if his throat is slit "like a lamb."[455] In March 2010, Irish authorities arrested a group of seven who were planning to kill Vilks.[456] Two American women were involved in the plot.[457] Vilks has been attacked while giving a lecture and arsonists have tried to burn his home.[458]

Even the satirical cartoon show *South Park* is not immune. The cartoonists did not draw Mohammed, but rather provided his voice from the back of a moving van and from inside a bear costume. An American Muslim[459] posted an Internet warning that the *South Park* cartoonists will probably end up dead like Theo Van Gogh, and put the cartoonists' addresses on the Internet.[460] The network broadcasting the show, Comedy Central, responded by bleeping out all references to

Mohammed in the second of two episodes that featured Mohammed's voice.[461] In response, an Internet user suggested that May 20, 2010 be declared "everybody draw Mohammed day," an idea others enthusiastically adopted.[462] The Secular Student Alliance posted advice and sample drawings on its Website.[463] Time will tell if this mass-response to religious censorship of art will be effective.

Killing for art is a uniquely religious characteristic. The Muslims have taken anger over perceived blasphemy and made it cause for international murder schemes. They are successfully censoring free speech in countries where it is protected. For example, Jytte Klausen wrote a book about the Danish cartoons titled, *The Cartoons that Shook the World*. Naturally, she included images of the cartoons. The publisher, Yale University Press, owned by Yale University, removed the cartoons from the book, as well as other images of Mohammed. Yale University Press announced, "The decision rested solely on the experts' assessments that there existed a substantial likelihood of violence that might take the lives of innocent victims."[464]

A storied American University allowed fear of superlegal violence by religious adherents to override freedom of speech. This is a dangerous aspect of religion.

And before Christian religionists start feeling too smug about their liberalism, an award winning photograph by Andres Serrano entitled "Piss Christ," which showed a plastic crucifix in hazy yellow liquid the artist said was his urine brought about violence, but not murder. When shown in Australia, on one day a patron tried to rip it off the wall and on another day, two men attacked it with a hammer, succeeding in getting the photo removed from the exhibition.[465]

Similarly, in the U.S., a portrait of Jesus' mother that included elephant dung and pornographic images was smeared with white paint at the Brooklyn Museum of Art because the vandal found it "blasphemous."[466] Admittedly, no one died in the actions of the Christians, yet they felt beliefs entitled them to violate the law to censor art.

Good art makes you think. But with their angry and sometimes violent response to thought-provoking art, it appears that religionists are afraid of thinking.

Fish legs and atheist riots.

Nowadays, when you hear about a suicide bomber, an airline hijacker, or a riot, as often as not, religion plays a role. When is the last time you heard of an atheist riot?

Religionists like to portray themselves as a defenseless minority being persecuted by powerful atheist groups. But as described in Chapter 2, it is really the other way around. A small but telling example of this is the fact that there is a need to sell plastic "fish legs" to replace the legs religionists feel entitled to break off "Darwin fish" on atheists' cars. Greater in number, greater in power, some religionists find it humorous to destroy another person's property and censor that person's right to free speech. Atheists are not trying to censor the religionists, religionists are trying to censor the atheists. Who acts like they are right?

If you published a political cartoon depicting an atheist, nothing would happen. A search on google results in countless atheist cartoons. Now perform the same search for Mohammed. There are only a few. The violent reaction of Muslim religionists censors free speech even in countries that guarantee it.

Religionists believe their myths give them superlegal powers to attack and even murder artists who produce work the religionists do not like. This dangerous perception of privilege is a disturbing symptom of the problems with religion.

Chapter 20. Religion and lies: necessarily intertwined.

Those who can make you believe absurdities can make you commit atrocities.[467] Voltaire

Religion is a lie. One need look no further than the four corners of the scriptures to find contradictions and impossibilities. For example, does the Bible say that god can be seen and heard? Well, yes and no. Here's what the Bible says:

> So Jacob called the place Peniel [the face of god], saying, "It is because I saw God face to face, and yet my life was spared."[468]

* * *

> The LORD would speak to Moses face to face, as a man speaks with his friend.[469]

* * *

> Then the man and his wife [Adam and Eve] heard the sound of the LORD God as he was walking in the garden in the cool of the day, and they hid from the LORD God among the trees of the garden. But the LORD God called to the man, "Where are you?" He answered, "I heard you in the garden, and I was afraid because I was naked; so I hid." And he said, "Who told you that you were naked? Have you eaten from the tree that I commanded you not to eat from?" The man said,

"The woman you put here with me--she gave me some fruit from the tree, and I ate it." Then the LORD God said to the woman, "What is this you have done?" The woman said, "The serpent deceived me, and I ate."[470]

Ignoring the issue of why an omnipotent god could not find the only man and woman on earth, the Bible story has god and man conversing.

Other parts of the Bible say that no man may see god's face:

And the LORD said, "I will cause all my goodness to pass in front of you, and I will proclaim my name, the LORD, in your presence" . . . "But," he said, "you cannot see my face, for no one may see me and live."[471]

Puzzlingly, Jesus, the putative son of god, said that god could be neither heard nor seen. The Bible reports Jesus said, "And the Father himself, which hath sent me, hath borne witness of me. Ye have neither heard his voice at any time, nor seen his shape."[472]

At least one of these statements in the "perfect book" is untrue. An atheist sees these inconsistencies as evidence the book was written by different men at different times, probably never knowing their tales would be assembled into a single book labeled the work of god. A religionist, on the other hand, is left supporting the lie that his holy book is perfect, when the imperfections are obvious.

The Koran has similar contradictions. For example, Muslims are prohibited from drinking alcohol in sura 2:219,[473] but another part of the "perfect book" says that among the good things Allah provides are, "the palm and the vine, from which you get wine and other healthful nutriment."[474] Other translations use the terms "intoxicants," "strong drink," and "inebriating liquor," although some change it to "wholesome drink."

Returning to the Bible, the story of god stopping the sun in the sky is instructive. The Bible says:

On the day the LORD gave the Amorites over to Israel, Joshua said to the LORD in the presence of Israel: "O sun, stand still over Gibeon, O moon, over the Valley of Aijalon." So the sun stood still, and the moon stopped, till the nation avenged itself on its enemies . . . The sun stopped in the middle of the sky and delayed going down about a full day. There has never been a day like it before or since, a day when the LORD listened to a man. Surely the LORD was fighting for Israel![475]

Making the sun and moon stand still in the sky must have been a great theatrical tool when men thought the sun rotated around the earth. But pictures of the earth from space and flights around the globe have convinced almost all the flat-earth-adherents that the earth is a planet that rotates around the sun. Therefore, to make the sun stand still in the sky, the earth would have needed to stop rotating, causing a loss of gravity and all the soldiers flying off into space! But no, lies are acceptable in the scriptures and the Bible story concludes with Joshua killing every person, young and old, and "all that breathed."[476]

Isaac Asimov said, "Properly read, the Bible is the most potent force for Atheism ever conceived."[477] Although the reasons that people leave religion have not been widely studied, a limited study by Altemeyer and Hunsberger agrees. They said, "If you want a 'nuclear' cause of [leaving religion] . . . it originates with this issue: Can you believe in the Bible, and its story of the existence of God?"[478] In a later study of atheists, the same authors reported, "atheists simply could not make themselves believe what most people believe. It was all too flawed, too self-contradictory, too unsupported, too illogical, [the atheists] said. They wanted the Truth."[479]

A Muslim man related a similar phenomenon about a colleague who insisted that he read the Koran to bring him closer to religion. It had the opposite effect:

He vouched that after I had comprehended the true messages of the Holy Scripture my life would change forever--for the better, he insisted. Reluctantly, I started to read the English translation--verse by verse, passage by passage. The more I read, the more I was shocked, disturbed, astonished, bewildered and resentful. I could not believe that a book which is supposed to be the handiwork of the most compassionate, the most merciful and the most forgiving Allah could contain such a terrible amount of hate, terror, call for murder, war, vengeance and most of all, a blanket plea for the destruction of all those who do not subscribe to the Qur'anic view of the world. . . . The more I learned about the Qur'an the more I became distraught, disturbed and angry--angry, because I felt that I was utterly let down by a killer religion which was imposed on me due to my birth.[480]

Religion is a lie. There is no bearded man in the sky. There was no virgin birth. Prayers are not answered. Jesus did not ascend bodily into heaven and Mohammed did not fly away on a winged horse. Thinking back to the Mormons described in Chapter 8, there were no golden plates, Mormons did not descend from an Israeli tribe that migrated to America, dark skin is not a punishment from god, and plural marriage is not a prerequisite to becoming a god yourself.

However, religious leaders repeatedly stand before their congregations and repeat these lies, and congregants repeatedly claim to believe them. Eventually, they build a house of cards composed of lies, so piling on more lies has little consequence.

Mark Twain said, "Faith is believing something you know ain't true."[481] A distinction between religionists and atheists is that religionists are more inclined to accept lies and atheists are more inclined to seek the truth. I have been continually amazed that religionists accept as true information that is demonstrably false. An

148

easy example is denying evolution science. Another example is believing untrue justifications for the war in Iraq. American religionists have consistently been the strongest supporters of war in Iraq.

Immediately following 9/11, only 3% of Americans suspected Iraq was behind the attacks. However, after a campaign by the Bush administration, by January 2003, 44% of Americans believed that most or some of the 9/11 attackers were Iraqi and 45% believed that Iraqi President Saddam Hussein was personally involved in the attacks.[482] Despite the fact that George W. Bush admitted in 2003, "No, we've had no evidence that Saddam Hussein was involved with September the 11th,"[483] religionists made it an issue of faith that Iraq had to be attacked. Support for the war in Iraq has been consistently highest among evangelical and born again Christians.[484] The more religious an American, the more likely that he supports the war. The least supportive group was those with no religion.[485]

The same preachers who stand before their congregation and lie from the scriptures adopted a faith-based approach to war. Sarah Palin's former pastor "has also preached that critics of President Bush will be banished to hell; questioned whether people who voted for Sen. John Kerry in 2004 would be accepted to heaven; charged that the 9/11 terrorist attacks and war in Iraq were part of a war 'contending for your faith;' and said that Jesus 'operated from that position of war mode.'" Palin herself made the war a religious issue, saying, "Pray for our military men and women who are striving to do what is right. Also, for this country, that our leaders, our national leaders, are sending (U.S. soldiers) out on a task that is from God."[486] Palin, a darling of the religious right, has declared that America is a "Christian nation" and that she opposes the separation of church and state.[487]

Sarah Palin was also at the heart of Politifact's 2009 Lie of the Year, "death panels."[488] As part of the dispute about President Obama's proposed health care changes, Palin coined the term "death panel" when she wrote on her Facebook page:

149

As more Americans delve into the disturbing details of
the nationalized health care plan that the current
administration is rushing through Congress, our
collective jaw is dropping, and we're saying not just no,
but hell no! . . . The America I know and love is not one
in which my parents or my baby with Down Syndrome
will have to stand in front of Obama's 'death panel' so
his bureaucrats can decide, based on a subjective
judgment of their 'level of productivity in society,'
whether they are worthy of health care. Such a system
is downright evil.

In truth, the bill proposed reimbursing medical doctors for
optional counseling to Medicare recipients about things like advance
directives and hospice care.[489] The lie took off and circulated widely in
right-wing religious circles. One poll found that only 50% of Americans
disbelieved the "death panel" lie, 45% believed it, and 5% were not
sure.[490] A poll with a larger sample confirmed that 50% of Americans
who had heard of death panels disbelieved the lie, but found 30%
believed it and 20% were not sure.[491] The polls did not inquire about
religion, but they did ask about party affiliation. Nearly half of
Republicans believed the death panel claims, but only 20% of
Democrats did.[492] In the end, the lie won. The Senate version of the bill
which eventually became law removed the counseling provisions.[493]

Another popular lie is that President Obama is not a U.S. citizen
(he is[494]). About 77% of the general population thinks Obama is
American, but only 42% of Republicans and 47% of Southerners are
sure Obama is American.[495] More research would be required to
correlate belief in these lies directly to religion, but indicators are there.
Belief is highest among Southerners and Republicans, both groups with
disproportionate numbers of religious adherents.

The issue of truth versus lies extends into the personal realm.
Chapter 17 discusses preacher Ted Haggard's fall from power due to
patronizing a male prostitute and using illegal drugs. Despite all of this,

his wife appeared on television and said he is completely heterosexual.[496] Similarly Suzanne Craig, wife of conservative Christian Larry Craig, an Idaho Senator who pled guilty to soliciting a male undercover officer for sex in a Minneapolis airport restroom, stood next to her husband while he told reporters he was not gay and mistakenly pleaded guilty to the charges.[497]

The relationship of lies and religion does not end with sexual scandals. Altemeyer and Hunsberger theorize that while atheists are characterized by low right-wing authoritarianism, religionists are typically high right-wing authoritarianists. Noting that authoritarian followers are more likely to copy their beliefs from others, instead of working things out for themselves, they say:

> [T]heir ideas could be more inconsistent, more self-contradictory, because they have not critically examined their beliefs very much. Their thinking may similarly show lots of double standards. They could prove more dogmatic than most people, because they reached their conclusions largely before they considered the evidence; their only refuge in the face of disconfirming facts may be dogmatism. They may also be readier than most people to accept invalid "evidence" that supports them. They may rely more upon social support for maintaining their beliefs, such as associating with people of like mind.[498]

Religion is a lie. Evidence shows that atheists and religionists differ in their willingness to accept lies and their willingness to question their leaders. This difference helps to explain why you rarely hear of an atheist riot or suicide bombing, while hardly a day goes by without hearing of a religiously motivated crime. A horrible example of this is motivating sexually frustrated young men to conduct suicide bombings with the promise that the religion that prohibits healthy access to women will reward them with the service of seventy-two virgins after their destructive death. Superlegal acts authorized by religious lies, described in the next chapter, constitute one of the most dangerous aspects of religion.

When I speak with a religionist who will not accept established facts–be it legislative language, tax impacts or evolution science, I often need to say to myself, "this is a person who believes in virgin birth, dead bodies coming back to life and a bearded man who lives in the sky and answers prayers." With this in mind, the religionist's acceptance of lies seems consistent with his overall lifestyle.

Religionists regularly attend services and listen to a professional telling lies. Since religionists are trained to accept lies, it is not surprising that they accept new lies on faith–lies like Iraq attacked the U.S., that a health care bill contains provisions to kill grandma, that Ted Haggard is completely heterosexual and that suicide bombers will be rewarded with seventy-two virgins. Religion, with its creation myth, miracles and far-out stories is simply a package of lies--practiced, repeated and refined over the years. Religion and lies are necessarily intertwined.

Chapter 21. Superlegal actions.

Here lies the saint, Dr. Baruch Kappel Goldstein, blessed be the memory of the righteous and holy man, may the Lord avenge his blood, who devoted his soul to the Jews, Jewish religion and Jewish land. His hands are innocent and his heart is pure. He was killed as a martyr of God on the 14th of Adar, Purim, in the year 5754 (1994).[499] Inscription on the grave of Baruch Goldstein

Men never do evil so completely and cheerfully as when they do it from religious conviction.[500] Blaise Pascal

One of the most disturbing effects of religion is that adherents feel it gives them authorization to violate the law, sometimes in the most horrific ways. Law represents a social contract–members of society agree to allow certain conduct and punish other conduct.[501] Religion is sometimes used as a justification for violating the law. Religion is belief in the "super-natural," things outside of nature. I call violations of law based on an imagined supernatural mandate "super-legal," supernaturally justified violations of the law. Superlegal actions range from the petty–breaking the legs off Darwin fish, to the extreme-- crashing airliners into the World Trade Center. But all share the same dangerous genesis, that religion provides a higher authority than law. All three of the major monotheisms have been used in recent years to justify murder.

For example, Dr. Baruch Goldstein was an American physician who emigrated to Israel. Goldstein adhered to a radical Jewish fundamentalism.[502] Serving in the Israeli military, he refused to treat an Arab and said he would only provide medical care to Jews. He was not discharged from the military for refusal to follow orders, but rather was transferred to another unit.[503]

One day, Goldstein put on his military reserve uniform and armed with a rifle and 140 rounds of ammunition, went to the Cave of the Patriarchs in Hebron, West Bank, Israel.[504] Both Muslims and Jews claim the Cave of the Patriarchs is the burial site of Abraham and others, and both religious groups maintain separate worship areas there.[505]

Using his military authority, Goldstein entered the Mosque, put on ear plugs, and began firing at the backs of Muslim worshipers.[506] He killed 29 and wounded 125, before being overpowered by the crowd and beaten to death. Goldstein had carefully chosen a day that was during the Muslim holiday of Ramadan, as well as the Jewish holiday of Purim.[507] Purim celebrates a story of the Jews escaping a Persian plot to kill them.[508]

Most readers would expect Goldstein's attack to be met with condemnation, which it did to a point. However, immediately after the massacre, friends and neighbors called Goldstein a hero and a martyr. Goldstein was given a massive funeral with streets closed in Jerusalem to allow the procession.[509] One observer of the procession said, "There are no innocent Arabs. These deaths were necessary and it is necessary to kill a lot more. Baruch was a hero, a hero of all the Jews. He was a perfect man, a kind man and a sweet man."[510]

Since the massacre, admirers have built a shrine to Goldstein,[511] written a book in praise of him,[512] and sung songs of his heroism.[513] The quote at the start of this chapter is from a memorial to Goldstein. Goldstein's acts were illegal, illegal in Israel and horrific in the eyes of most of the world. However, to some of his faith, his acts were heroic. Such is religion that it takes a criminal and makes him a hero. The use of religion to justify superlegal conduct is one of its most dangerous and disturbing functions.

Superlegal religious justifications for murder cross cultures and religions. Army Major Nidal Hasan was born in Virginia, of parents from Palestine. He volunteered for the U.S. Army and went to medical school on the taxpayers' dime. However, his religious beliefs radicalized and facing deployment to Iraq, he went to work with two guns and killed 13 and wounded 30, mostly soldiers.[514] He allegedly shouted "allahu akbar (god is great)" when he began shooting.[515] Most Americans label him a madman or a terrorist, but his coreligionists have other ideas. An American-born imam posted on his blog:

> Nidal Hasan is a hero. He is a man of conscience who could not bear living the contradiction of being a Muslim and serving in an army that is fighting against his own people. . . . How can there be any dispute about the virtue of what he has done? In fact the only way a Muslim could Islamically justify serving as a soldier in the US army is if his intention is to follow the footsteps of men like Nidal. . . . The fact that fighting against the US army is an Islamic duty today cannot be disputed. No scholar with a grain of Islamic knowledge can defy the clear cut proofs that Muslims today have the right-- rather the duty--to fight against American tyranny.[516]

Similarly, the "American Muslim," Adam Gadahn, released a video statement saying in part:

> Nidal Hasan has shown us what one righteous Muslim with an assault rifle can do for his religion and brothers in faith, and has reminded us of how much pride and joy a single act of resistance and courage can instill in the hearts of Muslims everywhere. . . . Nidal Hasan is a pioneer, a trailblazer and a role-model who has opened a door, lit a path and shown the way forward for every Muslim who finds himself among the unbelievers and yearns to discharge his duty to Allah and play a part in the defense of Islam and Muslims against the savage,

heartless and bloody Zionist Crusader assault on our religion, sacred places and homelands.[517]

Once again, from the perspective of law, he is a criminal. From the perspective of his religion, he is a hero and role model.

Christians engage in superlegal actions as well. Abortion, as of this writing, is legal in the United States. Yet, perhaps based on biblical directives encouraging procreation, many Christians condemn the procedure. Most operate within the law and seek change. But some have worked themselves into a frenzy and believe religion justifies killing abortion providers.

In 1993, Michael Griffin became the first religionist to murder an abortion provider. Before shooting Dr. David Gunn, Griffin said, "I felt like I had another word from the Lord for him: that he was accused and convicted of murder and that his sentence was Genesis 9:6 'Whosoever sheds man's blood, by man his blood shall be shed.'"[518]

Religionist Shelley Shannon thought Griffin's act was justified. She told a friend, "People cheered when Hitler was killed. And this abortionist was a mass murderer."[519] Shannon shot abortion provider Dr. George Tiller five times, but did not kill him.[520] Federal investigators found buried in her yard an "Army of God Manual" which said:

> [W]e, the remnant of God-fearing men and women of the United States . . . do officially declare war on the entire child killing industry. After praying, fasting, and making continual supplication to God for your pagan, heathen, infidel souls, we then peacefully, passively presented our bodies in front of your death camps, begging you to stop the mass murdering of infants. Yet you hardened your already blackened, jaded hearts. We quietly accepted the resulting imprisonment and suffering of our passive resistance. Yet you mocked God and continued the Holocaust. No longer! All of the

156

options have expired. Our Most Dread Sovereign Lord God requires that whosoever sheds man's blood, by man shall his blood be shed.[521]

The "Army of God" claims links to other violent extremists including Eric Robert Rudolph who not only murdered an off-duty police officer at an abortion clinic, but also bombed a lesbian bar and bombed the 1996 Olympics where he killed two and injured 100.[522]

Scott Roeder, who admired Shelley Shannon and visited her in prison,[523] murdered Dr. Tiller in 2009, an act praised by the Army of God, with whom Roeder now corresponds.[524]

The religiously motivated superlegal conduct that has garnered the most attention to date is the 9/11 attack on the World Trade Center and the Pentagon. Following the attacks, then President George W. Bush addressed the nation, but skirted around discussing the role of religion. Bush said:

> The enemy of America is not our many Muslim friends. It is not our many Arab friends. Our enemy is a radical network of terrorists and every government that supports them. . . . We have seen their kind before. They're the heirs of all the murderous ideologies of the 20th century. By sacrificing human life to serve their radical visions, by abandoning every value except the will to power, they follow in the path of fascism, Nazism and totalitarianism.[525]

Bush acted as if he did not see the role of religion in the attacks. He often sought photo opportunities with representatives of the three major monotheisms. Mere months after the 9/11 attack, Bush said, "Each year, the end of Ramadan means celebration and thanksgiving for millions of Americans. And your joy during this season enriches the life of our great country. This year, Eid[526] is celebrated at the same time as Hanukkah and Advent. So it's a good time for people of these great

157

faiths, Islam, Judaism and Christianity, to remember how much we have in common: devotion to family, a commitment to care for those in need, a belief in God and His justice, and the hope for peace on earth."[527] Bush also said, "I believe in an Almighty God, and I believe that all the world, whether they be Muslim, Christian, or any other religion, prays to the same God. That's what I believe. I believe that Islam is a great religion that preaches peace."[528]

Yet, the man who claims responsibility for the 9/11 attacks, Osama bin Laden, is clear about his religion's justification for his superlegal action:

> Why are we fighting and opposing you? . . . The answer is very simple: Because you attacked us and continue to attack us. You attacked us in Palestine. The creation and continuation of Israel is one of the greatest crimes, and you are the leaders of its criminals. . . . Each and every person whose hands have become polluted in the contribution towards this crime must pay its price, and pay for it heavily. . . . The people of Palestine are pure Arabs and original Semites. It is the Muslims who are the inheritors of Moses (peace be upon him) and the inheritors of the real Torah that has not been changed. Muslims believe in all of the Prophets, including Abraham, Moses, Jesus and Muhammad, peace and blessings of Allah be upon them all. If the followers of Moses have been promised a right to Palestine in the Torah, then the Muslims are the most worthy nation of this. . . . You have supported the Jews in their idea that Jerusalem is their eternal capital, and agreed to move your embassy there. With your help and under your protection, the Israelis are planning to destroy the Al-Aqsa mosque [on the Temple Mount]. Under the protection of your weapons, Sharon entered the Al-Aqsa

158

mosque, to pollute it as a preparation to capture and destroy it. . . .

It is commanded by our religion and intellect that the oppressed have a right to return the aggression. Do not await anything from us but Jihad, resistance and revenge. Is it in any way rational to expect that after America has attacked us for more than half a century, that we will then leave her to live in security and peace?

* * *

What are we calling you to [do], and what do we want from you? The first thing that we are calling you to is Islam[:] The religion of the Unification of God; of freedom from associating partners with Him, and rejection of this; of complete love of Him, the Exalted; of complete submission to His Laws; and of the discarding of all the opinions, orders, theories and religions which contradict with the religion He sent down to His Prophet Muhammad (peace be upon him). Islam is the religion of all the prophets, and makes no distinction between them--peace be upon them all.

It is to this religion that we call you; the seal of all the previous religions. It is the religion of Unification of God, sincerity, the best of manners, righteousness, mercy, honour, purity, and piety. It is the religion of showing kindness to others, establishing justice between them, granting them their rights, and defending the oppressed and the persecuted. It is the religion of enjoining the good and forbidding the evil with the hand, tongue and heart. It is the religion of Jihad in the way of Allah so that Allah's Word and religion reign

159

Supreme. And it is the religion of unity and agreement on the obedience to Allah, and total equality between all people, without regarding their colour, sex, or language.

It is the religion whose book--the Quran--will [remain] preserved and unchanged, after the other Divine books and messages have been changed. The Quran is the miracle until the Day of Judgment. Allah has challenged anyone to bring a book like the Quran or even ten verses like it. . . . We call you to be a people of manners, principles, honour, and purity; to reject the immoral acts of fornication, homosexuality, intoxicants, [gambling], and trading with interest . . . You are the nation who, rather than ruling by the Shariah of Allah in its Constitution and Laws, choose to invent your own laws as you will and desire. You separate religion from your policies, contradicting the pure nature which affirms Absolute Authority to the Lord and your Creator. You flee from the embarrassing question posed to you: How is it possible for Allah the Almighty to create His creation, grant them power over all the creatures and land, grant them all the amenities of life, and then deny them that which they are most in need of: knowledge of the laws which govern their lives?

* * *

If you fail to respond to all these conditions, then prepare for fight with the Islamic Nation. The Nation of Monotheism, that puts complete trust on Allah and fears none other than Him. The Nation which is addressed by its Quran with the words: "Do you fear them? Allah has more right that you should fear Him if you are believers. Fight against them so that Allah will punish them by

160

your hands and disgrace them and give you victory over them and heal the breasts of believing people. And remove the anger of their (believers') hearts. Allah accepts the repentance of whom He wills. Allah is All-Knowing, All-Wise." (Quran 9:13-1)

* * *

This is our message to the Americans, as an answer to theirs. Do they now know why we fight them and over which form of ignorance, by the permission of Allah, we shall be victorious?[529]

Osama bin Laden is not alone in this viewpoint. A survey in Muslim countries reported that respondents who say that violence against civilian targets in order to defend Islam is *never* justified ranged from only 28% of Nigerian Muslims, to 43% in Jordan, 45% in Egypt, 61% in Turkey, 69% in Pakistan and 71% in Indonesia.[530] Even in the least violence-prone Muslim nation, one in four respondents felt their religion justified violence against innocent people. Also surprising, since Osama bin Laden admits he was behind the 9/11 attacks,[531] majorities in Indonesia, Turkey, Egypt, and Jordan say that they do not believe groups of Arabs carried out the 9/11 terrorist attacks. Even 56% of British Muslims say they do not believe Arabs carried out the attacks.[532] It is a commonly held Muslim view that either Jews or the U.S. perpetrated the attacks[533] as an excuse to invade Afghanistan and start the "war on terror."[534] More than 90% of those surveyed in Arab nations have an unfavorable opinion of Jews.[535]

Americans and the media have spent a lot of time hating Osama bin Laden, but very little time listening to why he did what he did. His attacks on the U.S. and the U.S.'s responsive attacks on Afghanistan and Iraq have cost millions of lives and billions of dollars. It is about time we started thinking about the role of religion in the wars we are waging.

Also notable is Bin Laden's emphasis on the Temple Mount, a piece of land important to the mythology of Jews, Christians and Muslims. The next chapter looks at this ideological powder-keg and its role in the end times myths of the people of the book.

Although they seem to excel at it, superlegal activity is not the sole province of Muslims. It is a product of the religious mindset. Some killers would still kill without religion, but religion gives them the structure and justification for their illegal acts. Each of the bearded man in the sky myths contains a dangerous lie. The lie is that believers have supernatural authorization to kill unbelievers.

Religionists may argue that only a small minority of their number engage in superlegal conduct. They are right. Religionists may also point out that nonreligious people also engage in illegal conduct. That too is correct. However, illegal conduct by an atheist is just that–illegal. An angry software engineer who crashes his plane into an IRS building is simply a murderous bastard. By contrast, the religionists described in this chapter who engaged in superlegal actions are seen by a subset of their peers as heros and martyrs, and that group provides the structure and encouragement for others to follow the same path.

Think back to Chapter 19 about art and blasphemy. Simply drawing a bearded man with a bomb in his turban or a bearded man with the body of a dog has put the lives of the artists in danger. It is inconceivable that without religion the cartoon of Mohammed with a bomb in his turban by Kurt Westergaard would have lead to riots with 200 dead, and two attempts on his life in his home in Denmark. Religion creates situations where superlegal murder is authorized, that would not exist absent religion.

Also, it bears repeating that religious moderates empower religious radicals. For example, a kind and open-minded woman I know is a devout Catholic. She strongly favors gay rights, but she also attends and financially supports her Catholic church. When I told her that her scriptures call for killing gays, she did not believe it. When I showed her the passage, she was aghast. Yet the organization she supports had just successfully (and almost singlehandedly) defeated a statewide domestic partnership bill. Although she is a religious liberal, her organization used her funds and goodwill to pursue a more radical agenda. Similarly, religionists who could not imagine murdering others give money to their faith, encourage others to accept their scriptures as the word of god, then act shocked when some use the ancient texts to justify murder.

Tribalism.

One of the most recent attempted terrorist acts got me thinking about *why* religionists engage in superlegal conduct. Faisal Shahzad is a Muslim,[536] Pakistani-born, naturalized U.S. citizen who parked an SUV full of explosives in New York's Times Square outside of a theater featuring the play *The Lion King* on a busy Spring Saturday evening.[537] Luckily, the car did not explode as intended, but if it had, it would have hurt and killed pedestrians–primarily families attending *The Lion King*. I asked myself over and over, how anyone could plan such an act? How could someone intend to kill people, including innocent children attending a play? These men are for the most part not sociopaths–they do not indiscriminately kill people. In fact they limit their murderous acts to a specific group. Their killing is focused. Finally I realized that this man's mindset is not like mine. He does not think of the victims as people. Just like Osama bin Laden, his religion has dragged forward an ancient tribalism that does not belong in the modern world. In the eyes of a tribalist, he was not killing people, he was killing "others."

Tribalism likely evolved when small bands struggled to exist on limited resources. Back then, any other group that might use those resources was a threat and all means, including killing, were used in defense. To this end, indicators of other group membership–costumes, customs, and bearded-man ceremonies, could constitute incitement to violence.

The scriptures, written by men and fixed in time, drag forward ancient strategies–slavery, human and animal sacrifice, sexism, belief in demons and magical thinking, to name a few. The scriptures, written

163

by men and fixed in time, are full of endorsements of the ancient tribal lifestyle. The favored tribe is protected by a special covenant with their god, and part of that covenant is the entitlement and even the obligation to kill members of other tribes. The Old Testament of the Bible, applicable to Jews and Christians, provides, "They entered into a covenant to seek the LORD, the God of their fathers, with all their heart and soul. **All who would not seek the LORD, the God of Israel, were to be put to death, whether small or great, man or woman.**"[538] The entitlement to kill others does not just apply to individuals, but to whole towns, even including the livestock found there:

> If you hear it said about one of the towns the LORD your God is giving you to live in that wicked men have arisen among you and have led the people of their town astray, saying, "Let us go and worship other gods" (gods you have not known), then you must inquire, probe and investigate it thoroughly. And if it is true and it has been proved that this detestable thing has been done among you, **you must certainly put to the sword all who live in that town. Destroy it completely, both its people and its livestock**. Gather all the plunder of the town into the middle of the public square and completely burn the town and all its plunder as a whole burnt offering to the LORD your God. It is to remain a ruin forever, never to be rebuilt. None of those condemned things shall be found in your hands, so that the LORD will turn from his fierce anger; he will show you mercy, have compassion on you, and increase your numbers, as he promised on oath to your forefathers, because you obey the LORD your God, keeping all his commands that I am giving you today and doing what is right in his eyes.[539]

The Koran similarly encourages tribalism, authorizes the murder of unbelievers and sentences them to hell:

> Among the believers are men who have been true to their covenant with Allâh (i.e. they have gone out for Jihâd {holy fighting}, and showed not their backs to the disbelievers), of them some have fulfilled their obligations (i.e. have been martyred), and some of them are still waiting, but they have never changed (i.e. they never proved treacherous to their covenant which they concluded with Allâh) in the least. That Allâh may reward the men of truth for their truth (i.e. for their patience at the accomplishment of that which they covenanted with Allâh), and punish the hypocrites if He wills or accept their repentance by turning to them (in Mercy). . . . And those of the people of the Scripture who backed them (the disbelievers) Allâh brought them down from their forts and cast terror into their hearts, (so that) a group (of them) you killed, and a group (of them) you made captives. And He caused you to inherit their lands, and their houses, and their riches, and a land which you had not trodden (before).[540]

* * *

> Allah hath purchased of the Believers their persons and their goods; for theirs (in return) is the Garden (of Paradise): they fight in His cause, and slay and are slain: a promise binding on Him in Truth, through the Law, the Gospel and the Qur'an: and who is more faithful to his covenant than Allah? Then rejoice in the bargain

which ye have concluded: that is the achievement supreme.[541]

* * *

O Prophet! strive hard against the Unbelievers and the Hypocrites, and be firm against them. Their abode is Hell--an evil refuge indeed.[542]

* * *

[S]lay them wherever ye catch them, and turn them out from where they have turned you out; for tumult and oppression are worse than slaughter; but fight them not at the Sacred Mosque, unless they (first) fight you there; but if they fight you slay them. Such is the reward of those who suppress faith.[543]

From a tribal standpoint, the "us" is human, the "other" is inhuman. There are some ants that have been swarming on a wall near my house. I fear they are wood-eating ants and I intend to go to the store to get some poison to kill them so they will not eat the wood on my house. I take no joy in killing the ants, but I think it is necessary. If Faisal Shahzad intended to kill "people" attending *The Lion King*, his conduct is incomprehensible to me. However, if Faisal Shahzad is a true believer in a religion that has dragged tribalism into the modern world, then he was not trying to kill "people," he was trying to kill "others," with about as much concern as I feel for killing ants. Such ancient tribalism is exhibited again and again by terrorists.

End times beliefs, discussed more fully in the next chapter, magnify this tribalism. All of the people of the book believe that only those who subscribe to their religion, people who are members of their tribe, will survive the end times. Christians and Muslims condemn non-believers to eternity in hell. So from the perspective of a Christian or

166

Muslim believer, the "others" they are killing are already doomed to eternity in hell, the killers are just giving them a head start. Religion makes killing easier.

The "us" versus "other" distinction in modern religious conflicts is clear. Each of the superlegal actors described in this chapter labeled their victims as "others," as non-people. Osama bin Laden's viewpoint is overt, and Bush, with a bit more subterfuge, adopted a biblical quote[544] in creating his catchphrase, "you are either with us or with the terrorists,"[545] in launching his wars. But both Bush and bin Laden are essentially saying the same thing. Even the media is complicit. Soon after the Iraq war began, I read a newspaper headline, "90 Dead in Iraq." After seeing spectacular explosions on television, I could not believe so few had been killed. But when I read the article, the "people" who had been killed were Americans, there was no mention of the "others" who died–a number now as high as 1.3 million.[546]

We see the tribalism every day in the news reports of suicide bombers, religious terrorists and religiously fueled conflicts. Yet individuals, politicians and the media are too polite or too frightened to point a finger at the root cause of the carnage, religion. Even mention of Times Square bomber Faisal Shahzad's religion–Muslim–is left out of most news stories. When religion provides the motivation for murder, it is essential news. The only people served by omitting that news are other religionists. It is time to get honest.

Ancient tribalism + modern weapons = mass destruction.

Religion serves as a vehicle to bring ancient tribalism into the modern world, with deadly results. For example, when the Bible was made up, chariots, spears and swords were the most advanced weapons. Deaths were limited and sustainable territories were maintained. A tribe in the Middle East had no knowledge of, concern about, or impact on, a tribe in Europe. In modern times, spears and swords have evolved into nuclear bombs and missiles. The artwork of a tribe in Europe is transported instantaneously to the Middle East, nuclear fallout from Chernobyl drifts across Europe and Japan, and airplanes are commandeered as missiles. The 9/11 attacks on the U.S. and the responsive attacks on Afghanistan and Iraq have left more than a million people dead. But these massive deaths could be dwarfed by a nuclear attack and/or nuclear response to an attack. Religion drags forward an ancient tribalism that does not belong in the modern world. That tribalism, combined with modern weapons could lead to the destruction of the human race. It is time to stop the madness.

When millions die because "our" bearded-man myths and "their" bearded-man myths differ, it is time for tribalism to end and for the recognition that there is only one, interdependent tribe of man. This is where humanists, whom I criticize for imitating religionists, have a point. Think back to the mayonnaise jars in Chapter 1. The religionist's mayonnaise jar, in addition to things like miracles, virgin birth and people rising from the dead, contains the tribal belief that people of other religions may or must be killed. The humanist's jar, in contrast, contains the belief that there is only one human tribe. This is a big improvement over the "us" versus "other" sanctioned killings in the religionist's jar.

Religion's dragging ancient tribalism into the modern world is its most dysfunctional and dangerous characteristic. Tribalism magnifies the superlegal authority to kill others. When these factors combine with modern weapons of mass destruction, the result is indefensible insanity.

Chapter 22. The end times.

The LORD said to Moses and Aaron: This is a requirement of the law that the LORD has commanded: Tell the Israelites to bring you a red heifer without defect or blemish and that has never been under a yoke. Give it to Eleazar the priest; it is to be taken outside the camp and slaughtered in his presence. Then Eleazar the priest is to take some of its blood on his finger and sprinkle it seven times toward the front of the Tent of Meeting. While he watches, the heifer is to be burned--its hide, flesh, blood and offal.[547] The Bible

The combustive mixture of religion and politics, especially in the volatile Middle East, is frightening. That Christians and Jews see building a new temple on land now occupied by a Muslim Mosque as essential to bringing out their messiah is more frightening still.

Jews, Christians and Muslims have similar end times myths. Each predicts that soon world conditions will worsen, international leaders will rise, major battles will be fought and a messiah will appear, rewarding believers with everlasting heavenly life.

For Jewish people, a necessary step to bringing about the end times is a purification ritual using a red heifer born in Israel and conducted at a special new temple to be built on the Temple Mount, in an area now occupied by the Al-Asqa mosque–the same mosque Osama bin Laden mentioned in his letter in the previous chapter. As weird as it sounds, breeding and sacrificing a red heifer is considered essential. The Temple Institute says:

> Perhaps it would be difficult for some to believe that a cow could be so important. But in truth, the fate of the entire world depends on the red heifer. For G-d[548] has

169

ordained that its ashes alone are the single missing ingredient for the reinstatement of Biblical purity--and thereafter, the rebuilding of the Holy Temple. . . . [T]he ashes of the red heifer rectif[y] humanity's most basic flaw: despair. The despair brought about by the loss of the Temple and the Divine Presence amongst us.[549]

Around the time of building the temple, the story says, there will be a great battle involving Gog and Magog,[550] a messiah will be recognized, and 40 years later, all the dead in Israel will be resurrected.[551] All Jews will return "home" to Israel. Everyone will recognize the Jewish god and as the only god and Jewish religion as the correct religion. The world will live in peace.[552]

The Temple Institute, located in Jerusalem, already has prepared ritual vessels to be used at the new temple, as well as garments to be worn by the high priest. They also are working on raising a special group of boys, who have never touched the ground where people are buried, to serve at the temple.[553] An American Pentecostal preacher is helping the Israelis to breed a red heifer in their "holy land."[554]

The Temple Mount is home to the Dome of the Rock, where Muslims believe Mohammed departed the earth with the angel Gabriel and left behind a footprint. The FBI has warned, "A simple act of desecration, or even a perceived desecration of any of the holy sites on the Temple Mount is likely to trigger a violent reaction."[555] In 1990, a rumor that Jewish extremists would lay a cornerstone for the new temple resulted in riots with 17 dead. In 1996, Israel's opening a tunnel under the Temple Mount lead to riots with 80 dead.[556] The Dome of the Rock appears, crossed by swords, as part of the symbol of Hamas, the political party that calls for armed struggle with Israel and controls the Palestinian Parliament[557] (Figure 17). The end times myths

Figure 17. Hamas symbol, including the Dome of the Rock.

involving the Temple Mount show a great possibility of becoming a self-fulfilling prophesy, but with human destruction instead of everlasting life as the final result.

One might think that Christians have no motivation to help the Jews in this enterprise, especially since according to the Jewish myth, only Jews are spared in the end times. But, after Jews, evangelical Christians are the strongest supporters of Israel in the U.S., and 63% of them feel that Israel's establishment fulfills a biblical prophecy about Jesus' second coming.[558] In the Christian myth, the end times evolve in the same area, but the result is different:

When you see Jerusalem being surrounded by armies, you will know that its desolation is near. Then let those who are in Judea flee to the mountains, let those in the city get out, and let those in the country not enter the city. For this is the time of punishment in fulfillment of all that has been written. How dreadful it will be in those days for pregnant women and nursing mothers! There will be great distress in the land and wrath against this people. They will fall by the sword and will be taken as prisoners to all the nations. Jerusalem will be trampled on by the Gentiles until the times of the Gentiles are fulfilled.

There will be signs in the sun, moon and stars. On the earth, nations will be in anguish and perplexity at the roaring and tossing of the sea. Men will faint from terror, apprehensive of what is coming on the world, for the heavenly bodies will be shaken. At that time they will see the Son of Man coming in a cloud with power and great glory. When these things begin to take place, stand up and lift up your heads, because your redemption is drawing near.[559]

Christians believe the Jewish messiah is the anti-christ, but that his arrival is a necessary step to bring about the Christian end times. In the Christian version, Christians get to live with Christ and non-Christians go to hell.[560]

It will probably not surprise you that the Muslim end times story agrees on some of the details but has a different outcome from that of the Jews and Christians. The Muslim end times story gets confusing with a mixture of information from the Koran, Hadiths, and modern propaganda. Jews did not figure widely in the original story, but through a modern lens, they are a focus, as is the United States, which serves in some interpretations as the anti-christ (Dajjal).

In the Muslim end times story, the anti-christ, or Dajjal will arise from a road between Syria and Iraq and take on the characteristics of a god, but the legend says, he is a false god. Finally, after a period of forty days (in which time the first day will be a year), a battle will occur between the Dajjal and the Muslim forces near Syria, when Isa (Jesus or the messiah) will come down from heaven and kill the Dajjal and "destroy the cross, kill the swine and abolish the tax." This statement is seen to mean that Christians and Jews will not be accepted. Now, if they pay a tax, they are tolerated by Islam. But in the end times, only converting to Islam will allow a person to survive.[561] The Muslims will thereafter wipe out the Dajjal's army which may consist of 70,000 Jews. According to one source, "The Jews will not be able to hide behind anything on that day. Every time they try to hide behind a stone, a wall, a tree (except a boxthorn tree), or animal, Allah will make these things speak and they will say, 'O servant of Allah there is a Jew hiding behind me. Come kill him.'"[562]

An example of the modern spin on the Dajjal comes from the ilaam.net Website, whose author finds all Muslim prerequisites for the end times met by current events:

DAJJAL is not a person with one eye, "chained" at unknown islands (as claimed by many so-called Aalims, taken from Daeef-Hadiths). In fact, DAJJAL is an evil concept or mission (Anti-Allah and its commandments) which will be carried out by a powerful group, not by one country but almost every country of the world. A powerful leader whose string will be controlled by the Jews will be the leader of this group.

DAJJAL with "one eye" means "new world order," a concept initiated by former President of United States George Bush Senior during the war against Iraq. This concept works only in one direction. For example, whatever the United States says "is the law." No question, no argument. Hence this is considered the "one eye order."

If you compare the current situation of this world, it's clearly understood who are DAJJAL and its followers. This is the first time in the history of this world where all so-called civilized but in fact criminal minded people joined hands together to fight against Allah and his commandments. All former enemies joined together (Russia, China, India, Japan, Germany, virtually all so-called "Muslim States" (surprisingly even Iran)) with DAJJAL, [leaving] aside their differences. They changed their constitution if it [was] an obstacle to join DAJJAL (Example: Germany, Japan–were not permitted by their constitution[s] to send their troops overseas.)

Support for DAJJAL in not only within the Governments, but you may notice the attitude of the newspapers (even media from so-called Muslim countries), television, radio and all other media are supporting DAJJAL by providing one-sided stories.

DAJJAL was predicted to rain-down fire to its enemy and throw food to its supporters. This is exactly that was happening in Afghanistan. DAJJAL planes are throwing bombs (fire) and food side-by-side, one for the enemy and the other for "friends."[563]

Lest you think that such crazy interpretations are the sole province of Muslims, Christians produce similar evaluations.[564]

The details of the end times myth of each religion vary from sect to sect and even from time to time. What is important is that true believers think there will be a day of reckoning when believers are rewarded and non-believers are punished. For Christians and Muslims that punishment is eternity in hell.[565] In each religion, the end times are preceded by a time of turmoil and a great battle or Armageddon. For Christians and Muslims, the myth that non-believers spend eternity in hell magnifies the tribalism described in the previous chapter. If the non-believers are doomed to a life in hell anyway, adherents see little wrong in hurrying them to that end by killing them now.

The ultimate expression of religious tribalism is found in its end times stories. The monotheisms even warn that a single world government is a precursor to the end times. The Book of Revelation is the last book in the Bible and contains such gems as this, "[The antichrist] forced everyone, small and great, rich and poor, free and slave, to receive a mark on his right hand or on his forehead, so that no one could buy or sell unless he had the mark, which is the name of the beast or the number of his name. This calls for wisdom. If anyone has insight, let him calculate the number of the beast, for it is man's number. His number is 666."[566] Christians use this story to condemn organizations like the United Nations and unified currencies like the Euro. It is amazing that anyone repeats these myths, especially the incredible ones like the red heifer and the mark of the beast. What is even more frightening is that a survey of Americans showed that 59% believe that the Book of Revelation will come true.[567] A poll of Christians showed that 85% believe they are living in the end times.[568] These beliefs are dangerous.

Think back to the Mormons. They believe the end times will occur in the United States, and that they will take over the U.S. government and eventually the world. Mormons hold important political, military and civil service posts throughout the government including Senate Majority Leader (Harry Reid) and presidential candidate Mitt Romney, both of Utah's Senators (5% of the Senate is Mormon) and all three of Utah's Representatives, Utah's governor and Lieutenant Governor, and nine additional members of Congress.[569] The Mormons are preparing for their end times scenario–but the Mormon end times myths are not as widespread, frightening or imminent as the end times myths of the people of the book.

There are people at the highest levels of American government who say they believe the Christian end times myths. For example, born again Christian General William Boykin, Deputy Assistant Secretary for Intelligence, a key player in America's military strategy, believed god made George W. Bush President. He said he prevailed in a conflict with a Somali warlord because, "My God was bigger than his . . . I knew that my God was a real God and that his was an idol."[570] He said the "war on terror" is "a spiritual battle, it's a battle for our soul. And the enemy is a guy called Satan--Satan wants to destroy this nation. He wants to destroy us as a nation and he wants to destroy us as a Christian army."[571] A man who believed these religious myths helped plan American strategy in the volatile Middle East. It actually makes you thankful for the hypocrites who say they believe but really do not. The true believers are the most frightening.

Religionists and the media seem afraid to discuss the role religion plays in the horrible strife in the Middle East. Perhaps they are afraid that discussing the religious motivation of the "infidels" will necessitate a similar examination of their own beliefs. Every time I hear a report about religiously influenced violence, I yell at the radio or TV, "talk about the role of religion!" But they never do.

The largest danger to the health and safety of the world comes not from the incidental acts of terrorism religionists have performed to date, but from the monumental acts they may commit in the future. The false beliefs that threaten the lives of virtually everyone on earth cannot continue unchallenged. The time has come to stop looking through the lens of ancient tribalism and seeing enemy tribes and instead start seeing a world composed of humans just like ourselves. Instead of seeing the world as "win-lose," let us start searching for "win-win." Regarding the Temple Mount, it would be nice if everyone would behave like atheists and think of it as a historical piece of real property. But if they cannot, then maybe for the advancement of world peace, it should be closed to everyone and left as a monument to madness.

End times myths are a bizarre element of religion. What is truly terrifying is picturing end times believers with their fingers on the buttons that activate nuclear weapons. The U.S., India, Pakistan and likely Israel possess nuclear weapons and Iran appears to be seeking them. Such weapons in the hands of people who truly believe in the end times could hasten their use and heretofore unknown levels of destruction. The most horrific aspect of ancient tribalism dragged into the modern world is that end times believers might use nuclear weapons to bring about what they hope is the rapture. To an outsider, end times myths sound like a joke as laughable as the flying spaghetti monster. Unfortunately to a number of religionists, including those in positions of power, the end times are a deadly serious reality. Atheists should challenge religious myths not only because they are lies, but because the lies could result in the destruction of the human race. Religious violence is not a joke. It affects our lives every day and with the wrong combination of belief, superlegal action and potent weapons, it could end life as we know it. The time for action is now.

Roadmap.
The second section of this book is dedicated to illustrating problems with religion, small and large. I started out with silly things, like the "miracle" of the image of Jesus on a tortilla. The following

176

chapters looked at bigger problems, issues like religion's unfairness to women and gays, Finally, I have shared my views on the dangers of superlegal actions, especially when combined with modern weapons and end times myths. From my perspective, these are the strongest arguments against religion and for atheist action.

I have a few more points to make about religion before returning my focus to atheism. The next chapter contains my thoughts about how deeply religionists believe, and finally I speculate why religion is still around after the rise of evolution science. That will complete my comments on religion and I will conclude the book with a few thoughts about the atheist movement.

Chapter 23. How deep is your love?

How deep is your love? The Bee Gees

One would like to think that . . . devout Christians would also behave in a manner that is in accord with Christian ethics. But pastorally and existentially, I know that that is not the case--and never has been the case.[572] Reverend Richard John Neuhaus

I want religionists to become atheists. Because of this, I am interested in how deeply they believe in their religion and therefore how open they may be to a different point of view. To a religious outsider such as me, it is difficult to imagine that even one person believes in religion. However, I cannot ignore conduct that demonstrates belief, such as flying airliners into buildings. But I remain convinced that a large number of people who say they believe, do not. My guess is that more than 50% of them have a "soft" belief in religion. They go through the motions of demonstrating belief, but in their hearts they know it is not so. If you were their best friend and they confided in you, they would admit that they do not believe in god. One way of examining the depth of belief is to look at what religionists do, another is to look at what they say.

What they do.

The way many religionists conduct themselves shows soft belief. One example is birth control. The Catholic Church condemns birth control and makes its users subject to eternal damnation in hell.[573] However, a study reveals that 97% of sexually active Catholic women have used church-prohibited birth control.[574] Either they do not believe it condemns them to hell or they do not believe their god evaluates their every move. But whatever the reason, it means they do not believe a major tenet of their faith. Their conduct with regard to birth control shows that their belief is not very deep.

Another example is sex before marriage. Although most religions condemn premarital sex, one study estimates that 95% of Americans have sex before marriage and this has been going on for quite some time. For women born in the 1940's, nine out of ten reported having sex before marriage.[575] In a nation where about 80% of the people claim to be religious and 95% engage in premarital sex, the numbers show that conduct and belief are inconsistent.

Another angle, true believers should be happy to die. In their belief system, death leads to an eternal paradise. That is one of the most effective sales gimmicks religion offers. Yet, very few religious people welcome death.[576] Surprisingly, atheists, who accept that they will cease to be when they die, are more comfortable with death than religionists.[577] The fact that most religionists fear death, rather than celebrate it, shows a lack of belief in one of the most important aspects of their faith. Similarly, when religionists are ill, most call for a doctor before they call a religious practitioner. It seems they find religion fine for ceremonies and holidays, but when their health is at stake, the majority of them prefer science.

Looking at morality and criminality, many religionists engage in conduct that, if they believed in their religious doctrine, would condemn them to hell. Clergy who sexually abuse children are an example. Ted Haggard's story (Chapter 17) indicates he was much more concerned about being caught by his spouse and parishioners than answering to the god he claims to serve. The willingness of religionists to engage in patterns of illegal conduct shows both that they do not think their god is watching them and that they do not expect their god to punish them.

An interesting anecdote about what religionists do is one atheist's challenge to proselytizers who show up at his door. A sign on his front door says, "If your purpose is religious, to tell us about your God's love for us or to convince us that we need Jesus to be our

179

personal savior, please don't knock. Instead, bow your head and pray as sincerely and intently as possible for this door to disappear. When it does, feel free to come on in . . . we will definitely want to hear what you have to say!" He relates his experience, "But no one tries. If they really believed, at least they would give it a try."[578] Although many religionists are dramatic about their faith in public, in private they act as if they have no belief at all.

What they say.

According to a Gallup survey, 56% of church attendees say they are "spiritually committed," but only 15% answer individual questions the surveyors believed showed commitment.[579] A Pew survey of church attendance similarly shows that only about 56% of Americans find their religion "very important" and only about 54% attend church once a month or more. About 49% say they receive answers to their prayers yearly or more frequently (and a full 43% seldom or never receive answers to their prayers).[580] Only 32% of the U.S. population thinks the Bible should have more influence on U.S. laws than the will of the people.[581] Although about 40% of Americans report they attend church weekly, studies show they overstate their church attendance and only about 20% actually attend weekly (providing another interesting comparison of what they say and what they do).[582]

In response to an open-ended question of what was the most important reason they attended church or synagogue in a Gallup survey, only about 28% said they did so because of a belief in god or religion, 23% said they attended for spiritual growth and guidance and 20% because it grounded or inspired them. Thirteen percent responded that they attended church for the opportunity for fellowship or to be part of a community, 12% responded they were brought up that way or that it was a family value or tradition, and finally, 15% responded with the enigmatic, "It's my faith."[583] These self-reported numbers are a bit like the pattern of darts on a dart board. No single dart is definitive, but they demonstrate a pattern. Here the pattern shows that many religionists have a soft belief.

180

An expert, Robert Wuthnow, Director of the Center for the Study of Religion at Princeton University, agrees. He estimates that only 25% of the U.S. population is devoutly religious, 25% is secular, and 50% is mildly interested.[584] This expert opinion supports in general numbers my guess that more than 50% of religionists have a soft belief. Although people tell pollsters they are religious, both examination of their conduct and deeper questioning of their replies shows otherwise.

Why do religionists run away?

Since starting work on this book, I have discussed religion with a wide variety of friends, acquaintances and strangers. One of the most surprising results has been the number of religionists who refuse to discuss the subject and run away from the conversation. If the religionists possess a life-saving secret, especially considering that their religion encourages them to share the good word, they should jump at the opportunity to share their knowledge. To me, this would be a demonstration of the strength of their belief. But the majority of them run away. I think the people who refuse to discuss the issue know in their hearts that they do not believe. They are afraid an atheist will illuminate their non-belief. It is the people with strong belief who listen politely to the atheist and then present their life-saving knowledge. I have met very few of these.

Religion, for some, is as considered as wearing socks.

Recently, I went to lunch with a friend I have known for decades. I asked her if a pollster telephoned and inquired about her religion, how would she reply? "Christian," she said. I was shocked because I have never known her to attend church, pray, or mention religion in any form. After talking about some of the issues in this book, and with no prompting or encouragement from me, she said, "I guess I would more classify myself as a 'none.'" Although a pollster would have categorized her as a Christian, her response was not deeply considered.

Most atheists have thought long and hard about religion. For many of us, atheism is a cause, or at least a sport. But the majority of people have spent little time on the issue. Many spend as little time thinking about religion as I think about wearing socks. Socks are a part of my daily routine. I lay them out when I dress, I change them when they are dirty, but I spend very little time analyzing why I wear them and what they mean to me. Since my mother put socks on my feet as a child, I have worn them. It is likely I will continue to wear them for the rest of my life. But, I do not think much about socks.

Similarly, most people were provided a religion by their parents. They participate in religious ceremonies throughout their lives, but they rarely think about why or what they could do alternatively. They think about religion about as much as I think about wearing socks. In the example of my lunch companion, a pollster would have categorized her as a Christian, but her response reflected a belief soft enough to be changed by a passing conversation. Religion is almost never questioned or discussed, not by the media, not by "polite" company and not by the religionists themselves. This deference to religion helps to perpetuate it. But breaking the silence and discussing religion provides atheists with fertile ground for sowing the seeds of freethought.

Religion without belief.

There are countless reasons people participate in religion even if they do not believe it. For some it is a tradition, their family has always attended church, they have always attended church, and they indoctrinate their children into the church. It is the way things have always been done and will continue to be done. The lack of belief is inconsequential, tradition is preserved.

Others have no strong objection to religion and they go to church to appease a spouse, parent or other loved one. An hour or so a week of philosophical reflection does no harm, they think, and sometimes the music is nice, so they call themselves religionists even though they lack belief. They wear the religionist label just to get along.

Still others participate in religion for business reasons. Many Realtors, insurance salespeople and business owners make a good living serving members of their religious group. Religion provides a ready-made community to which they can hawk their goods and services. Whether they never had a belief to start with or if that belief has faded, the business reason for feigning belief continues.

In some rural communities, religious houses provide a rare opportunity to socialize. As a child, you meet your friends there. As a youth, you may meet your future spouse at a religious function. The house of worship serves as a community center where you meet your friends and neighbors. It marks the births, courting, marriage and death of each member. People who do not believe may continue to attend because they like the opportunity to socialize with their neighbors.

Additionally, some may stick with religion because they fear the social stigma of being labeled an atheist or non-believer. Atheists are one of the most despised minorities in the United States. In a small study by Altemeyer and Hunsberger, a solid majority of the people who left religion to become atheists said their decision "cost them a great deal."[585] Religionists who become atheists may face broken relationships and social condemnation. Some people call themselves religionists despite their lack of belief because they do not see the alternative as more appealing.

Are non-believing religionists liars?

I have labeled people who frequent temples, churches and mosques but do not believe as having a "soft" belief. But I have also asked myself, are they liars? To attend church and profess a belief you do not have seems dishonest. But on further thought, I could easily conceive of myself professing belief. For example, if a religionist pointed a gun at me and threatened to shoot unless I said, "allah is great," I would do it. I would not believe it, but I would say it. Similarly, if I were hungry and homeless and the mission kitchen insisted I say a prayer before eating, I would do it. I would not believe it, but I would do it. If I had no job but had a family to support, I could

183

see myself professing faith if it were the only way to get a job. In each case I would be lying, but with a reason. Lots of people lie, and some have good reasons for doing so. Further, considering that religionists with soft belief are an audience that is likely to be open to the atheist message, using strong labels like "liar" will do little to forward our cause.

Philosopher Daniel Dennett coined the term "belief in belief" to describe religionists who do not believe in god but yet profess belief. To my understanding, Dennett says they think it would be good to believe, so therefore they say they believe.[586]

To me, it matters little whether you call them liars, soft believers or believers in belief. The functional result is that a large number of religionists are like the crowd in *The Emperor's New Clothes* before the child's call, "he's naked" filtered to them. They know the emperor is naked, but they still profess to admire his nonexistent splendid clothes.

Soft belief provides fertile soil for atheists who want to see religionists become atheists. It is up to us atheists to point out the emperor is naked, to get religionists to consider religion more deeply than they consider putting on socks, and to provide examples that life is better without religion. And it is up to us to change the negative image of atheism that religionists have propagated over the years. The potential audience for atheist action goes beyond nones, agnostics, deists and the generally spiritual. Many of those sitting in the pews of the houses of worship are amenable to the atheist message. Avoiding answering the question of "how deep is your love" with an analogy using "soft" belief, let me use the analogy of the Platte river.[587] For the majority of American religionists, their belief is a mile wide but only an inch deep. And after considering the specter of true believers using superlegal means to bring about their end times myths, the likelihood that many religionists have a soft belief is encouraging.

Chapter 24. Darwin should have done it.

I am bewildered . . . I own that I cannot see, as plainly as others do, and as I should wish to do, evidence of design and beneficence on all sides of us. There seems to me too much misery in the world. I cannot persuade myself that a beneficent and omnipotent God would have designedly created the . . . [parasitic wasps] with the express intention of their feeding within the living bodies of caterpillars.[588] Charles Darwin

I am a strong advocate for free thought on all subjects, yet it appears to me (whether rightly or wrongly) that direct arguments against christianity & theism produce hardly any effect on the public; & freedom of thought is best promoted by the gradual illumination of men's minds, which follows from the advance of science. It has, therefore, been always my object to avoid writing on religion, & I have confined myself to science. I may, however, have been unduly biassed [sic] by the pain which it would give some members of my family, if I aided in any way direct attacks on religion.[589] Charles Darwin

Evolution science, begun by Charles Darwin, should have dealt a death blow to Judaism, Christianity and Islam. That is what I mean by the title of this chapter, "Darwin should have done it." Judaism, Christianity and Islam were invented by men before the rise of modern science. Sure, pre-Darwinian scientists like Copernicus and Galileo challenged the scriptures by declaring that the earth revolved around the sun, but scriptural statements that the earth is fixed in space are few and are unessential to the religionists' myths. But evolution science shoots an arrow straight through the heart of the religious creation myth.

185

The monotheisms have essentially the same creation story. The Koran does not have the creation myth all in one section, it jumps around. But the essence is the same as the Torah/Bible. For example:

> Your Guardian-Lord is Allah, Who created the heavens and the earth in six Days, then He established Himself on the Throne (of authority): He draweth the night as a veil O'er the day, each seeking the other in rapid succession: He created the sun, the moon, and the stars, (all) governed by laws under His command. Is it not His to create and to govern? Blessed be Allah, the cherisher and sustainer of the Worlds![590]

* * *

> And indeed We created man (Adam) out of an extract of clay (water and earth).[591]

* * *

> It is He Who has created you from a single person (Adam), and (then) He has created from him his wife [Hawwa (Eve)], in order that he might enjoy the pleasure of living with her.[592]

* * *

> And it is He Who spread out the earth, and set thereon mountains standing firm, and (flowing) rivers: and fruit of every kind He made in pairs, two and two. . . . And in the earth are tracts (diverse though) neighbouring, and gardens of vines and fields sown with corn, and palm trees growing out of single roots or otherwise: watered

with the same water, yet some of them We make more excellent than others to eat.[593]

In contrast, the creation myth in the Torah/Bible is organized and linear:

In the beginning God created the heavens and the earth.

Now the earth was formless and empty, darkness was over the surface of the deep, and the Spirit of God was hovering over the waters.

And God said, "Let there be light," and there was light. God saw that the light was good, and He separated the light from the darkness. God called the light "day," and the darkness he called "night." And there was evening, and there was morning--the first day.

And God said, "Let there be an expanse between the waters to separate water from water." So God made the expanse and separated the water under the expanse from the water above it. And it was so. God called the expanse "sky." And there was evening, and there was morning--the second day.

Then God said, "Let the land produce vegetation: seed-bearing plants and trees on the land that bear fruit with seed in it, according to their various kinds." And it was so. The land produced vegetation: plants bearing seed according to their kinds and trees bearing fruit with seed in it according to their kinds. And God saw that it was good. And there was evening, and there was morning--the third day.

And God said, "Let there be lights in the expanse of the sky to separate the day from the night, and let them serve as signs to mark seasons and days and years, and let them be lights in the expanse of the sky to give light on the earth." And it was so. God made two great lights--the greater light to govern the day and the lesser light to govern the night. He also made the stars. God set them in the expanse of the sky to give light on the earth, to govern the day and the night, and to separate light from darkness. And God saw that it was good. And there was evening, and there was morning--the fourth day.

And God said, "Let the water teem with living creatures, and let birds fly above the earth across the expanse of the sky." So God created the great creatures of the sea and every living and moving thing with which the water teems, according to their kinds, and every winged bird according to its kind. And God saw that it was good. God blessed them and said, "Be fruitful and increase in number and fill the water in the seas, and let the birds increase on the earth." And there was evening, and there was morning--the fifth day.

And God said, "Let the land produce living creatures according to their kinds: livestock, creatures that move along the ground, and wild animals, each according to its kind." And it was so. God made the wild animals according to their kinds, the livestock according to their kinds, and all the creatures that move along the ground according to their kinds. And God saw that it was good.

Then God said, "Let us make man in our image, in our likeness, and let them rule over the fish of the sea and the birds of the air, over the livestock, over all the earth, and over all the creatures that move along the ground."

So God created man in his own image, in the image of God he created him; male and female he created them.

God blessed them and said to them, "Be fruitful and increase in number; fill the earth and subdue it. Rule over the fish of the sea and the birds of the air and over every living creature that moves on the ground."

Then God said, "I give you every seed-bearing plant on the face of the whole earth and every tree that has fruit with seed in it. They will be yours for food. And to all the beasts of the earth and all the birds of the air and all the creatures that move on the ground--everything that has the breath of life in it--I give every green plant for food." And it was so.

God saw all that he had made, and it was very good. And there was evening, and there was morning--the sixth day.

Thus the heavens and the earth were completed in all their vast array.

By the seventh day God had finished the work he had been doing; so on the seventh day he rested from all his work. And God blessed the seventh day and made it holy, because on it he rested from all the work of creating that he had done.[594]

As an aside, the Jewish/Christian creation myth has some internal inconsistencies. To start with, why does an all-powerful god need to rest after six days work? The Muslims improved on that aspect of the myth by giving their god boasting rights for not having to rest after creating the world. Further, the Genesis creation myth neglects to explain how light was created on day one but the sun was not created until day four. But inconsistencies like these are the smallest of problems.

Darwin's discoveries went to the heart of religion. Evolution science shows our world is the result of natural selection and evolution over thousands and millions of years and the scriptures are wrong. A bearded man in the sky did not create the earth in six days, the plants and animals were not created in their current form, and the house of cards that is religion should come tumbling down.

Darwin published *On the Origin of the Species* in 1859, 151 years before this book. Darwin may be the father of evolution science, but the field has grown so enormously that he would unlikely recognize it. Over the past 151 years, countless scientific discoveries have supported Darwin and disproved the scriptures.

Despite the enormous weight of fact supporting evolution, a 2009 Gallup poll reported that only 39% of those surveyed believed in evolution, while 25% did not, and 36% had no opinion either way.[595] Another poll found that 44% of respondents believed that the world was created in six days.[596]

Religionists label the teaching of their scriptural creation myth "creationism." A 1987 U.S. Supreme Court ruling prohibited teaching creationism in schools, but the Court left the door open to other approaches by saying "teaching a variety of scientific theories about the origins of humankind to schoolchildren might be validly done with the clear secular intent of enhancing the effectiveness of science instruction."[597] The new strategy of teaching "intelligent design," that a creator rather than natural selection is responsible for modern life, is an attempt to teach religion while complying with U.S. law. Even though prohibited by judicial ruling, 58% of Americans favor teaching creationism along with evolution in public schools.[598]

190

A complete industry has sprung up trying to support the scriptural creation theory. For example, Answers in Genesis (named after the chapter of the Bible with the creation story) built a $27 million creationism museum that opened in May 2007 and had more than 900,000 visitors by the end of 2009.[599] Charity Navigator reports Answers in Genesis had $22 million income in 2008.[600] The organization says, "The Bible is divinely inspired and inerrant throughout. Its assertions are factually true in all the original autographs. It is the supreme authority in everything it teaches. Its authority is not limited to spiritual, religious, or redemptive themes but includes its assertions in such fields as history and science. The final guide to the interpretation of Scripture is Scripture itself. The account of origins presented in Genesis is a simple but factual presentation of actual events and therefore provides a reliable framework for scientific research into the question of the origin and history of life, mankind, the earth and the universe."[601] The modern success of a project based solely on an ancient myth that has been completely discredited by science is a testament not to the truth of the myth but to the power of religion.

To someone raised without religion, it is inconceivable that religious belief persists contrary to all scientific fact. However, this ignores the powerful position from which religion operates and the slow pace of social change. As demonstrated by Answers in Genesis and as discussed in Chapter 2, religion is incredibly powerful. It has worked its way into the psyche of believers over thousands of years. It is not about to let go without a fight. However, the fact that religionists spend so much time and money denying evolution shows that they know it is a threat.

Broad social changes occur slowly. Religions rise and fall over periods of thousands of years. Humans have created the term "dog years" to describe a dog's age in relationship to humans, using a factor of 1:7 (10 years for a dog's life and 70 years for a human's) so a three-year-old dog is called "21 years old" for relative comparison. Creating a similar comparison for religion, if the average religion lasts 3,000 years, and a human lives 70 years (70:3000 or .023), then the 151 years since Darwin's book is only 3.5 "religion years." Broad social changes like the elimination of religion will likely take place at a much slower pace than the duration of one human life.

The Emperor's New Clothes.

Most people are familiar with the story of *The Emperor's New Clothes*, written by Danish author Hans Christian Andersen. I have referred to it a number of times in this book, and now I will take the time to refresh your recollection of its contents. In that story, two con men undertake making the emperor clothes that "had a wonderful way of becoming invisible to anyone who was unfit for his office, or who was unusually stupid." Although no one can see the clothes, all say they do. The emperor tries on his new clothes before his advisors, and:

> His whole retinue stared and stared. One saw no more than another, but they all joined the Emperor in exclaiming, "Oh! It's *very* pretty," and they advised him to wear clothes made of this wonderful cloth especially for the great procession he was soon to lead. "Magnificent! Excellent! Unsurpassed!" were bandied from mouth to mouth, and everyone did his best to seem well pleased. The Emperor gave each of the swindlers a cross to wear in his buttonhole, and the title of "Sir Weaver."

The emperor marches before the people with his noblemen carrying a nonexistent train of cloth behind him. Andersen concludes his story with:

> "But he hasn't got anything on," a little child said.
>
> "Did you ever hear such innocent prattle?" said its father. And one person whispered to another what the

192

child had said, "He hasn't anything on. A child says he hasn't anything on."

"But he hasn't got anything on!" the whole town cried out at last.

The Emperor shivered, for he suspected they were right. But he thought, "This procession has got to go on." So he walked more proudly than ever, as his noblemen held high the train that wasn't there at all.[602]

In rereading the story, I was struck by how Andersen ended it. Even though the emperor knows he is naked, he concludes "this procession has got to go on," and continues to parade naked before the people more proudly than ever, followed by his noblemen holding high the nonexistent train. The application to religion is clear. The falsity of religion must be obvious to its participants, but each supports the other by marveling at its truth. And even when the leaders understand that they are promoting lies, they conclude, "this procession has got to go on" and forge forward despite their knowledge. Religion is a lie. Yet the majority of people go on acting as if it is true.

In Andersen's story, it took a while for the child's cry to circulate among the crowd. And even when the emperor shivers and realizes the crowd is probably right, he continues marching proudly. To me, Darwin is like the child who pointed out the emperor has no clothes. In "religion years," this happened recently, so the word is only now circulating around the crowd. But eventually, just like the crowd in the story, we will all recognize that religion is a lie. Until then, it is up to atheists to keep repeating that the emperor has no clothes.

So, going back to the title of this chapter, "Darwin should have done it," the premise stands. However, the statement needs to be seen in the slow context of social change, especially when considering a social institution as powerful as religion. There are encouraging signs that change has begun. In countries like Sweden, Denmark, Norway and

Japan, the majority of the population is nonreligious. The United States stands alone among rich nations in having such a high degree of religious belief.[603] However, even within the United States, atheism is rising. In 1966, 2% of Americans had no religion. In 1972, 5% of Americans had no religion. In 1981, 7% of Americans had no religion. In 2002, 10% of Americans had no religion.[604] In 2008, 16.1% of Americans had no religion.[605] And among the youth, who represent the future of our country, in 2008, 25% had no religion.[606] Although change has begun in America, religion retains a powerful hold. In order to open the minds of the remainder of the crowd to the fact that the emperor has no clothes, atheists should repeat Darwin's cry and take other action to hasten the crowd's realization.

SECTION III.

Atheist action.

Chapter 25. Atheists have an image problem.

We show not only that atheists are less accepted than other marginalized groups but also that attitudes toward them have not exhibited the marked increase in acceptance that has characterized views of other racial and religious minorities over the past forty years. . . . Americans are less accepting of atheists than of any of the other groups we asked about, and by a wide margin.[607] University of Minnesota study of atheists as "other."

Atheism has always been hostile to religion, such as in its arguments that freedom of or for religion should include freedom from religion. Atheism's threat rises as its proponents grow in numbers and aggressiveness. . . . [A]theism's spokesmen are aggressive [and] have developed great skills in demonizing those who disagree with them, turning their opponents into objects of fear, hatred and scorn.[608] Mormon Elder Dallin Oaks

      Atheists are one of the most unpopular minorities in America. Surveys consistently show that atheists are ranked less favorably than any religious group in America.[609] Atheists are rated 18 points *below* Muslims, who are in the public eye because of the 9/11 attacks, their treatment of women and their superlegal attacks on cartoonists who draw Mohammed. Atheists are ranked 26 points *below* Mormons, who only 152 years ago stood off the American Army, who only outlawed polygamy in 1890, and who only allowed Blacks to become ministers in 1978. Atheists are ranked 39 points *below* Catholics, who still will not allow women to be church leaders, who deny members access to birth control and who are rocked by child-abuse cover-up scandals (Figure 18). Answering the question, "This group does not at all agree

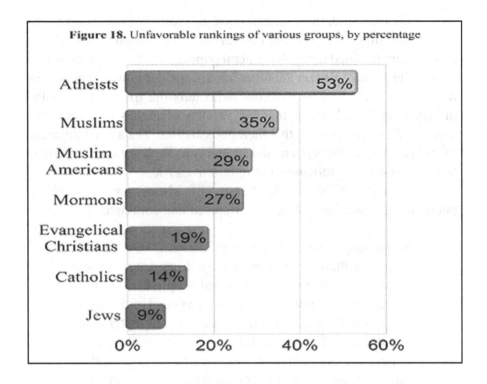

Figure 18. Unfavorable rankings of various groups, by percentage

with my vision of American society," atheists are rated the highest, named by 39.6% of respondents, followed by Muslims at 26.3% and gays at 22.6%. In a similar vein, 47.6% of respondents would disapprove of their child marrying an atheist, while only 33.5% would disapprove of marrying a Muslim.[610] Think of that, Muslims conducted:

• the 9/11 attacks in the United States which killed almost 3,000,
• train bombings in Spain that killed 191 and wounded 1,800,
• subway bombings in England that killed 52 and injured 700,
• an assault in Mumbai, India that killed 173 and injured 308,

and yet Americans think more highly of Muslims than they do of atheists.

197

On one hand, these statistics are shocking because atheists are not committing suicide bombings or massive criminal acts. As an atheist, I am inclined to ask the general population, "what has an atheist done to hurt you?" But on the other hand, consider how threatened the religionists must feel by someone who tells the truth. The Muslim merely tells the Christian that his version of god is incorrect. The atheist tells all religionists that their gods are lies. The atheist threatens the religionist's belief system and strangely enough is more feared than a coreligionist who threatens the religionist's life.

Researchers at the University of Minnesota explored the phenomena of why atheists are so despised and commented:

> Some people view atheists as problematic because they associate them with illegality, such as drug use and prostitution--that is, with immoral people who threaten respectable community from the lower end of the status hierarchy. Others saw atheists as rampant materialists and cultural elitists that threaten common values from above--the ostentatiously wealthy who make a lifestyle out of consumption or the cultural elites who think they know better than everyone else. Both of these themes rest on a view of atheists as self-interested individualists who are not concerned with the common good.[611]

* * *

> To be an atheist in such an environment is not to be one more religious minority among many in a strongly pluralist society. Rather, Americans construct the atheist as the symbolic representation of one who rejects the basis for moral solidarity and cultural membership in American society altogether. Over our history, other groups have, perhaps, been subject to similar moral concerns. Catholics, Jews, and communists all have

198

been figures against which the moral contours of American culture and citizenship have been imagined. We suggest that today, the figure of the atheist plays this role.[612]

The atheist image problem is also reflected in the gap between the number of people who say they do not believe in god and the number who call themselves atheists. Five to ten percent of Americans say they do not believe in god, yet only .7 to 1.6% of Americans identify themselves as atheists. There are powerful disincentives to self-identifying as an atheist. The negative image of atheism is likely a major factor in the disparity between the number of those who do not believe in god and the number of those who call themselves atheists.

Over the years, poll takers have asked the public if a presidential candidate were otherwise well qualified but belonged to a certain group, would you vote for him or her? During the most recent presidential election, the results were as follows:[613]

Group	Percent who would refuse to support
Catholic	4%
Black	5%
Jewish	7%
Woman	11%
Hispanic	12%
Mormon	24%
Homosexual	43%
Atheist	53%

Although gays were the lowest on the scale for years, recently they have gained more public approval, leaving atheists in dead last place. Figure 19 shows that while gays were ranked about 10% lower than atheists in the 70's and 80's, they improved by 20 percentage points in recent years, leaving atheists with a 10% lower approval rating than gays for the past two decades. Figure 19 also shows that atheists have done little to change their perception by the general public. Disapproval of atheists was 53% in 1978 and 53% in 2007. In contrast, gays have made great strides, dropping from a disapproval rating of 66% in 1978 to 43% in 2007. Obviously, the gay rights movement knows something that atheists do not. The next chapter looks at what the atheist movement can learn from the gay rights movement.

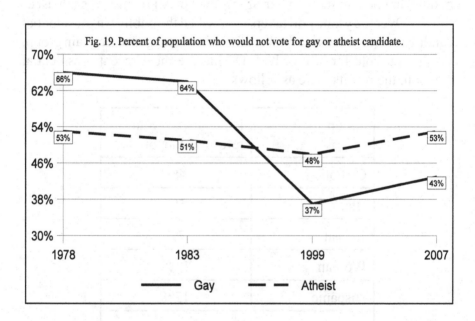

Fig. 19. Percent of population who would not vote for gay or atheist candidate.

Among atheists, the fear of prejudice and discrimination is real. Atheists are excluded from membership and leadership roles in organizations like the Boy Scouts of America[614] and the Salvation

200

Army.[615] Atheists can also be excluded from employment in programs financed through the government's "faith-based initiatives."[616] Even Census workers are administered an oath ending with the religious promise, "so help me god."[617]

Discrimination against atheists surfaces in child custody cases. For example in overturning a trial court's transfer of sole custody to the nonreligious parent and ordering continued joint custody, a Michigan Appellate court said:

> [W]e find that the evidence presented below clearly preponderates against the trial court's determination that neither party displayed a greater capacity and disposition to continue [the child's] religious upbringing. There was ample testimony that defendant regularly took [the child] to church and Sabbath school, taught [the child] how to pray and read him Bible stories, while plaintiff testified that she did not regularly attend church and presented no evidence demonstrating any willingness or capacity to attend to religion with [the child]. Thus, the trial court should have found that the disposition to continue [the child's] religious upbringing weighed in favor of defendant.[618]

Atheist children are regularly subjected to cruel treatment by their religious peers.[619] Atheists in the military face systematic discrimination.[620] While atheism precludes hiring by a few employers such as the Boy Scouts and the Salvation Army, it subtly affects the work environment and promotion opportunities in countless others. Atheist-owned small businesses risk losing customers if their disbelief is publicized. Atheists are excluded from recovery programs like Alcoholics Anonymous which require belief in a "higher power," and also face a dilemma when, for example, court sentencing programs offer AA programs as an alternative to imprisonment. Atheists are largely ignored by the media and the media provides few positive atheist role models.

However, considering the breadth and depth of public sentiment against atheists, it is surprising that there are not more reported cases of discrimination. One explanation may be that Americans take seriously the phrase "freedom of religion" and control their prejudices in the workplace and the marketplace. Another explanation may be that atheists are largely invisible unless they identify themselves and that they avoid self-identification in arenas where prejudice prevails. However, discrimination against atheists is not my main concern in discussing this topic–welcoming more people to identify themselves as atheists is. And from this perspective it is obvious that atheists have an image problem. That is why as few as 10% of the people who do not believe in god label themselves "atheists."

The negative image of atheists, built and perpetuated by religionists, serves its intended function. It not only discourages religionists with soft belief from declaring themselves to be atheists, it discourages them from listening to and considering the atheist message. From a public safety perspective, atheists are a small and harmless minority, but from the perspective of perpetuating religion, they are a deadly threat. Rather than telling the truth about atheists, that we are a small minority, generally kind, intelligent and as a movement disorganized and largely ineffective, religionists tell the lie that atheists are powerful, dangerous and agents of the devil. That is how frightened they are of the atheist message. To effectively convey the atheist message we must overcome thousands of years of unchallenged myths that demonize us. If your audience is watching for the devilish horns they expect to pop from your head it is unlikely they will hear your message. To effectively convert religionists to atheists, truth must prevail over lies. A preliminary step is convincing the religionist that the atheist is not evil, is not the "other" and is a source worth trusting.[621]

As a primary matter, we should learn from other groups that have improved their public image. Gays are a group with many characteristics similar to atheists and the next chapter examines how we can learn from the gay rights movement.

A second strategy is to use our skills to change public perception. Probably the strongest strategy is to change the "unidentified other" the general public pictures when they think of an atheist, to a specific person. For example, Heinerman and Shupe relate that the most effective recruitment tool for Mormons is *not* the scrubbed young people riding bicycles through your neighborhood in a missionary program. The missionaries are actually being taught to distinguish themselves from the general population and to be bound tighter to the Mormon church, but they convert few. The most effective recruitment tool the Mormons use is the "home mission program." The Mormon neighbor helps the elderly person cut the lawn, volunteers as a baby sitter, lends tools and works their way into the good graces of their neighbors in thousands of little ways, slowly introducing their status as Mormons and building interest in the Mormon church. Heinerman and Shupe recount that missionaries are effective one-tenth of one percent of the time, while the home mission technique is effective 50% of the time.[622] Mormons set a goal of bringing one new person into the church a year. This is a technique that atheists, by being open, proud and helpful in our community, can utilize as well.

Finally, we cannot ignore the media. Atheist characters are largely absent from the media, just as gays were a few decades ago. But as we live more openly and call on our friends in the media to portray us accurately, our image can change.

Paid advertising can also have a positive effect. Groups like the Freedom from Religion Foundation, American Humanist Association, United Coalition of Reason and others have recently purchased billboards and bus ads with messages like:

- Imagine no religion. (Freedom from Religion Foundation)
- In good we trust. (American Humanist Association)
- Don't believe in god? You are not alone. (United Coalition of Reason)

As the atheist movement builds, we can use professionally designed and tested campaigns to convey our message. And for free, we can make up our own campaigns. The back cover of this book shows my attempt, a surfing dinosaur introducing an element of fun and calling, "Atheism is up, catch the wave!"

Atheists have an image problem. This is important to me *not* because of the effects of discrimination against atheists, we are a pretty tough lot, but because it makes the goal of spreading the atheist message more difficult. More than 50% of the American religious population should be open to the atheist message, but entrenched attitudes and powerful religious institutions make it hard to effectively reach our audience. However, atheist action, as I describe in the upcoming chapters and which we can refine over the upcoming years, will make spreading the word easier.

Chapter 26. Learning from the gay rights movement.

The Boy Scouts of America maintains that no member can grow into the best kind of citizen without recognizing an obligation to God. . . . The recognition of God as the ruling and leading power in the universe and the grateful acknowledgment of His favors and blessings are necessary to the best type of citizenship and are wholesome precepts in the education of the growing members. No matter what the religious faith of the members may be, this fundamental need of good citizenship should be kept before them. The Boy Scouts of America . . . is absolutely nonsectarian in its attitude toward that religious training.[623] Declaration of Religious Principle, Bylaws of Boy Scouts of America

We believe that homosexual conduct is inconsistent with the requirements in the Scout Oath that a Scout be morally straight and in the Scout Law that a Scout be clean in word and deed, and that homosexuals do not provide a desirable role model for Scouts. Because of these beliefs, the Boy Scouts of America does not accept homosexuals as members or as leaders, whether in volunteer or professional capacities.[624] Boy Scouts of America Position Statement: Homosexuality and the BSA.

The parallels between atheists and gays are many. Both atheists and gays can "pass" as heterosexuals or religionists if they do not identify themselves. Absent that self-identification, they will often be assumed to be heterosexual or religious, as the case may be. Further, both gays and atheists are raised in a society where most presume they will grow up to be heterosexual or religious. An atheist child in a religious family may feel a similar sense of isolation and loneliness to that of a gay child. Growing up, the gay or atheist child must often learn to reject the assumptions of the dominant culture and to stand on his own with pride.

Both "gay" and "atheist" are affirmative identities. There are many people who have homosexual relations (Ted Haggard for example, see Chapter 17) who do not assume the identity of being gay. Similarly, there are many more people who do not believe in religion than the few who affirmatively identify themselves as atheists. One of the distinguishing elements of identity is pride. Gays have been building their pride for more than 40 years, atheists have some catching up to do.

Additionally, both gays and atheists suffer from social stigma and discrimination. Five hundred years ago, both atheism and homosexuality were crimes punishable by death. Even in some countries today, both homosexual activity and apostasy (specifically, renouncing the Muslim faith) remain punishable by death. The Boy Scouts of America singles out both gays and atheists as people unfit for membership. The Christian right attacks gays and atheists with equal fervor. The general public views gay and atheist candidates as the least desirable to serve as president.[625] An old proverb counsels, "the enemy of my enemy is my friend." There are natural parallels between the gay and atheist movements.

The path of the gay rights movement over the past 50 years has lessons for atheists. Think about it, 50 years ago, gay relations were illegal in all states. However, gays have taken concrete steps to improve their lot. Now a U.S. Supreme Court decision affirms their right to relationships,[626] 21 states prohibit discrimination against gays,[627] 8 states have domestic partnership laws[628] and 5 states plus the District of Colombia recognize gay marriage.[629] Gays, once a horribly stigmatized minority, are now ranked ahead of atheists in a poll asking who the electorate might choose to be president.[630]

Fighting for gay rights.

The birth of the modern gay rights movement, the Stonewall Rebellion, was marked by three days of riots which started when police tried to harass the patrons of a New York City gay bar, the Stonewall Inn, on June 28, 1969. The patrons and protestors labeled themselves "homosexuals." But that was about to change.

In the fertile civil rights environment of the era, the Gay Liberation movement began. On the first anniversary of the Stonewall Rebellion, thousands of New Yorkers marched in a gay pride parade. Parades were also held in Chicago and Los Angeles. Each year the number of cities and countries conducting "pride" parades has grown–all on or around the anniversary of the Stonewall Rebellion. The world's largest celebration occurs in Sao Paulo, Brazil, with over 3 million attending,[631] the largest celebration in the U.S. is in San Francisco, with over a million attending.[632]

The people previously known as "homosexuals" adopted a new name, "gay." Formerly a derisive term, it became both a name and an identity. Slogans like "gay is good" and "gay and proud" were popularized.

Gay Liberation also used symbols. One early symbol was the Greek letter lambda (λ), for liberation. Some gay organizations still have "lambda" in their names. Others used an inverted pink triangle ($\blacktriangledown$)–the symbol used by Nazis to identify gays in the concentration camps where they were exterminated along with the Jews. But in 1978 a San Francisco artist designed the rainbow flag,[633] which has become the most recognized symbol of gay pride. If you live in a larger city, you will likely see rainbow flags, or variations of rainbow flags, on many vehicles and businesses.

The gay rights movement identified itself from its inception as a civil rights movement. As such, it built coalitions with other groups. Women's liberation was a natural ally, but other coalitions formed as well. For example, in San Francisco, unions wished to boycott Coors beer. Gay politician Harvey Milk worked to get Coors removed from gay bars, thereby earning him union support in his run for political office.[634]

Gay Liberation worked with the political system to recognize gay rights. From ending police harassment, the movement quickly moved to affirmative rights. Policies and laws against discrimination were promoted in businesses and cities. San Francisco, Ann Arbor and East Lansing first adopted gay rights ordinances in 1972.[635] In 1974 AT&T became the first major national company to adopt an equal opportunity policy for gays.[636] Such small steps have led to statewide anti-discrimination laws in 21 states,[637] plus anti-discrimination laws and policies in countless cities and companies nationwide.

Gays and their allies have also worked in the fields of art and entertainment to create more positive gay images. One of the first Hollywood movies with central gay characters, 1970's *The Boys in the Band*, opened the floodgates for numerous others that followed. Ellen DeGeneres' disclosure she was a lesbian in 1997, and the incorporation of her character as a lesbian on the *Ellen* show were big news. Gay characters are now so common in television and movies that the review I read before seeing the 2009 movie *Taking Woodstock* did not even mention that the main character was gay. And on TV, talk show host Wanda Sykes speaks of her wife without anyone blinking an eye. Even the all-American comic book, *Archie* has added a gay character.[638] Gays have come a long way and the media has helped.

The gay rights movement has not only worked on the social side of the spectrum, but on the legal side as well. Victories include the 2003 U.S. Supreme Court decision in *Lawrence v. Texas*,[639] overruling the few state laws that still prohibited gay sex, as well as state court decisions in Vermont, Massachusetts, Iowa and California authorizing gay marriage.[640]

The gay rights movement has also become an economic force. In the early days, activists marked their bills "gay money" to make the point that gays are a strong economic force. Some advertisers caught on early–Subaru successfully marketed its automobiles to lesbians. The liquor industry was a pioneer in advertising to the gay market. Coors beer, once subject to a boycott by unions and gay rights activists, later began sponsoring gay events and advertising in the gay media. Today, advertising to the gay market is frequent and occurs without much notice or comment. The power of the gay dollar has been recognized.

Many strategies have worked effectively for the gay rights movement, but probably the most effective is "coming out." Within the gay world, not disclosing your status is known as "being in the closet," while becoming open is known as "coming out of the closet," or simply "coming out." Early in the gay rights movement, activists insisted that being "out" was essential to recognition of gay rights. They reasoned that everyone knows someone gay, even if they do not realize it. It would be easy to oppose gay rights if you had never met a gay person, but if you know your favorite elementary school teacher is gay, your grocer is gay, your barber is gay, your neighbor is gay, and each of them is a fine and likeable person, then it is much harder to oppose gay rights. Seventy-seven percent of Americans say they know a gay person, an increase of 35 percentage points since 1992.[641]

The gay rights movement established a "national coming out day," October 11, to encourage gay people to be more open.[642] A coming out brochure reads, "Gay . . . Americans are sons and daughters, doctors and lawyers, teachers and construction workers. We serve in Congress, protect our country on the front lines and contribute to the well-being of the nation at every level. In all that diversity, we have one thing in common: we each make deeply personal decisions to be open about who we are with ourselves and others--even when it isn't easy. We express that openness by telling our friends, family, co-workers and even strangers that--among all the other things we are--we're also gay."[643]

The brochure lists advantages of coming out:

- Living an open and whole life.
- Developing closer, more genuine relationships.
- Building self-esteem from being known and loved for who we really are.
- Reducing the stress of hiding our identity.
- Connecting with others who are GLBT.[644]
- Being part of a strong and vibrant community.

- Helping to dispel myths and stereotypes about who GLBT people are and what our lives are like.
- Becoming a role model for others.
- Making it easier for younger GLBT people who will follow in our footsteps.

If you reread the preceding paragraphs about coming out and substitute "atheist" for "gay," almost every provision applies to atheists as well.

Over the years, you probably have met a gay person who takes the coming out strategy quite seriously. He will have a rainbow flag on his car, a gay button on his jacket, a T-shirt that says "how dare you presume I am straight," and still he will find a way to speak about being gay in just about every conversation. It can be a bit amusing, but it is a necessary process, and it is a process that atheists should consider. How many times have you heard of a loud, out and proud atheist? We need more of them.

At one point, openly gay celebrities were few and far between. Quentin Crisp's publication of *The Naked Civil Servant* in 1968 pushed him to the fore, and Elton John's public declaration he was bisexual in 1988 was big news. Now, entire books and Websites contain seemingly endless lists of gay celebrities. But the impact of role models is important. Celebrities who are open about their status help to reduce discrimination and serve as role models for younger people. Atheist celebrities currently seem more secretive about their lack of religion than they do about their sexuality.

Of course, the analogy between gays and atheists has its limits. To a large degree, gays need each other to find love and support. Gay bars have been a gathering point for centuries. But to be honest, I have never heard of an atheist bar. Also, living honestly with one's sexual orientation may be more key to the happiness of an individual than atheism. At first this seemed obvious to me. But the more I think about it, the more I am unsure. Atheism is a key element of my personality and I could no more comfortably attend church, sing hymns and pray, than a gay person could marry a spouse of the opposite sex. Nonetheless, I do think that sexual orientation is a more core distinguishing factor than the lack of religion.

That said, the number of gay people in the world is relatively fixed. Heterosexuals, despite the claims of the Christian right, do not convert to homosexuals and homosexuals do not convert into heterosexuals. Religion, however, can be changed. A large number of atheists were once religious and each year the number of atheists grows. We are not limited to remaining 1% or 20% of the population. Eventually, we will be the majority.

The correlation between the gay rights movement and the atheist movement is not complete. Nonetheless, the movements are similar. Gays have significantly improved their rights and societal standing in America over the past 40 years, while atheists have not. The gay rights movement has adopted valuable strategies that the atheist movement can use as well; strategies like agreeing on a name, choosing a symbol, developing an identity and most importantly, coming out. The next chapter discusses actions atheists may wish to consider to improve the effectiveness of the atheist movement.

Chapter 27. Atheist action.

Coming out as an atheist is the single most important step you can take.[645]

When compared to religion, atheism is an immature and poorly defined movement. But the time has come for us to stop complaining and instead to take action. In this chapter I suggest a few action steps. Hopefully, this list will seem pitifully inadequate as the movement grows. However, from my review of the literature, few atheists are even trying to make specific suggestions. It is not enough to say we should rage against the religious machine, we must act.

Choose one name.

Nonreligious people toss around dozens of names to identify ourselves. We call ourselves brights, evolutionists, freethinkers, godless, heathens, heretics, humanists, infidels, irreligious, materialists, non-believers, non-theists, nones, pagans, rationalists, secularists, skeptics, unbelievers and more. Some day religion will fade and we will not need a name, but until then, we do. Choosing a name is a first step to defining an identity and building pride. Let us stop dividing our energies among numerous names. Let us stick with the term "atheist."

"Atheist" has been used as a derogatory name and it carries a fair amount of baggage. But it is the most widely recognized term to signify a lack of religious belief. Just as homosexuals claimed the name "gay" as their own, we can claim "atheist" as ours and redefine it. Let us gather under one name, one banner, and define ourselves positively.

Find a symbol.

As the gay rights movement grew, the rainbow flag became a unifying symbol. When a gay person is behind a car with a rainbow flag, he knows he is behind family. When a lesbian stays at a hotel flying a rainbow flag, she knows her patronage is welcome. No atheist symbol has achieved wide recognition. To me, combining the word "atheist" with the footed evolve fish is the most functional symbol that has emerged so far. Using a single common symbol will help us to recognize one another and to build our movement.

Create an identity.

Atheism is more than non-belief. It encompasses a willingness to self-identify as nonreligious, combined with a desire to counteract the negative aspects of religion. Atheists are more open to new experiences than the general population, less inclined to be prejudiced against minorities, and more vocal about their opinions. Look back at the predicted characteristics of atheists in Chapter 4. Part of creating an identity is recognizing what makes us different and celebrating it. We can best counter the negative image religionists have of atheists when we know what is right about us. We will most effectively celebrate our strength when we know what brings us together. When there are five to ten times as many nones as there are atheists, there is an obvious failure to create a positive atheist identity. As we remedy this, our numbers will grow.

Make atheism a civil rights issue.

Atheists are despised minority. Discrimination against atheists is considered to be more acceptable than discrimination against women, older people, Jews, Muslims, and gays. The negative view of atheists, just as with other minorities, is based on prejudice. It is time to challenge that prejudice.

Religion is the first protected category in the Bill of Rights,[646] it is listed along with race, color, sex, and national origin in Title VII of the Civil Rights Act of 1964,[647] and the Supreme Court has held that "government should not prefer one religion to another, *or religion to irreligion*."[648] In the eyes of the law, atheism receives the same protection as religious belief. The civil rights of atheists should be seen no differently than the civil rights of Jews, Muslims and Quakers.

Atheists should clarify in both the legal and social spheres that freedom *of* religion includes freedom *from* religion. Only by increasing awareness will we change perception. Identifying atheism as a civil rights issue will bring partnerships with other civil rights advocates. It is time we speak up and take our place at the table. Prejudice against atheists is widespread, but it is unjust, unreasonable and often illegal. Let us use legal and social channels to bolster and enforce our civil rights.

Link with others.

Popular culture pokes a lot of fun at liberals. But shockingly enough, liberals tend to side with religionists when it comes to issues of religious tolerance. It makes me want to shout, "how could you lose the liberals?" In part, I believe, we have lost the liberals because we do not make freedom from religion a civil rights issue, we are not open about our atheism, and we do not ask them for support. It is time that atheists start linking with other groups to build support for our cause.

The women's movement is another group that should be sympathetic. Both women and atheists are colored bad by religionists. Additionally, without religion, atheists have no basis for opposing women's rights and equality. We should let women know that we support them and ask them to support us.

Gays are another group. The Christian scripture is unambiguous that gays should be stoned to death. Muslims are even worse. Trying to fit homosexuality into religion is like trying to fit a square peg in a round hole. The fact that so many gays try is a testament to the power of religion. But atheists can offer an alternative. Absent religion there is no reason atheists are concerned about who dates whom, or who marries whom. We should let gays know that we welcome them and that we seek their support.

214

Jews have suffered horribly at the hands of their co-religionists and therefore are forever vigilant about encroachments in the area of the separation of church and state. Additionally, a large number of people are culturally Jewish, but have no belief in god. Court opinions that effectively hold, for example, that a cross is not a religious symbol, are just as offensive to Jews as to atheists. Jewish people have spent years in the trenches supporting the separation of church and state and battling Christian bias. We should learn from them and link with them where our interests are the same.

As atheists build coalitions, our progress will become stronger and faster.

Engage in political activity.

People widely assume that America's history of separation of church and state and freedom of religion are all that atheists need to achieve equality. That is not the case. Just as gay rights activists needed to explicitly put their group into anti-discrimination laws and policies, atheists should as well. Start with your employers, ask them to add atheism[649] to their anti-discrimination policy. This will raise awareness that atheists are here and that we have rights. Then, take it to your municipal, city and state governments. It is time atheists have visibility and recognition of our rights.

The fact only one member of Congress admits to being atheist is pitiful. Yet, candidates know of the prejudice against atheists and therefore avoid being identified as such. (Gay politicians suffer similar prejudice, but there are three openly gay people in Congress now.[650]) Let us support atheist candidates and encourage hidden atheist politicians to "come out." As the environment changes, more and more politicians will be openly atheist.

Additionally, as discussed more in the "coming out" section of this chapter, write to your elected representatives and let them know your concerns. When you volunteer for political campaigns, be clear about your atheist status. Atheists should become a political force to be reckoned with.

215

Atheists are falling all over themselves thanking Barack Obama for mentioning us in a speech or two. This is a start, but our goals should be much higher. Just as gays progressed politically from ending harassment to gaining acceptance and are finally working on achieving equality, atheists should demand no less.

Pursue legal remedies.

Lawsuits are one area in which atheists seem to be doing pretty well. Organizations like the American Civil Liberties Union, Americans United for Separation of Church and State, and the Freedom From Religion Foundation as well as individual atheists and attorneys nationwide seem skillful in bringing their claims.

However, it is likely that there will be some setbacks in this area. Fifty-six percent of the judges nationwide were appointed by Republicans.[651] The George W. Bush administration was famous for its litmus test for appointees–god, guns and gays. The recent 9th Circuit decision upholding the inclusion of "under god" in the Pledge of Allegiance is an example.[652] The author of the opinion was a Bush appointee. The U.S. Supreme Court is stacked with six Republican appointees, only three were appointed by Democrats. The 2010 decision in *Salazar v. Buono*, upholding the transfer of federal park land to private ownership to maintain a cross, is an example of the shift in the courts. In that decision, Reagan appointee Justice Kennedy, writing for the plurality, seems to use "because I said so" as his justification that a cross is not a predominantly religious symbol:

> [A] cross is not merely a reaffirmation of Christian beliefs. It is a symbol often used to honor and respect those whose heroic acts, noble contributions, and patient striving help secure an honored place in history for this Nation and its people. Here, one Latin cross in the desert evokes far more than religion. It evokes thousands of small crosses in foreign fields marking the

216

graves of Americans who fell in battles, battles whose tragedies are compounded if the fallen are forgotten.[653]

State constitutions may provide another resource if the federal judiciary falters. However, even if we face temporary setbacks in the courts, the rising tide of atheist social change will provide an alternate avenue for success. Look at the gay rights movement, with limited dollars and members, they have made great strides. With larger potential numbers and resources, atheists should do even better.

Seek visibility in arts and entertainment.

Because atheism is virtually invisible, it seems that our friends in the arts and entertainment community have neglected us. Just as the media ignored gays 50 years ago, we are ignored today. It is time for us to use the media to create more recognition and a positive image for the atheist community. We need more atheists to come out, and we need the inclusion of atheist characters in the media. Popular media has enormous impact on public sentiment. The progress made by gay characters over the past 50 years can be duplicated by atheists.

Oppose religious myths.

As discussed in Chapter 20, religionists have little problem telling lies. Once people adopt belief in a bearded man in the sky who answers prayers, it is not hard to rewrite U.S. history to say it is a Christian nation or to ignore evolutionary science and not only say the earth is less than 10,000 years old, but to also try to teach it to all school children. Even if you are not "out" as an atheist, you can fight against religious myths and try to limit their impact on society.

At this point in history, the religious mythologists are winning. Only 39% of Americans believe in evolution,[654] 67% believe America is a Christian nation[655] and 55% think the U.S. Constitution establishes the U.S. as a Christian nation.[656] It is time that we organize and speak out against these baseless religious myths.

•

Build organizational strength.

The Freedom from Religion Foundation has 14,000 members and claims to be the largest atheist organization in the United States. It has eight full-time employees[657] and a budget of $2 million.[658] It pales in comparison to religious organizations–the Catholic Church has 68 million members in the U.S., and more than 40,000 working priests.[659]

In general, atheist organizations are disorganized, territorial, and dependent on the personalities and efforts of a limited number of leaders. Religion has millions of employees and billions in assets. For atheists to present a powerful message we need to develop professionally staffed and managed organizations with national scope so that they may become successful agents of change. Donating money, time and leadership will move us toward this goal.

Develop economic power.

The gay rights movement gained ground when businesses recognized the economic power of the gay community. There is almost no recognition of the economic power of atheists. Some atheist activists are starting at the grass-roots level by marking "god" off the paper currency, or changing the phrase "in god we trust" to "in reason we trust." Of course, marking money is likely an illegal act,[660] so it might be wise to consult an attorney if you choose to engage in this activity.

Religionists have great economic power. However, atheists can let businesses know that they choose to go elsewhere because of their religious assertions. For example, since 1997 Hobby Lobby has placed full page Christian ads in newspapers on Easter and other holidays. The Easter 2010 ad included three crosses, a biblical quote and an invitation to come to Jesus.[661] Although I am not a regular customer, I wrote the store to tell them I would no longer do business with them and transferred my business to a locally owned store. The least we can do is let them know they are losing customers. If this were a battle on which we chose to focus, a coalition with gays and Jews could potentially triple the impact on Hobby Lobby.

218

Similarly, some businesses put a Jesus fish in their ads or on their service trucks. To me, this is a sign that they are liars and I never do business with them. If there were a local directory of atheist businesses (like there is for gay businesses), I would use them. As the atheist community grows in size and visibility, the business community will start to respond. We can start small, if you have a business and are not afraid of religious backlash, sponsor a local atheist group or place an ad in their publication. The gay rights movement started with the same small steps and now they have significant national sponsors for their activities.

Additionally, open your wallet for local and national atheist organizations. Religion has become powerful by directing adherents to give 10% of their income to their group. Atheists do not seek to duplicate this madness, but making a few donations of $50 or $100 will help atheist groups grow and give you a feeling of participation in the process. The creationist project "Answers in Genesis" alone had $22 million in revenue in 2008. In contrast, The Freedom From Religion Foundation had $2 million. We are gaining ground, but we have a long way to go to be on an equal financial footing with the religionists.

Create Radio Free Religion.

The 9/11 attacks served as a wake up call for atheists. The attacks were religiously motivated and killed more than 3,000 people. As a direct result of 9/11, the United States initiated wars in Afghanistan and Iraq killing a million or more people. Now religion is not just a matter of creationism and the ten commandments in public places, it is a matter of life and death.

So far, the military approach has had limited success. Guns, planes, bombs and torture have only added fuel to the fire of religious extremists. My suggestion is that we try to erode the religious basis for their violence.

During the cold war, the United States created Radio Free Europe to broadcast anticommunist information to the East Bloc. Let us update the concept and promote antireligious messages by radio,

Internet and new media to the world. If only political leaders had the will to question *all* religion, they could speak to religious extremists, in their own language, about the fallacies of their positions. A friend of mine suggests that if the oppressed women of the Muslim world would all at once tie up (or worse) their sleeping spouses, the region could be freed of religious oppression. The concept is simplistic but powerful. Radio Free Religion could erode the foundations of religious violence and bring about a more peaceful world. This could be done at a fraction of the cost of war and with the impact of words instead of bombs.

Use new media.

Admittedly, I am from a generation that grew up before the advent of the personal computer. But even a primitive like me sees the power of the new media. The Internet, MySpace, Facebook, Twitter, podcasts, blogs, and other tools allow people to privately learn about issues, as well as to find socialization and support. Rural atheists can access the same information and support as city folks. Atheist Nexus bills itself as the largest social networking site exclusively for atheists.[662] MySpace had an atheist group of 35,000, the world's largest atheist group, until MySpace (owned by Rupert Murdoch's News Corporation) deleted it in 2007.[663] Ex-Mormons, ex-Muslims, ex-Scientologists and ex-Catholics all find custom-tailored support online. Meetup.com can tell you where like-minded people are gathering face-to-face in your area. You can watch your favorite authors delivering video lectures (as well as religionists making horrible mis-characterizations of us) on YouTube. The Internet allows us to reach across the world to people oppressed by religion. The Internet is a valuable source of information, interaction and support for atheists. We should make the most of it.

Talk with your ex's.

The atheist community has a valuable resource in its former religionists. Ex-Mormons, ex-Muslims and ex-Scientologists can, for example, speak more accurately to specific issues that will help convert their brethren into ex-religionists. It would be nice to have a set of pamphlets next to the front door specially tailored to offer to the various brands of religionists who knock. That way we could ask the Mormons to promise to read our brochure if we promise to read theirs. An ex-Mormon could best draft such a pamphlet. The former members of religions provide atheists a valuable window into how and why people leave their religion and we should tap this resource to help duplicate their experiences.

Be inclusive.

Atheist organizations seem to be dominated by older, college-educated, white men. We need to be sure that the full spectrum of atheists feel welcome within our group. Women, young people and people of color should all have a role. Where are our American Indian members? Where are our Arab members? Where are the laborers and the rural residents? Class and education should not be seen as membership criteria for our club. For example, Vietnam has one of the highest percentages of atheists in the world. Is the waitress or dishwasher at your favorite Vietnamese restaurant aware of your local atheist organization? Does she feel welcome there? Or will she go from an atheist perspective to believing America is a Christian nation and concluding her children should be churched in order to assimilate? Let us make every effort to reach out to the rainbow spectrum of atheists and potential atheists and strive to make them feel welcome in our movement. People from all backgrounds should serve as role models and leaders and further expand our diversity.

Be international.

The phrase, "we are everywhere" should be more than an empty statement.[664] Atheists around the world are seeking to obtain support or to give it. In places like Egypt, Saudi Arabia and Iran, atheists exist at all levels, they are just waiting for the environment to become safe so they can make their non-belief known. We should help to create the environment where they feel comfortable expressing their views.

Pressure can be placed on oppressive regimes to recognize the right to freedom from religion.

Additionally, we can learn from progressive countries like Sweden, Denmark, Norway and Japan about social change that lessens the danger and influence of religion. Studies of atheism can be translated and shared via the Internet. Atheists are not limited by religious borders or cultures. We are everywhere, and we will gain strength through mutual support and information sharing.

Develop science.

Religion is powerful and atheism is despised. Perhaps this explains why there is very little scientific study of atheism and religion from an atheist perspective.[665] Right now, atheism is a movement of armchair philosophers, me included. We sit around making guesses about why atheists are a minority and religion prevails. Pollsters give us numbers to look at, but they rarely get to the reasons for conduct. It is time that we demand and fund studies that show what factors make some of us atheists and others religionists. Let us study why some Muslims reject their religion and its violent tenets. How can we help others to duplicate the process? How can we assist religionists to see the lie in the bearded man myth and start living a life based on reason? It is time for atheists to move from guessing and philosophizing and apply the science of which we claim to be so proud.

Talk with religionists.

Religionists are not the enemy. They are simply people infected with the religious virus, usually at a young age. Knowledge and rational thought are the cures. In order to stop the destructive effects of religion—anti-intellectualism, subjugation of women and the environment, murder, suicide bombing and the threat of myth-motivated nuclear war, we must accelerate the rising tide of atheism. Polite people *do* talk about religion. The longer religionists can insulate themselves, the longer religion will last. Atheism is not broadly accessible to those who are not looking for information about it. But by being open and discussing atheism and religion, we make it more accessible and more human.

Hunsberger and Altemeyer found that a majority of religionists who became atheists were motivated by intellectual honesty about the inconsistencies of their scriptures.[666] In order to accelerate the change, we should talk to religionists about this. It may entail learning a bit about their scriptures, listening politely to their perspectives and planting the seeds of rational thought and skepticism. In their limited study, Hunsberger and Altemeyer found it took religionists from six to fourteen years to become atheists after they first felt doubt in their religion.[667] So we should not be surprised when religionists do not change after one conversation. We should study how and why religionists adopt rational thought and seek to duplicate and refine our strategies. There is too much at stake not to do so. It is not enough to sit back and say, "religionists are crazy and there is no use talking to them." They are crazy, but they are crazy and in control, with their hands on the triggers of guns and the detonators of weapons of mass destruction. The time for deference is over. The time for action is now.

Come out.

The most important action step of all is both simple and complex, that is to come out as an atheist. Just as with gays, everyone knows an atheist, everyone respects an atheist, they are just unaware that the person is an atheist.

It is time that we tell people who we are. Does your spouse know you are an atheist? Does your family know? Do your neighbors know? If not, tell them.

The same cautions that apply to gays coming out apply to atheists as well. Young atheists should think carefully about whether their revelation will threaten their physical or financial well-being. It is not that an atheist student should never risk having his family's financial support cut off because of his disclosure, but he should carefully evaluate if it is worth the risk.

Atheists should also carefully consider how coming out may affect their work. Discrimination on the basis of irreligion is illegal, but as other minorities know, discrimination can be quietly invidious. Unless your boss says, "I did not promote him because he is an atheist," it may be difficult to prove discrimination.

But after giving the issue careful thought and protecting your financial and emotional position, I encourage you to have at it. I have been openly atheist for all of my adult life and I have found the gains far outweigh the losses.

When you come out, consider the following:

Write letters. When is the last time you wrote to your elected officials, told them you are an atheist, and expressed your concern about an issue within their control, for example, not using government money to fund religious institutions (such as the "faith based" federal initiatives or many school voucher programs)? We will never gain visibility and power unless we speak up and insist that we be heard.

Join organizations. Numerous atheist and atheist friendly organizations work hard every day to protect and promote the rights of atheists. Join one, two or more. Your efforts will assist them in their cause and their meetings and publications will help keep you aware of issues and remind you to remain out and active.

Display a bumper sticker, button, or T-shirt. Your automobile, bicycle or body can serve as a mobile atheist billboard. Put an atheist fish on your car, stick a button on your coat and decorate your coffee mug with a message. Your statement will support other out atheists, encourage those not yet out to consider taking the plunge, and educate the general public that we are here, and in many instances, we have a sense of humor. And when you see an atheist stating her opinion, give her a wave, a thumbs-up, or an encouraging comment. We are everywhere, we just have not yet learned to show it.

Educate around the religious holidays. Religious holidays offer an excellent opportunity to educate the public that atheists exist and that our beliefs may be different from theirs. At a minimum, when someone wishes you "Merry Christmas," wish them a "Seasonal

Solstice," say "ho, ho, ho," or something that does not create the impression that you share their belief. Around Christmas time, I do not have time to give everyone the long version of why I do not celebrate, but usually about one in five times I do. People have been surprised, but never have I had a bad reaction and sometimes it has lead to interesting conversations. This has been an especially easy way for me to educate my neighbors that I am an atheist, after all, they brought up religion.

Choose a day. The gay rights movement anchors gay pride day (and now often gay pride week) to the start of the Stonewall Rebellion, June 28. National coming out day for gays is on the anniversary of their largest march on Washington, October 11. These events provide an opportunity for activities, media coverage and a special place on the calendar to consider how much you are out and to whom. Atheists should not pass up the opportunity to pick a day and do the same. Any day will do. Charles Darwin was born on February 12, the same day as famous American skeptic Abraham Lincoln who said, "The Bible is not my book nor Christianity my profession."[668] Interestingly, a notable book concludes that Lincoln was gay.[669]

But back to the subject at hand, let us declare February 12th Freedom from Religion Day,[670] a day to discuss our atheist predecessors, atheist beliefs, to remind ourselves to come out, and to educate the media and the public about our issues. Let us have the Mayor and the Governor recognize our day by proclamation (in less progressive areas you could call it "Freedom of Religion Day," while still emphasizing atheist issues). February 12 can be our atheist pride day and national coming out day, all rolled into one.

Teach your children. One of the most surprising conclusions in Hunsberger and Altemeyer's book *Atheists* is that most atheists surveyed would not teach their children to be atheists.[671] The parents said they would just allow the children to figure it out on their own. On one hand, *not* teaching your children shows great confidence that the truth will prevail and they will grow up atheist. The good news is that children of atheists tend to grow up as atheists, no matter what their parents say. However, this strikes me a little bit like saying you will not teach your children about drugs and alcohol, you will just let them figure it out on their own. Why take a chance that children will experiment unadvised with drugs, alcohol or religion? In our lifetimes, we have learned something about powerful forces. I believe it is our obligation to teach our children what we have learned.

Exhibit pride. Gay people were once a hated minority. Over the years, societal perception of gays has changed so that being gay has become, for most people, an interesting aspect of an individual's personality, not a stigmatized status. Part of the reason for the change is gay pride.

Atheists should learn a lesson from this. Atheists have engaged in rational analysis of religious claims and rejected them. Atheists have chosen a harder road. Where religionists pray, atheists analyze and decide. Where religionists give responsibility for their decisions to their bearded sky father, atheists take responsibility for themselves. Where religionists are expected to sin and be forgiven, atheists expect themselves to do right and to analyze and learn from mistakes. Atheists have not taken the easy way out. Further, atheists have gone beyond the agnostics and "nones" to stand up and be counted as people who reject religion, despite the social costs. Rather than keeping this aspect of your personality in the closet, display it with pride. We are atheists, out, loud and proud.

Coming out conclusion. Coming out is an individual process. Only you can determine how and when to do it. But if the experience of the gay rights movement is predictive, coming out will accelerate our agenda more than any other strategy. And our membership is not limited to 3% or 5% or 10% of the population, once the ball is rolling, atheists will become the majority. Coming out as an atheist is the single most powerful step you can take to change the world.

Conclusion.

Religion is a man-made phenomenon. Religion is represented by a cross, a sword and a stone building. If we make atheism a religion, or if we allow religionists to convince us it is a religion, we will only be making a better symbol, a better weapon and a better building.

Islam represents religion in perhaps its purest, most primitive and most powerful form. Ibn Warraq quotes Ayatollah Khomeini saying:

> Islam makes it incumbent on all adult males, provided they are not disabled and incapacitated, to prepare themselves for the conquest of (other) countries so that the writ of Islam is obeyed in every country in the world.

> But those who study Islamic Holy War will understand why Islam wants to conquer the whole world. . . . Those who would know nothing of Islam pretend that Islam counsels against war. Those (who say this) are witless. Islam says: Kill all the unbelievers just as they would kill you all! Does this mean that Muslims should sit back until they are devoured by (the unbelievers)? Islam says: Kill them (the non-Muslims), put them to the sword and scatter (their armies). Does this mean sitting back until (non-Muslims) overcome us? Islam says: Kill in the service of Allah those who may want to kill you! Does this mean we should surrender to the enemy? Islam says: Whatever good there is exists thanks to the sword and in the shadow of the sword! People cannot be

227

made obedient except with the sword! The sword is the key to Paradise, which can be opened only for Holy Warriors! There are hundreds of other (Koranic) psalms and Hadiths (sayings of the Prophet) urging Muslims to value war and to fight. Does all that mean that Islam is a religion that prevents men from waging war? I spit upon those foolish souls who make such a claim.[672]

But the response of atheism should not be to build a stronger army or more virulent ideology, but rather to let truth erode the man-made structure of religion. Yes, we should try to help it along, but the erosion is inevitable.

Atheism is a natural phenomenon. It is a rising tide that will wash away religious symbols, weapons and structures. It will cleanse people of their man-made religion and leave them in their natural state--curious, rational and flawed. And once that natural state is achieved, there will be no more need for an imaginary god and the dangerous dogma that surrounds him.

The rising tide of atheism is inevitable. We should help it by building channels to erode religious structures. Religious violence makes this necessary. And hopefully the tide and our efforts will succeed before religionists bring about their imagined end times with nuclear destruction.

Religionists are not the enemies of atheists. Religionists are simply people who are mis-educated or mistaken. Because of indoctrination or desperation, they follow an inflexible code that hurts them as well as us. They have been prejudiced against atheists by their powerful institutions. It is up to us to educate them. We will not combat them with their own techniques, we will lead by example and convert by rational discourse.

Our action is necessary, but the rising tide of atheism is inevitable. When the tide recedes, both religion and atheism will recede with it. Man will continue. Wars will not end, hate will not end, but neither will they be assisted by religious dogma. When religion and atheism are gone, man will continue in a cleaner, more natural state.

Author's closing note.

If you enjoyed *Born Atheist*, please do not put it on a bookshelf. Give this copy to a friend or relative. If you would like a copy available for reference, ask your public library to buy one, then it will always be there when you want to look at it.

If you would like to buy additional copies, visit iUniverse.com, Amazon.com, or your local bookseller.

For updates on topics discussed in the book, visit BornAtheist.com.

A note about the endnotes.

      I have elected to use a pared-down style for the endnotes in this book. In the modern world, people use the Internet more than the library, so I have included information that will make locating these resources easier for the Internet user. For these reasons, I have left out the names and cities of book publishers, but I have added, wherever possible, Websites that contain the information cited. In most endnotes, I have not used punctuation at the end of the Website address so that the punctuation will not get accidentally copied, invalidating the Website address. However, in endnotes with more than one citation, I have separated the information with a semicolon or a period. The unique characteristics of Website addresses preclude using full justification in the endnotes and result in odd line breaks, however I think the utility of including them outweighs the formatting compromises they require.

      All Websites cited were accessed in the first half of 2010 and were active at that time.

1. As with so many issues in atheism, there is scant research on even this most basic question. Bruce Hunsberger and Bob Altemeyer, in their 2006 book *Atheists*, studied small samples of atheists in San Francisco, Idaho, Alabama and Manitoba. They concluded that most of the atheists they studied had "little or no" religious training in childhood. However, they additionally found that about 25% had a moderate or considerable indoctrination to religion. *Atheists* at 42. Conversely, Luke Galen, in his larger sample of organizational atheists, found 15% grew up in a household where religion was mildly or not at all emphasized and 35% grew up in a home with a strong emphasis on religion, with 50% falling into an intermediate category. Galen, Luke, "Profiles of the Godless," Free Inquiry, Aug/Sept 2009, at 43,
http://www.centerforinquiry.net/uploads/attachments/Profiles_of_the
_Godless_FI_AugSept_Vol_29_No_5_pps_41-45.pdf. A look at the Pew Research Center Data from 2008 shows that less than a third of atheists were raised as atheists. Pew Forum on Religion and Public Life, U.S. Religious Landscape Survey, February 2008, at 26,

http://religions.pewforum.org/pdf/report-religious-landscape-study-c
hapter-2.pdf. Analyzing the same data in a later release, Pew found
that 21% of the unaffiliated (which includes atheists, as well as about
40% of the unaffiliated who say they believe in god) were raised
unaffiliated. "Faith in Flux," Pew Forum on Religion and Public
Life, April 2009,
http://pewforum.org/uploadedfiles/Topics/Religious_Affiliation/fullr
eport.pdf. The American Religious Identification Survey looked at
"nones" (of whom, only a small percentage are atheists), and found
that 73% came from religious homes while 23% had a nonreligious
parent. Kosmin, Barry and Keysar, Ariela "American Nones:The
Profile of the No Religion Population," *American Religious
Identification Survey* 2008, at 6,
http://www.americanreligionsurvey-aris.org/reports/NONES_08.pdf.
Part of the problem may be the definition of a "religious
upbringing." For example, I categorize myself as *not* having a
religious upbringing since there was no emphasis on religion in my
home, however I was sent to Sunday school weekly for most of my
childhood. Atheists come from both strongly religious and
nonreligious families. I suspect that a large number of atheists had
less religious emphasis than average, and the surveys support this,
however, there is no clear support at this time to say, for example,
that 50% of atheists had little or no religious upbringing.

2. I will follow the usual conventions for capitalizations in this book
with a few exceptions. I will capitalize the names of religions, like
Christianity; books, like the Bible, and religious characters for whom
an argument can be made for their existence, like Mohammed and
Jesus. I will not capitalize the name of god, for whose existence no
credible argument can be made. Further, I will not capitalize
"atheist." One could argue that atheism deserves just as much respect
as Christianity and therefore should be capitalized. But, as you will
see in this book, I argue that atheism is broader than religion, and
therefore I treat the term more like I treat the term "human," that is
without capitalization. Finally, I recognize that alternative spellings
for Mohammed and the Koran have become popular, but I have

elected to stick with the more traditional spellings of those terms.

With regard to the titles of books, for most books I will use italics. However, for the Bible, the Koran and the Book of Mormon, I will forgo the italics because I cite these books so often that the frequent italics might interrupt the flow of the text.

3. Hemingway, Earnest, *A Farewell to Arms*, 1988, at 7.

4. The Website, Godchecker.com provides information about 2850 gods. http://www.godchecker.com/

5. Incredibly, I could not find a quote of someone who has said this before, so I am saying it for myself now.

6. Heinerman, John and Shupe, Anson, *The Mormon Corporate Empire*, 1985, at 125.

7. "Archbishop of Westminster attacks atheism but says nothing on child abuse," The Times, March 22, 2009, http://www.timesonline.co.uk/tol/comment/faith/article6334837.ece

8. The World Fact Book, Central Intelligence Agency, updated May 27, 2010, https://www.cia.gov/library/publications/the-world-factbook/geos/vt.html

9. "Bush To Roll Out Red Carpet For Pope," CBS News, April 14, 2008, http://www.cbsnews.com/stories/2008/04/14/national/main4012614.shtml

10. The new Dalai Lama is selected randomly on the death of a previous leader by dreams, watching smoke, looking in a lake, and seeing if a child plays with the possessions of a prior Dalai Lama. "Q&A: The Dalai Lama, Tibet and China," MSNBC, undated, http://www.msnbc.msn.com/id/21321374/

11. "Obama, McCain talk issues at pastor's forum," CNN, August 17, 2008, http://www.cnn.com/2008/POLITICS/08/16/warren.forum/

12. "Why Rick Warren's Invocation at Obama's Inauguration Matters," U.S. News and World Report, December 17, 2008, http://www.usnews.com/blogs/god-and-country/2008/12/17/why-ric k-warrens-invocation-at-obamas-inauguration-matters.html

13. "God's business," The Orange County Register, November 12, 2006, http://www.ocregister.com/news/-46304--.html

14. "God and Money - The Church and the IRS," Charity Navigator Blog, July 24, 2008, http://blog.charitynavigator.org/2008/07/god-and-money-church-and -irs.html

15. "U.S. charitable giving estimated to be $307.65 billion in 2008," Giving USA, 2009, http://www.philanthropy.iupui.edu/News/2009/docs/GivingReaches 300billion_06102009.pdf

16. The World Fact Book, The Central Intelligence Agency, updated May 19, 2010, https://www.cia.gov/library/publications/the-world-factbook/geos/us. html

17. Kosmin, Barry and Keysar, Ariela, *American Religious Identification Survey*, (hereinafter, ARIS 2008), March 2009, http://b27.cc.trincoll.edu/weblogs/AmericanReligionSurvey-ARIS/re ports/ARIS_Report_2008.pdf

18. "Our Mission," National Religious Broadcasters, undated, http://nrb.org/index.php/about/our_mission/

19. "Catholic Education Questions," National Catholic Education Association, undated, http://www.ncea.org/FAQ/CatholicEducationFAQ.asp

20. "About CCCU," Council for Christian Colleges & Universities (CCCU), undated, http://www.cccu.org/about

21. "Transcript: Mitt Romney's Faith Speech," NPR, December 6, 2007, http://www.npr.org/templates/story/story.php?storyId=16969460

22. "Many Americans Say Other Faiths Can Lead to Eternal Life," The Pew Forum on Religion & Public Life, December 18, 2008, http://pewforum.org/Many-Americans-Say-Other-Faiths-Can-Lead-to-Eternal-Life.aspx

23. "Being Good for Goodness' Sake?" The Pew Forum on Religion & Public Life, December 11, 2008, http://pewforum.org/Being-Good-for-Goodness-Sake.aspx

24. "Some Americans Reluctant to Vote for Mormon, 72-Year-Old Presidential Candidates," Gallup News Service, February 20, 2007, http://www.gallup.com/poll/26611/Some-Americans-Reluctant-Vote-Mormon-72YearOld-Presidential-Candidates.aspx

25. Edgell, Penny, Gerteis, Joseph, and Hartmann, Douglas, "Atheists As 'Other': Moral Boundaries and Cultural Membership in American Society," American Sociological Review, 2006, Vol. 71, at 218, http://www.soc.umn.edu/~hartmann/files/atheist%20as%20the%20other.pdf

26. "Rep. Stark applauded for atheist outlook," MSNBC, March 13, 2007, http://www.msnbc.msn.com/id/17594581/

27. Arkansas Constitution, Article 19, Section 1, 1874, http://www.arkleg.state.ar.us/assembly/Summary/ArkansasConstitution1874.pdf

28. "History of 'In God We Trust,'" U.S. Department of the Treasury, undated,

http://www.ustreas.gov/education/fact-sheets/currency/in-god-we-tru
st.shtml

29. 100 Cong. Rec. 2, 1700, February 12, 1954, (Statement of Rep. Louis C. Rebaut, chief sponsor of the Act of 1954).

30. "The U.S. Pledge of Allegiance," Religious Tolerance.org, February 7, 2010, http://www.religioustolerance.org/nat_pled1.htm

31. "Atheists sue to keep 'In God We Trust' off Capitol Visitor Center," McClatchy Newspapers, July 18, 2009, http://www.mcclatchydc.com/2009/07/18/72058/atheists-sue-to-keep-in-god-we.html; "'In God we trust': Should it be on new visitor center?" Lodi News Sentinel, July 23, 2009, http://www.lodinews.com/articles/2009/07/23/news/5-visitors-center-090723.txt

32. "Can George Bush, with impunity, state that atheists should not be considered either citizens or patriots?" Positive Atheism.org, undated, http://www.positiveatheism.org/writ/ghwbush.htm

33. "Barack Obama invokes Jesus more than George W. Bush," Politico.com, June 9, 2009, http://www.politico.com/news/stories/0609/23510.html; "White House Faith Office to Expand," The New York Times, February 5, 2009, http://www.nytimes.com/2009/02/06/us/politics/06obama.html?_r=1

34. Clarke, Arthur, *The Exploration of Space*, 1951.

35. The Koran, 4:89, (parentheticals omitted, emphasis added), (Mohsin Khan).

36. "Ibn Warraq" is the pen name of an undisclosed activist, critic of Islam and author. To protect his safety, he has adopted a pen name used by past critics of Islam. The fact that he fears for his life despite living in Europe highlights the danger of informal enforcement of

235

Muslim apostasy rules. "Ibn Warraq," Absolute Astronomy, undated, http://www.absoluteastronomy.com/topics/Ibn_Warraq

37. Warraq, Ibn, "Islam, Apostasy, and Human Rights," Jihad Watch, April 17, 2004, (quotation marks omitted), http://www.jihadwatch.org/2004/04/islam-apostasy-and-human-right s.html

38. Id.

39. "Afghan Christian Convert Granted Asylum in Italy," The New York Times, March 29, 2006, http://www.nytimes.com/2006/03/29/international/asia/29cnd-afghan .html?scp=20&sq=apostasy&st=cse

40. "Islamic Scholars Wrestle With Death-For-Apostasy Issue," Cybercast News Service, April 30, 2009, http://www.cnsnews.com/news/print/47401

41. "Muslim 'apostates' in U.S. ask for protection," The Washington Times, September 25, 2009, http://www.washingtontimes.com/news/2009/sep/25/muslim-apostat es-in-us-ask-for-protection/?page=2

42. Warraq, Ibn, *Why I am not a Muslim*, 1995, at 217.

43. The Bible, Deuteronomy 13:6-10, (emphasis added).

44. The Bible, Luke 19:27, (emphasis added); see also Matthew 13:40-22.

45. The Bible, Psalms 14:1.

46. Altemeyer, Bob and Hunsberger, Bruce, *Amazing Conversions*, 1997, at 117.

47. Id. at 200.

48. Id.

49. For example, Catholic Cardinal Murphy-O'Connor said, "the inability to believe in God and to live by faith is the greatest of evils." "Archbishop of Westminster attacks atheism but says nothing on child abuse," The Times, March 22, 2009, http://www.timesonline.co.uk/tol/comment/faith/article6334837.ece

50. Parentheticals and ellipses omitted, as quoted in *The autobiography of Charles Darwin and selected letters*, edited by Francis Darwin, 1958, at 60.

51. *U.S. Religious Landscape Survey, Religious Affiliation: Diverse and Dynamic*, February 2008, The Pew Forum on Religion & Public Life (hereinafter, Pew 2008), at 93, http://religions.pewforum.org/pdf/report-religious-landscape-study-full.pdf. Luke Galen's study found that 74% were male. Galen, Luke, "Profiles of the Godless," Free Inquiry, August/September 2009, at 43, http://www.centerforinquiry.net/uploads/attachments/Profiles_of_the_Godless_FI_AugSept_Vol_29_No_5_pps_41-45.pdf. Hunsberger and Altemeyer found that 69% were male. Hunsberger, Bruce and Altemeyer, Bob, *Atheists*, 2006, at 25.

52. Pew 2008 at 81.

53. Hunsberger and Altemeyer found an average age of 60. Hunsberger, Bruce and Altemeyer, Bob, *Atheists*, 2006, at 25. Galen found an average age of 48. Galen, Luke, "Profiles of the Godless," Free Inquiry, August/September 2009, at 43, http://www.centerforinquiry.net/uploads/attachments/Profiles_of_the_Godless_FI_AugSept_Vol_29_No_5_pps_41-45.pdf

54. Id.

55. Id at 93. Another large survey shows similar results, with 60% of nones being male and 40% being female. Kosmin, Barry, and

Keysar, Ariela, *American Nones: The Profile of the No Religion Population, A Report Based on the American Religious Identification Survey 2008*, 2008, http://www.americanreligionsurvey-aris.org/reports/NONES_08.pdf

56. Pew 2008 at 75.

57. "People with 'no religion' gain on major denominations," USA Today, September 22, 2009, http://www.usatoday.com/news/religion/2009-09-22-no-religion_N.htm

58. Pew 2008 at 78, 84.

59. Id at 72.

60. "U.S. divorce rates for various faith groups, age groups, & geographic areas," Religious Tolerance .org, (reporting on a no longer available survey from Barna Research Group), July 20, 2009, http://www.religioustolerance.org/chr_dira.htm

61. "Spiritual Profile of Homosexual Adults Provides Surprising Insights," Barna Group, June 20, 2009, http://www.barna.org/barna-update/article/13-culture/282-spiritual-profile-of-homosexual-adults-provides-surprising-insights?q=homosexual

62. "State of the States: Importance of Religion," Gallup News, January 28, 2009, http://www.gallup.com/poll/114022/state-states-importance-religion.aspx

63. Segal, David and Wechsler Segal, Mady, *Population Bulletin: America's Military Population*, December 2004, at 25, http://www.prb.org/Source/ACF1396.pdf; see also, "Military Chaplain Support: Demographics study of Defense Manpower Data Agency data," Military Association of Atheists & Freethinkers,

February 2010,
http://www.maaf.info/resources/MAAF%20DoD%20Demo%20201
0.pdf

64. Religious Affiliations of Inmates, data as of January 30, 2010,
U.S. Department of Justice, Federal Bureau of Prisons, data provided
in response to a freedom of information act request by the author. In
March, 1997, a freedom of information act request by Rod Swift
resulted in a response of .2% of federal prison inmates identified as
atheist. "The results of the Christians vs. atheists in prison
investigation," Holysmoke.org, undated,
http://www.holysmoke.org/icr-pri.htm. For additional discussion of
this topic, see Chapter 7.

65. "Leading scientists still reject God," Nature, Vol. 394, No. 6691,
1998, at 313, http://www.stephenjaygould.org/ctrl/news/file002.html

66. *U.S. Religious Landscape Survey, Religious Beliefs and
Practices: Diverse and Politically Relevant*, June 2008 (hereinafter
Pew Social 2008), at 90, 92.
http://religions.pewforum.org/pdf/report2-religious-landscape-study-
full.pdf

67. Pew Social 2008 at 83.

68. Galen, Luke, "Profiles of the Godless," Free Inquiry,
August/September 2009, at 42,
http://www.centerforinquiry.net/uploads/attachments/Profiles_of_the
_Godless_FI_AugSept_Vol_29_No_5_pps_41-45.pdf

69. Baker, Joseph and Smith, Buster, "The Nones: Social
Characteristics of the Religiously Unaffiliated," Social Forces 87(3),
March 2009,
http://www.isreligion.org/publications/recent/documents/smith_none
s.pdf

70. From Bruce E. Hunsberger and Bob Altemeyer, *Atheists: A Groundbreaking Study of America's Nonbelievers* (Amherst, NY: Prometheus Books, 2006), p. 110. Copyright © 2006 by the estate of Bruce E. Hunsberger and by Bob Altemeyer. All rights reserved. Used with permission of the publisher; www.prometheusbooks.com.

71. The Pew 2008 poll puts atheists at 1.6%, but "unaffiliated" at 16.1%. ARIS 2008 puts "nones" at 15% of the population.

72. Pew 2008 reports 1.6% (Pew 2008 at 5), while ARIS 2008 comes up with a figure less than half that, .7% (ARIS 2008 at 5).

73. Pew 2008 at 5.

74. Pew 2008 finds 5% of Americans do not believe in god, http://pewforum.org/Not-All-Nonbelievers-Call-Themselves-Atheist s.aspx; a Harris poll found that 10% did not believe in god and 9% were not sure; "More Americans Believe in the Devil, Hell and Angels than in Darwin's Theory of Evolution," December 10, 2008, http://www.harrisinteractive.com/vault/Harris-Interactive-Poll-Resea rch-Religious-Beliefs-2008-12.pdf;

75. See Chapter 25.

76. ARIS 2008 at 8.

77. The numbers on the graph do not equal a perfect 100% because some survey respondents refused to answer the question or responded, "I don't know." This number was 5.2% in ARIS 2008 and .8% in Pew 2008.

78. "One-Third of Americans Believe the Bible is Literally True," Gallup News, May 25, 2007, http://www.gallup.com/poll/27682/onethird-americans-believe-bible -literally-true.aspx

79. "Religion," Gallup News, undated,
http://www.gallup.com/poll/1690/Religion.aspx

80. Dennett, Daniel, *Breaking the Spell*, 2006, at 200-246.

81. "Christian? or Secular Humanist?" Abounding Joy, 2005,
http://www.aboundingjoy.com/humanism_chart.htm

82. Huxley, Aldous, *Words and Their Meanings*, 1940, at 9.

83. "Humanism vs. Christianity, The Greatest Battle of Our Times,"
theBible1.net, 2000,
http://www.thebible1.net/biblicaltheism/humanchrist.htm;
"Christianity v. Secular Humanism," Fundamentalist Baptist Church,
undated, http://www.fightingsecularhumanism.com/; "Apologist:
Christianity Losing Out to Secular Humanism?" The Christian Post,
February 17, 2010,
http://www.christianpost.com/article/20100217/apologist-christianity
-losing-out-to-secular-humanism/index.html

84. "Humanism and its Aspirations, Humanist Manifesto III,"
American Humanist Association, undated,
http://www.americanhumanist.org/who_we_are/about_humanism/H
umanist_Manifesto_III

85. "Secular Humanism Defined," Council for Secular Humanism,
undated,
http://www.secularhumanism.org/index.php?section=main&page=sh
_defined

86. Pew 2008 at 5,
http://religions.pewforum.org/pdf/report-religious-landscape-study-f
ull.pdf

87. "Enthusiastic Brights," the brights, undated,
http://the-brights.net/people/enthusiastic/index3.html#paul-geisert

241

88. "What is a bright?" the brights, undated, http://the-brights.net/

89. Merriam-Webster Dictionary Online, undated,
http://www.merriam-webster.com/dictionary/freethinker

90. "Freethinker Cenotaph," theinfidels.org, 2002,
http://www.theinfidels.org/freethinkercenotaph.htm

91. Critics label authors such as Sam Harris (*The End of Faith* and
Letter to a Christian Nation), Daniel Dennett (*Breaking the Spell*),
Richard Dawkins (*The God Delusion*) and Christopher Hitchens
(*God Is Not Great*) "new atheists." "The New Atheists," The Nation,
June 7, 2007, http://www.thenation.com/doc/20070625/aronson

92. "History," The Freethinker, undated, (italics added, capitalization
omitted and spelling altered for standardization),
http://freethinker.co.uk/history/

93. "Atheism vs. Freethought," about.com, undated,
http://atheism.about.com/od/atheismquestions/a/freethinker.htm

94. Coulter, Ann, *Godless, The Church of Liberalism*, 2007.

95. ARIS 2008 at 2,
http://religions.pewforum.org/pdf/report-religious-landscape-study-f
ull.pdf; Pew 2008 at 181,
http://religions.pewforum.org/pdf/report-religious-landscape-study-f
ull.pdf

96. "Humanist Manifesto III," American Humanist Association,
undated,
http://www.americanhumanist.org/who_we_are/about_humanism/H
umanist_Manifesto_III

97. Humanist Manifesto I, 1933. That manifesto provided in part,
"While this age does owe a vast debt to the traditional religions, it is
none the less obvious that any religion that can hope to be a

synthesizing and dynamic force for today must be shaped for the needs of this age. To establish such a religion is a major necessity of the present. It is a responsibility which rests upon this generation. We therefore affirm the following . . . "
http://www.americanhumanist.org/who_we_are/about_humanism/Humanist_Manifesto_I

98. "Atheist," podictionary, January 29, 2007, http://podictionary.com/?p=449

99. Galen, Luke, "Profiles of the Godless," Free Inquiry, August/September 2009, at 42-45, http://www.centerforinquiry.net/uploads/attachments/Profiles_of_the_Godless_FI_AugSept_Vol_29_No_5_pps_41-45.pdf

100. "The American Humanist Association: building on momentum," American Humanist Association, November 4, 2009, http://www.iheu.org/american-humanist-association-building-momentum

101. "2009 Year in Review," Freedom from Religion Foundation, undated, http://ffrf.org/about/year-in-review/2009-year-in-review/

102. "Ellen Johnson No Longer President of American Atheists," American Humanist Association, May 7, 2008, http://americanhumanist.org/hnn/archives/index.php?id=347&article=0

103. "Secular Coalition for America," Secular Coalition for America, undated, http://www.secular.org/

104. "Atheist Alliance Member Organizations," Atheist Alliance International, December 27, 2007, http://www.atheistalliance.org/Member-Organizations.html

105. "Campus Group List," Secular Student Alliance, November 27, 2005 (but appears to be more recently updated), http://www.secularstudents.org/affiliates

106. "The National Association of Evangelicals' Questions for Obama's Faith-Based Office," U.S. News and World Report, February 11, 2009, http://www.usnews.com/blogs/god-and-country/2009/02/11/the-national-association-of-evangelicals-questions-for-obamas-faith-based-office.html

107. "About American Atheists," American Atheists, undated, http://atheists.org/about

108. "AA Logo," American Atheists, undated, http://atheists.org/about/AA_Logo

109. "Atheist symbols," Religious Tolerance.org, November 11, 2009, http://www.religioustolerance.org/atheist6.htm

110. "The Out Campaign," outcampaign.org, undated, http://outcampaign.org/blogroll

111. "New Atheist Symbol," Friendly Atheist, October, 23, 2007, http://friendlyatheist.com/2007/10/23/new-atheist-symbol/

112. "Parodies of the ichthys symbol," Wikipedia, May 10, 2010, http://en.wikipedia.org/wiki/Darwin_fish

113. "Origins of the Happy Human Symbol," Humanists of Utah, February 1996, http://www.humanistsofutah.org/1996/artfeb96.htm

114. "Welcome to the Church of the Flying Spaghetti Monster," Church of the Flying Spaghetti Monster, undated, http://www.venganza.org/

115. "Faith in America," Speech by presidential candidate Mitt Romney, NPR, December 6, 2007, http://www.npr.org/templates/story/story.php?storyId=16969460

116. "The Religion of Atheism," Patriot.net, February 3, 2009, http://patriot.net/~bmcgin/atheismisareligion.html

117. "Biblical Christianity vs. Secular Humanism, Why Should I Worry about Secular Humanism?" Dr. Justin Imel, undated, http://justinimel.com/biblicalchristianitysecularhumanismwhyshould iworryaboutsecularhumanism.html

118. The footnote reads, "Among religions in this country which do not teach what would generally be considered a belief in the existence of God are Buddhism, Taoism, Ethical Culture, Secular Humanism and others." The text of the case, accompanying the footnote, provided, "We repeat and again reaffirm that neither a State nor the Federal Government can constitutionally force a person 'to profess a belief or disbelief in any religion.' Neither can constitutionally pass laws or impose requirements which aid all religions as against non-believers, and neither can aid those religions based on a belief in the existence of God as against those religions founded on different beliefs." *Torcaso v. Watkins*, 367 U.S. 488 (1961), http://caselaw.lp.findlaw.com/cgi-bin/getcase.pl?court=US&vol=367 &invol=488#f11

119. "Is the religion of Secular Humanism being taught in public school classrooms?" Christian Answers.net, undated, http://www.christiananswers.net/q-sum/sum-g002.html

120. "About," Church of the Flying Spaghetti Monster, undated, http://www.venganza.org/about/

121. "Our World View is Real Reality," Church of Reality, undated, http://www.churchofreality.org/wisdom/welcome_home/

122. "IRS Tax Exempt Status," Church of Reality, undated,
http://www.churchofreality.org/wisdom/irs_tax_exempt_status/

123. "About Humanism: Humanist Manifesto I," American
Humanist Association, 1933,
http://www.americanhumanist.org/who_we_are/about_humanism/H
umanist_Manifesto_I

124. "'Millions are Good Without God,' Moscow, ID Billboard
Declares," American Humanist Association, September 16, 2009,
http://www.americanhumanist.org/news/details/2009-09-millions-are
-good-without-god-moscow-id-billboard-dec

125. "Dan Barker: Minister Turned Atheist," Freedom from Religion
Foundation, undated,
http://ffrf.org/about/getting-acquainted/dan-barker/

126. "Secularist group posts 'Praise Darwin' billboards," USA
Today, February 10, 2009,
http://www.usatoday.com/news/religion/2009-02-10-darwin-secular
_N.htm

127. "Does not the very nature of things teach you that if a man has
long hair, it is a disgrace to him, but that if a woman has long hair, it
is her glory?" The Bible, 1 Corinthians 11:14-15.

128. "What's a Natural Disaster Without Pat Robertson to Explain?"
Time Magazine, January 13, 2010,
http://swampland.blogs.time.com/2010/01/13/whats-a-natural-disast
er-without-pat-robertson-to-explain/

129. "Second Trial Rejected for Abortion Shooter," Time Magazine,
April 1, 2010
http://www.time.com/time/nation/article/0,8599,1977072,00.html

130. "The Fort Hood Killer: Terrified . . . or Terrorist?" Time Magazine, November 11, 2009, http://www.time.com/time/nation/article/0,8599,1938415,00.html

131. "Emperor Has No Clothes Award," Freedom from Religion Foundation, 1999, http://www.ffrf.org/outreach/awards/emperor-has-no-clothes-award/s teven-weinberg/

132. Governor Daniels is a bit confused, Hitler was a Catholic. For example, in one speech Hitler said, "In this hour I would ask of the Lord God only this: that, as in the past, so in the years to come He would give His blessing to our work and our action, to our judgement and our resolution, that He will safeguard us from all false pride and from all cowardly servility, that He may grant us to find the straight path which His Providence has ordained for the German people, and that He may ever give us the courage to do the right, never to falter, never to yield before any violence, before any danger . . . I am convinced that men who are created by God should live in accordance with the will of the Almighty. . . If Providence had not guided us I could often never have found these dizzy paths… Thus it is that we National Socialists, too, have in the depths of our hearts our faith. We cannot do otherwise: no man can fashion world-history or the history of peoples unless upon his purpose and his powers there rests the blessings of this Providence." Adolf Hitler, in a speech at Wurzburg on June 27, 1937, as quoted at http://www.catholicarrogance.org/Catholic/Hitlersfaith.html

133. "Daniels talks candidly about his faith," WANE-TV, December 24, 2009, http://www.wane.com/dpp/news/politics/Daniels-talks-candidly-abo ut-his-faith

134. Arkansas Constitution, Article 19, Section 1, 1874, http://www.arkleg.state.ar.us/assembly/Summary/ArkansasConstituti on1874.pdf

135. *Torcaso v. Watkins*, 367 U.S. 488 (1961),
http://caselaw.lp.findlaw.com/cgi-bin/getcase.pl?court=us&vol=367
&invol=488

136. "Atheist Revival in Arkansas," The Washington Post, February
13, 2009,
http://newsweek.washingtonpost.com/onfaith/undergod/2009/02/an_
advocate_for_atheists_in_ar.html; "Status, HJR1009," Arkansas
State Legislature, 87th General Assembly 2009,
http://www.arkleg.state.ar.us/assembly/2009/R/Pages/BillInformatio
n.aspx?measureno=HJR1009

137. Warraq, Ibn, "Democracy vs. Theocracy--Islamic Human
Rights and the Universal Declaration," International Humanist and
Ethical Union, May 26, 2009,
http://www.iheu.org/democracy-vs-theocracy-islamic-human-rights-
and-universal-declaration

138. "One-Third of Americans Believe the Bible is Literally True,"
Gallup News Service, May 25, 2007,
http://www.gallup.com/poll/27682/onethird-americans-believe-bible
-literally-true.aspx

139. The Bible, Genesis 19:1-36.

140. The man is described as a "Levite." The Bible, Joshua 3:3
(King James Version) says "When ye see the ark of the covenant of
the LORD your God, and the priests the Levites bearing it, then ye
shall remove from your place, and go after it." In some contexts,
Levites are not priests, but are holy assistants. "Levites," Bible
Dictionary (Mormon), undated, http://scriptures.lds.org/en/bd/l/26

141. The Bible, Judges 19:22-29.

142. "The Sacrament of Penance," The Catholic Encyclopedia,
undated, http://www.newadvent.org/cathen/11618c.htm

143. The Bible, Luke 23:39-43.

144. "Did Dahmer Find God?" TruTV/Turner Broadcasting System, undated,
http://www.trutv.com/library/crime/serial_killers/notorious/dahmer/22.html

145. "Saving a Serial Killer," Christian Broadcasting Network, undated,
http://www.cbn.com/entertainment/books/elliott_Jeffrey.aspx

146. "Dahmer Is Baptized in Prison Tub," The Milwaukee Sentinel, May 12, 1994, republished at
http://www.adherents.com/people/pd/Jeffrey_Dahmer.html

147. The Bible, Exodus 20:7.

148. For example, one priest abused as many as 200 deaf children over a period of 24 years. "For Years, Deaf Boys Tried to Tell of Priest's Abuse," The New York Times, March 26, 2010, http://www.nytimes.com/2010/03/27/us/27wisconsin.html. The long duration of his depraved conduct demonstrates that there is no supernatural punishment for violating the rules of the sky god.

149. Paul, Gregory, "Cross-National Correlations of Quantifiable Societal Health with Popular Religiosity and Secularism in the Prosperous Democracies," Journal of Religion and Society, Volume 7, 2005, (citations omitted),
http://moses.creighton.edu/JRS/2005/2005-11.html

150. "World's Happiest Places," Forbes, May 5, 2009,
http://www.forbes.com/2009/05/05/world-happiest-places-lifestyle-travel-world-happiest.html

151. "U.S. divorce rates for various faith groups, age groups, & geographic areas," Religious Tolerance.org, July 20, 2009,
http://www.religioustolerance.org/chr_dira.htm

152. Id.

153. "George Barna," The Barna Group, undated,
http://www.barna.org/about/george-barna

154. "New Marriage and Divorce Statistics Released," The Barna
Group, March 31, 2008,
http://www.barna.org/barna-update/article/15-familykids/42-new-ma
rriage-and-divorce-statistics-released

155. The Barna group notes distinctions between religionists and
atheists in opinions about issues like gambling, cohabitation and
abortion. "Morality Continues to Decay," The Barna Group,
November 3, 2003,
http://www.barna.org/barna-update/article/5-barna-update/129-moral
ity-continues-to-decay?q=generational+differences. However,
atheists and religionists would likely disagree as to whether these are
moral issues.

156. Rate is per 100,000 of population.

157. Crime data from the FBI, Uniform Crime Report, 2008,
http://www.fbi.gov/ucr/cius2008/data/table_05.html; religiosity data
from Gallup Polls, "State of the States: Importance of Religion"
January 28, 2009,
http://www.gallup.com/poll/114022/State-States-Importance-Religio
n.aspx;

158. Religious Affiliation of Inmates Data as of January 30, 2010,
report produced in response to the author's freedom of information
act request to the U.S. Department of Justice, Federal Bureau of
Prisons.

159. Pew 2008,
http://religions.pewforum.org/pdf/affiliations-all-traditions.pdf

160. "Emperor Has No Clothes Award," Freedom from Religion Foundation, 1999, http://www.ffrf.org/outreach/awards/emperor-has-no-clothes-award/steven-weinberg/

161. The Book of Mormon, 1 Nephi 12:22-23

162. Second Mormon President, Brigham Young, in Heinerman, John, and Shupe, Anson, *The Mormon Corporate Empire*, 1985, at 21.

163. Pew 2008, http://religions.pewforum.org/affiliations

164. "Style Guide - The Name of the Church," The Church of Jesus Christ of Latter-day Saints, undated, http://www.newsroom.lds.org/ldsnewsroom/eng/style-guide

165. Abanes, Richard, *One Nation under Gods a History of the Mormon Church*, 2002, (hereinafter, Abanes) at 1.

166. Abanes at 11-16.

167. Hill, Marvin, "Joseph Smith and the 1826 Trial: New Evidence and New Difficulties," BYU Studies Vol 12, Winter 1972, at 223-234, republished at http://www.lightplanet.com/response/1826Trial/1826Trial_Hill.html

168. Abanes at 41-46.

169. Abanes at 23-25.

170. Abanes at 54.

171. Letter of Professor Charles Anthon, published in E. D. Howe's Book, *Mormonism Unvailed* [sic], 1834, pp. 270-272, reprinted at http://www.lds-mormon.com/anthon.shtml; Abanes at 55.

172. "Weight of Gold Plates," Mormon Fortress, 1998,
http://www.mormonfortress.com/gweight.html

173. Smith, Joseph, The Book of Mormon, 1830, at 588,
http://www.archive.org/stream/bookofmormonacco1830smit#page/5
88/mode/2up

174. BCE is an acronym for "before common era," and CE is an
acronym for "common era," used in place of the religious
abbreviations BC, for "before Christ" and "AD" for "anno domini"
or "in the year of our lord."

175. Sperry, Sidney, *Answers to Book of Mormon Questions*, 1976,
http://www.shields-research.org/Books/Sperry/AChap17.PDF

176. Abanes at 59-62.

177. Abanes at 71.

178. Abanes at 73-4.

179. "The Stolen Manuscript: The lost 116 Pages of the Book of
Mormon," Excerpt from Rev. M. T. Lamb, *The Golden Bible*, 1887,
at 118-126, reprinted at
http://www.utlm.org/onlineresources/bom_early_problems/goldenbi
ble_stolenmanuscript.htm

180. The preface to the 1830 Book of Mormon reads:

> As many false reports have been circulated respecting
> the following work, and also many unlawful measures
> taken by evil designing persons to destroy me, and also
> the work, I would inform you that I translated, by the
> gift and power of God, and caused to be written, one
> hundred and sixteen pages, the which [*sic*] I took from
> the Book of Lehi, which was an account abridged from
> the plates of Lehi, by the hand of Mormon; which said

account, some person or persons have stolen and kept from me, notwithstanding my utmost exertions to recover it again--and being commanded of the Lord that I should not translate the same over again, for Satan had put it into their hearts to tempt the Lord their God, by altering the words, that they did read contrary from that which I translated and caused to be written; and if I should bring forth the same words again, or, in other words, if I should translate the same over again, they would publish that which they had stolen, and Satan would stir up the hearts of this generation, that they might not receive this work: but behold, the Lord said unto me, I will not suffer that Satan shall accomplish his evil design in this thing: therefore thou shalt translate from the plates of Nephi, until ye come to that which ye have translated, which ye have retained; and behold ye shall publish it as the record of Nephi; and thus I will confound those who have altered my words. I will not suffer that they shall destroy my work; yea, I will shew [*sic*] unto them that my wisdom is greater than the cunning of the Devil. Wherefore, to be obedient unto the commandments of God, I have, through his grace and mercy, accomplished that which he hath commanded me respecting this thing. I would also inform you that the plates of which hath been spoken, were found in the township of Manchester, Ontario county, New-York.

Smith, Joseph, The Book of Mormon, 1830, text from the original 1830 edition,
http://www.archive.org/stream/bookofmormonacco1830smit#page/n3/mode/2up

181. Smith, Joseph, The Book of Mormon, 1830, text from the original 1830 edition,

http://www.archive.org/stream/bookofmormonacco1830smit#page/n
3/mode/2up

182. Twain, Mark, *Roughing It*, 1913, at 110-111.

183. Abanes at xvii.

184. Abanes at 138-9.

185. Abanes at 147.

186. Abanes at 145-169.

187. Abanes at 171-195.

188. Abanes at 196-201.

189. "The Mormons: The Church's Growth, Structure and Reach,"
PBS, April 30, 2007,
http://www.pbs.org/mormons/faqs/structure.html

190. "The Mormons: Dissent/Excommunication/Controversies,"
PBS, April 30, 2007,
http://www.pbs.org/mormons/faqs/controversies.html#4

191. "Public Expresses Mixed Views of Islam, Mormonism," The
Pew Forum on Religion & Public Life, September 25, 2007,
http://pewforum.org/surveys/religionviews07/

192. Pew 2008 reports that 1.7% of the U.S. population is Mormon,
while 1.6% is atheist. http://religions.pewforum.org/affiliations

193. Simon Southerton posted an excellent analysis of DNA on his
blog, as well as this telling statement of his difficulty breaking ties
with the Mormon Church:

> I didn't leave the LDS Church and stop believing
> because it was easy. I desperately wanted the

comforting teachings of the Church to be true. I don't have any brilliant insight to offer about the meaning of life, and I haven't found another "true Church." Curiously, in some conversations with Mormons the fact that I haven't resolved these problems seems to reassure them that I am wrong. I realized recently that for most of my life my family was the most powerful force motivating me to stay in the Church. Honestly telling my family of my concerns over the years was almost unthinkable. I think back to the time on my mission when I was pleading for a witness that the Book of Mormon was true. As with all young Mormons searching for the truth, there was a lot riding on those prayers. It was not simply a matter between God and me. There were going to be many people enormously disappointed in me if I didn't get the right answer, including parents, family, friends, companions and my mission president. Most young men gain their testimony of the Church when they are a missionary. Not surprisingly, I have never heard of a missionary returning from his mission early because he didn't believe the Church was true. The fear of hurting the feelings of those you love the most is an extremely powerful motivation to not rock the boat.

"DNA Genealogies of American Indians and the Book of Mormon," exmormon.org, December 2004,
http://www.exmormon.org/whylft125.htm

194. "Statement Regarding the Book of Mormon," 1988, godandscience.org, (minor grammatical changes made),
http://www.godandscience.org/cults/smithsonian.pdf

195. Smith, George (ed.) *An Intimate Chronicle: The Journals of William Clayton*, 1991, at 100 (emphasis added),
http://www.irr.org/MIT/kinderhook-plates.html.

196. "Kinderhook Plates Brought to Joseph Smith Appear to Be a Nineteenth-century Hoax," Ensign Magazine, August 1981, http://www.lds.org/ldsorg/v/index.jsp?hideNav=1&locale=0&source Id=b6a8aeca0ea6b010VgnVCM1000004d82620a___&vgnextoid= 2354fccf2b7db010VgnVCM1000004d82620aRCRD

197. Bales, James, *The Book of Mormon?* 1958, at 98, excerpted at http://www.utlm.org/newsletters/no46.htm

198. "The Book of Abraham Translation," The Watchman Expositor, 2000, http://www.watchman.org/lds/abraham2.htm; http://www.mrm.org/book-of-abraham; "Dr. Ritner Debunks Mormon Claim," Mormon Doctrine.net, undated, http://www.mormondoctrine.net/articles/BoA_Dr_Ritner_debunks_LDS_claim.htm

199. Dawood, N.J., The Koran, 1990, at 87.

200. U.S. Central Intelligence Agency, *The World Factbook*, Religion, undated, https://www.cia.gov/library/publications/the-world-factbook/fields/2122.html

201. Pew 2008 at 5, http://religions.pewforum.org/pdf/report-religious-landscape-study-full.pdf

202. "The Big Religion Chart," Religion Facts, August 9, 2009, http://www.religionfacts.com/big_religion_chart.htm

203. "Elohim," New Advent, undated, http://www.newadvent.org/cathen/05393a.htm

204. Wright, Robert, *The Evolution of God*, 2009, excerpt from Chapter 14, http://evolutionofgod.net/allahphonetics/

205. The Koran, 19:19-20.

206. "Atheists Promote Bible Reading?!" Thank God for Evolution, undated, http://thankgodforevolution.com/archive/201001

207. Twain, Mark, *The Works of Mark Twain, What is a Man?* Vol. 19, 1997, at 71-75.

208. Advertisement in Life Magazine, March 18, 1946, page 142 (ellipses omitted, commas substituted).

209. "On the day the LORD gave the Amorites over to Israel, Joshua said to the LORD in the presence of Israel: 'O sun, stand still over Gibeon, O moon, over the Valley of Aijalon.' So the sun stood still, and the moon stopped, till the nation avenged itself on its enemies, as it is written in the Book of Jashar. The sun stopped in the middle of the sky and delayed going down about a full day. There has never been a day like it before or since, a day when the LORD listened to a man. Surely the LORD was fighting for Israel!" The Bible, Joshua 10:12-14.

210. Bible stories allowed characters to see from one side of the flat earth to the other, something impossible on a sphere: "Thus were the visions of mine head in my bed; I saw, and behold a tree in the midst of the earth, and the height thereof was great. The tree grew, and was strong, and the height thereof reached unto heaven, and the sight thereof to the end of all the earth." The Bible, Daniel 4:10-11 (King James Version). "[T]he devil took him to a very high mountain and showed him all the kingdoms of the world and their splendor. 'All this I will give you,' he said, 'if you will bow down and worship me.'" The Bible, Matthew 4:8.

211. The winged horse does not appear in the Koran, but was added by later legend. The Bible provides a bit of contradiction about flying up to heaven. One verse says that only Jesus could do it, "No one has ever gone into heaven except the one who came from heaven--the Son of Man." The Bible, John 3:13. However, other parts tell a different story, "As they were walking along and talking together, suddenly a chariot of fire and horses of fire appeared and

separated the two of them, and Elijah went up to heaven in a whirlwind." The Bible, 2 Kings 2:11.

212. "And he dreamed, and behold a ladder set up on the earth, and the top of it reached to heaven: and behold the angels of God ascending and descending on it. And, behold, the LORD stood above it, and said, I am the LORD God of Abraham thy father, and the God of Isaac: the land whereon thou liest, to thee will I give it." The Bible, Genesis 28:12-13 (King James Version).

213. The earth is seen as a two dimensional circle, like a pancake, not a three dimensional object like a globe.

214. The Bible, Isaiah 40:22. Some thought the clouds could block god's view: "Is not God in the heights of heaven? And see how lofty are the highest stars! Yet you say, 'What does God know? Does he judge through such darkness? Thick clouds veil him, so he does not see us as he goes about in the vaulted heavens.'" The Bible, Job 22:12-14.

215. The Bible, Leviticus 25:44-46.

216. The Bible, Exodus 21:7-11.

217. The Bible, Exodus 21:20-21.

218. The Bible, 1 Timothy 6:1-2.

219. Gunasekara, Victor, *Slavery and the Infidel in Islam*, undated, http://uqconnect.net/slsoc/manussa/tr05manu.htm

220. The Bible, Genesis 22:2.

221. The Bible, Judges 11:29-40.

222. "How old is the earth?" Answers in Genesis, May 30, 2007, http://www.answersingenesis.org/articles/2007/05/30/how-old-is-earth

223. The Bible, Genesis 6-9:17; "The Date of Noah's Flood," Answers in Genesis, March 1981, http://www.answersingenesis.org/creation/v4/i1/noahs_flood.asp

224. "Dendrochronology Fact and Creationist Fraud," EvC Forum, January 11, 2007, http://www.evcforum.net/cgi-bin/dm.cgi?action=msg&f=25&t=2612&m=1

225. The Bible, Genesis 7:14.

226. "Insects: Beetle," San Diego Zoo, undated, http://www.sandiegozoo.org/animalbytes/t-beetle.html

227. The Bible, Matthew 17:20.

228. Paine, Thomas, *The Age of Reason*, Part First, Section 14, 1794, http://www.ushistory.org/paine/reason/reason14.htm

229. de Fleury, Maurice, Translated from French by Collins, Stacy, *Medicine and the Mind*, 1900, at 45.

230. "Belief in miracles is matter of faith," The Arizona Republic, December 25, 2006, http://www.azcentral.com/arizonarepublic/news/articles/1225miracle1221main.html?&wired

231. Moss, Claude, *The Christian Faith: an Introduction to Dogmatic Theology*, 1943, http://www.katapi.org.uk/ChristianFaith/master.html?http://www.katapi.org.uk/ChristianFaith/XVIII.htm

232. Pew Social 2008 at 34,
http://religions.pewforum.org/pdf/report2-religious-landscape-study-full.pdf

233. The Bible, Mark 9:14-29.

234. The Bible, John 2:11.

235. The Bible, Matthew 14:13-21.

236. "What's Mother Teresa Got to Do with It?" Time Magazine,
October 21, 2002,
http://www.time.com/time/magazine/article/0,9171,1003488-1,00.html

237. "Indian Rationalists Question Mother Teresa's Ovarian
Miracle," Rationalist International, undated,
http://www.rationalistinternational.net/article/se_en_14102002.htm;
"Mother Teresa: Miracle or Myth?" Truth Evangelical Assistance
Ministries, March 30, 2009,
http://teamtruth.com/articles/art_motherteresa.htm

238. "History of the Sanctuary of Our Lady of Lourdes," Sacred
Destinations, undated,
http://www.sacred-destinations.com/france/lourdes-history.htm

239. de Fleury, Maurice, Translated from French by Collins, Stacy,
Medicine and the Mind, 1900, at 45.

240. "Is God real, or is he imaginary?" Why won't God heal
amputees? undated, http://whywontgodhealamputees.com/

241. "Hungry for Miracles? Try Jesus on a Fish Stick," ABC News,
November 30, 2004,
http://abcnews.go.com/Entertainment/WolfFiles/story?id=307227&page=1

242. McMahon, Matthew, *The Miracle of the Resurrection*, A Puritan's Mind, undated, http://www.apuritansmind.com/Apologetics/McMahonMiraclesAnd TheResurrection.htm

243. "Pope Benedict on the Resurrection," Catholic Online, May 1, 2006, (sub-quotation marks omitted), http://www.catholic.org/featured/headline.php?ID=3246

244. "One-Third of Americans Believe the Bible is Literally True," Gallup News Service, May 25, 2007, http://www.gallup.com/poll/27682/onethird-americans-believe-bible -literally-true.aspx

245. "Quotes by Will Rogers," Good Reads, undated, http://www.goodreads.com/author/quotes/132444.Will_Rogers

246. "Inscription on The Monument of a Newfoundland Dog, A Memorial to Boatswain by Lord Byron," November 30, 1808, http://readytogoebooks.com/LB-dog63.htm

247. "Muhammad and the Dogs," Answering Islam, January 25, 2007, http://www.answering-islam.org/Silas/dogs.htm

248. "Cabbie refuses ride to guide dog," The Cincinnati Enquirer, April 3, 1999, http://www.enquirer.com/editions/1999/04/03/loc_cabbie.html

249. The Bible, Revelation 21:1.

250. The Bible, Romans 10:9.

251. "Pets in Heaven?" Global Catholic Network, undated, http://www.ewtn.com/expert/answers/pets_in_heaven.htm

252. The Bible, Genesis 1:28-30.

253. The Bible, 1 Corinthians 15:42-44.

254. Congressman John Shimkus of Illinois, testifying before the U.S. House Subcommittee on Energy and the Environment, YouTube, March 25, 2009, http://www.youtube.com/watch?v=_7h08RDYA5E

255. "Congresswoman Michele Bachmann Talks Openly About Jesus and Policy," Christian Broadcasting Network, December 4, 2009, http://blogs.cbn.com/thebrodyfile/archive/2009/12/04/congresswoman-michele-bachmann-talks-openly-about-jesus-and-policy.aspx

256. "Religious Groups' Views on Global Warming," The Pew Forum on Religion and Public Life, April 16, 2009, http://www.pewforum.org/docs/?DocID=238

257. "Born Again Christians Remain Skeptical, Divided About Global Warming," Barna Group, September 17, 2007, http://www.barna.org/barna-update/article/20-donorscause/95-born-again-christians-remain-skeptical-divided-about-global-warming

258. Sherk, James, "Christians and Climate Change: Should Followers of Christ Concern Themselves with the Threat of Global Warming?" Evangel Society, January 8, 2004, http://www.evangelsociety.org/sherk/wwjd.html

259. "Mississippi is the fattest state for 5th straight year, Colorado still leanest," CalorieLab (Utilizing Center for Disease Control statistics), July 28, 2010, http://calorielab.com/news/2008/07/02/fattest-states-2008/; "State of the States: Importance of Religion," Gallup Polls, January 28, 2009, http://www.gallup.com/poll/114022/State-States-Importance-Religion.aspx#2

260. Id.

261. The correlation is not as startling as with the most religious and most obese states, but the trend is still apparent. The environmental differences of Alaska (long winters, short days, cold weather) may in part explain why it has relatively high obesity despite low religiosity.

State	Religion Ranking	Obesity Ranking
Vermont	50	46
New Hampshire	49	34
Maine	48	29
Massachusetts	47	48
Alaska	46	24

262. "Trust in God," Newsweek, July 8, 2009,
http://www.newsweek.com/id/205705/page/1

263. "Faith Healing Couple Acquitted of Manslaughter Charges,"
KPTV News, July 23, 2009,
http://www.kptv.com/news/20158093/detail.html

264. "Jury finds Beagleys guilty in faith-healing case," Clackamas
Review, January 30, 2010
http://www.clackamasreview.com/news/story.php?story_id=126491
397548985800

265. "Child deaths test faith-healing exemptions," The Associated
Press, November 23, 2008, reprinted at
http://www.firstamendmentcenter.org/news.aspx?id=20915

266. Id.

267. "Trials for Parents Who Chose Faith Over Medicine," The New York Times, January 20, 2009,
http://www.nytimes.com/2009/01/21/us/21faith.html

268. "Wisconsin's faith-healing law faces fresh scrutiny," Isthmus, March 26, 2008,
http://www.thedailypage.com/daily/article.php?article=22061

269. "Dale & Leilani Neumann's Sentencing Tuesday," WSAW News, October 4, 2009
http://www.wsaw.com/home/headlines/63477647.html

270. "Dale and Leilani Neumann Sentenced To Spend Time In Jail, On Probation, and Serve Community Service," KASW News, October 6, 2009,
http://www.wsaw.com/karaneumann/headlines/63630282.html

271. Benson, Herbert, M.D., et al. "Study of the Therapeutic Effects of Intercessory Prayer (STEP) in Cardiac Bypass Patients: A Multi-Center Randomized Trial of Uncertainty and Certainty of Receiving Intercessory Prayer," The John Templeton Foundation, May 5, 2005
http://www.templeton.org/pdfs/press_releases/060407STEP_paper.pdf

272. "Long-Awaited Medical Study Questions the Power of Prayer," The New York Times, March 31, 2006,
http://www.nytimes.com/2006/03/31/health/31pray.html?

273. Order of the Circuit Court of Pinellas County, February 11, 2000, http://abstractappeal.com/schiavo/trialctorder02-00.pdf

274. "Abstract Appeal's posts from 2005 regarding the Terri Schiavo saga," Abstract Appeal, 2005,
http://abstractappeal.com/schiavo/schiavoposts2005.html

275. The Bible, 1 Corinthians 11:7-9.

276. The Koran, 24:31 (Shakir).

277. *Eisenstadt v. Baird,* 405 U.S. 438 (1972),
http://caselaw.lp.findlaw.com/cgi-bin/getcase.pl?court=us&vol=405
&invol=438

278. "Milestones in U.S. Women's History," America.gov, February
25, 2009,
http://www.america.gov/st/diversity-english/2008/April/2008032519
0828liameruoy0.3090631.html

279. "Perpetual Minors: Human Rights Abuses Stemming from
Male Guardianship and Sex Segregation in Saudi Arabia," Human
Rights Watch, April 2008,
http://www.hrw.org/en/reports/2008/04/19/perpetual-minors-0

280. "Saudi Arabia: Country Reports on Human Rights Practices,"
U.S. Department of State, February 25, 2004,
http://www.state.gov/g/drl/rls/hrrpt/2003/27937.htm

281. "An Iranian Village Mob and a Wife's Execution," The New
York Times, June 26, 2009,
http://movies.nytimes.com/2009/06/26/movies/26stoning.html

282. "Promiscuous women cause earthquakes, Iran cleric says,"
CNN, April 20, 2010,
http://www.cnn.com/2010/WORLD/meast/04/20/iran.promiscuity.ea
rthquakes/

283. "Iranian Cleric: Promiscuous Women Cause Quakes," NPR,
April 20, 2010,
http://www.npr.org/templates/story/story.php?storyId=126128371

284. U.S. Central Intelligence Agency, *The World Factbook*, May
27, 2010,
https://www.cia.gov/library/publications/the-world-factbook/geos/ir.
html

285. ARIS 2008 at 3,
http://b27.cc.trincoll.edu/weblogs/AmericanReligionSurvey-ARIS/re
ports/ARIS_Report_2008.pdf

286. The Bible, 1 Timothy 2:11-14.

287. The Bible, Genesis 3:16.

288. The Bible, Ephesians 5:22-24.

289. The Bible, Leviticus 15:19-30.

290. "Introduction to the Laws of Niddah," Jewish Women's Health,
undated, http://www.jewishwomenshealth.org/article.php?article=12

291. "The History Behind the Equal Rights Amendment," Equal
Rights Amendment, National Council of Women's Organizations,
undated, http://www.equalrightsamendment.org/era.htm

292. Id.

293. Utah is about 72% Mormon, Nevada is 7.1% and Arizona is
6%. "The truth about the number of Mormons," All About
Mormons, undated,
http://www.allaboutmormons.com/number_of_mormons.php

294. The States which have not ratified the Equal Rights
Amendment are: Alabama, Arizona, Arkansas, Florida, Georgia,
Illinois, Louisiana, Mississippi, Missouri, Nevada, North Carolina,
Oklahoma, South Carolina, Utah, and Virginia. "Frequently Asked
Questions," Equal Rights Amendment, National Council of
Women's Organizations, undated,
http://www.equalrightsamendment.org/faq.htm

295. "Eagle Forum," Eagle Forum, undated,
http://www.eagleforum.org/misc/descript.html

266

296. "Equal Rights Amendment," *Utah History Encyclopedia,* undated, http://historytogo.utah.gov/utah_chapters/utah_today/equalrightsame ndment.html

297. Concerned Women for America's Website says, "CWA affirms the Bible's unmistakable standard that there is right and wrong; that God is the Authority who established right and wrong by creation and by revelation in His Word, the Bible; that He has sent a Savior, Jesus Christ, to free us from our sin (wrong) by simple repentance and to enable us through the Holy Spirit to do what is right." "Biblical Support for CWA Core Issues," Concerned Women for America, undated, http://www.cwfa.org/coreissues.asp. They continue to oppose the Equal Rights Amendment because they say it would, "Aid in the killing of millions of unborn babies . . . Usher in homosexual rights . . .[and] Suppress true femininity and womanhood." "The "Second Wave's" Last Hurrah," Concerned Women for America, November 3, 1999, http://www.cwfa.org/articles/1068/CWA/family/1999-11-03_era_sb-not-ratified.shtml

298. Granberg, Donald, "The Abortion activists (profiles of typical members of the National Abortion Rights Action League and the National Right to Life Committee)," Induced Abortion, Volume 1: Politics and Policies, January 1, 2000, reprinted at http://www.highbeam.com/doc/1G1-80541714.html

299. "Christian Coalition of America," Right Wing Watch, September 2006, http://www.rightwingwatch.org/content/christian-coalition

300. "Christian Coalition is Splintering," The Los Angeles Times, September 5, 2006, http://articles.latimes.com/2006/sep/05/nation/na-coalition5

301. "Media Pioneer," The Official Website of Pat Robertson, 2009, http://www.patrobertson.com/mediapioneer/

302. "Host Bio: Pat Robertson," Christian Broadcasting Network, undated, http://www.cbn.com/700club/showinfo/staff/patrobertson.aspx

303. "Spotlight: The 700 Club: Show History, Format, and Highlights," Christian Broadcasting Network, undated, http://www.cbn.com/700club/ShowInfo/About/about700club.aspx

304. "Christian Broadcasting Network/ CBN/ 700 Club/ Pat Robertson," Ministry Watch, undated, http://www.ministrywatch.com/profile/christian-broadcasting-networ k.aspx

305. "Uphill fight forecast for Equal Rights Amendment," The Boston Globe, April 4, 2007, http://www.boston.com/news/nation/washington/articles/2007/04/04 /uphill_fight_forecast_for_equal_rights_amendment/

306. Initially approved, but later repealed. "Senate Signals More Time for ERA," The Toledo Blade, October 5, 1978, http://news.google.com/newspapers?nid=1350&dat=19781005&id=- g0wAAAAIBAJ&sjid=gwIEAAAAIBAJ&pg=2029,3693470

307. On a personal note, I wonder if the men who subjugate women had mothers? Perhaps this is colored by my respect for my mother, but I still wonder. For example, Catholic priests may not know women as wives and lovers, but they all had mothers. How can they look their mothers in the eye and say that women are less valuable than men? I wonder even more about Muslims in countries where women are treated like property. How can a Muslim man tell his mother that her testimony in court is only worth half that of a man? How can he subject a woman to violence and abuse and still face his mother? Does religion and tradition have a stronger hold on these men than respect for the woman that bore them? I suppose the answer is sadly, yes.

308. The Bible, 1 Corinthians 6: 9-10 (King James Version).

309. The Bible, Genesis 1:28 (King James Version).

310. "Historical Estimates of World Population," U.S. Census Bureau, undated, http://www.census.gov/ipc/www/worldhis.html

311. Id., using lower range population estimates.

312. "Current World Population," About.com, August 12, 2009, http://geography.about.com/od/obtainpopulationdata/a/worldpopulation.htm

313. "Water shortages will leave world in dire straits," USA Today, January 26, 2003, http://www.usatoday.com/news/nation/2003-01-26-water-usat_x.htm

314. "The natural law purpose of sex is procreation. . . . But sexual pleasure within marriage becomes unnatural, and even harmful to the spouses, when it is used in a way that deliberately excludes the basic purpose of sex, which is procreation. God's gift of the sex act, along with its pleasure and intimacy, must not be abused by deliberately frustrating its natural end--procreation." "Birth Control," August 10, 2004, Catholic Answers, http://www.catholic.com/library/Birth_Control.asp

315. *Griswold v. Connecticut*, 381 U.S. 479 (1965), http://caselaw.lp.findlaw.com/scripts/getcase.pl?court=us&vol=381&invol=479

316. *Eisenstadt v. Baird,* 405 U.S. 438 (1972), http://caselaw.lp.findlaw.com/cgi-bin/getcase.pl?court=us&vol=405&invol=438

317. "Pope claims condoms could make African AIDS crisis worse," The Guardian, March 17, 2009, http://www.guardian.co.uk/world/2009/mar/17/pope-africa-condoms-aids

318. "Pope says condoms are not the solution to AIDS-- they make it worse," The Times, March 17, 2009, http://www.timesonline.co.uk/tol/comment/faith/article5923927.ece; "Pope: Condoms Not The Answer To AIDS," The Huffington Post, March 17, 2009, http://www.huffingtonpost.com/2009/03/17/pope-condoms-not-the-a nsw_n_175623.html;

319. A 1970's Mormon pamphlet on the "evils" of masturbation is reprinted at: http://www.affirmation.org/learning/steps_in_overcoming_masturbat ion.shtml. Ironically, some Christian groups have adopted the same text, as far as I can tell in all seriousness. For example: http://www.turnbacktogod.com/steps-in-overcoming-masturbation-1/ and http://www.landoverbaptist.net/showthread.php?t=20129

320. "Indicators of Marriage and Fertility in the United States from the American Community Survey: 2000 to 2003," U.S. Census Bureau, May 2005, http://www.census.gov/population/www/socdemo/fertility/mar-fert-s lides.html#abstract

321. "CBS' Janet Jackson 'Wardrobe Malfunction' Super Bowl Fine To Be Reconsidered," The Huffington Post, February 23, 2010, http://www.huffingtonpost.com/2010/02/23/cbs-janet-jackson-wardr ob_n_472851.html

322. "'Fatwa' forbids Muslims going through full-body scanners," USA Today, February 12, 2010, http://content.usatoday.com/communities/ondeadline/post/2010/02/f atwa-forbids-muslims-going-through-full-body-scanners/1

323. "Pope enters airport body scanners row," The Guardian, February 21, 2010, http://www.guardian.co.uk/world/2010/feb/21/pope-benedict-naked- scanners-airports

324. "Full-body scans at airports might violate teachings of some faiths," The Vancouver Sun, March 17, 2010, http://www.vancouversun.com/travel/Full+body+scans+airports+mi ght+violate+teachings+some+faiths/2692829/story.html

325. The Bible, Matthew 5:27-30.

326. "Morality Continues to Decay," Barna Group, November 3, 2003, http://www.barna.org/barna-update/article/5-barna-update/129-moral ity-continues-to-decay?

327. "Flight 253 terror suspect Umar Farouk Abdulmutallab bemoaned his 'loneliness' in online postings," NY Daily News, December 29, 2009, http://www.nydailynews.com/news/national/2009/12/29/2009-12-29 _flight_253_terror_suspect_.html

328. "Allah's Messenger (peace be upon him) said, 'The martyr receives six good things from Allah: he is forgiven at the first shedding of his blood; he is shown his abode in Paradise; he is preserved from the punishment in the grave; he is kept safe from the greatest terror; he has placed on his head the crown of honour, a ruby of which is better than the world and what it contains; he is married to seventy-two wives of the maidens with large dark eyes; and is made intercessor for seventy of his relatives.'" Mishkat Al-Masabih (Hadith) quoted in "What is Islam," Truthnet.org (Christian site), undated, http://www.truthnet.org/islam/whatisislam.html

329. Warraq, Ibn, "Virgins? What virgins?" The Guardian, January 12, 2002, http://www.guardian.co.uk/books/2002/jan/12/books.guardianreview 5

330. "Muttaqûn" are the pious and righteous who fear and love allah. "As-Salaam u Alaikum," undated, http://www.ehtesham.com/

331. The Koran, 78:31-34 (Mohsin Khan).

332. A "Jinn" is a demon or evil spirit.

333. The Koran, 55:54,56 (parentheticals from the translator, Yusuf Ali).

334. "Do Liberals, Atheists Have Higher IQs?" U.S. News and World Report, March 9, 2010, http://health.usnews.com/health-news/family-health/brain-and-behav ior/articles/2010/03/09/do-liberals-atheists-have-higher-iqs.html?Pag eNr=1

335. "U.S. Teen Sexual Activity," Kaiser Family Foundation, January 2005, http://www.kff.org/youthhivstds/upload/U-S-Teen-Sexual-Activity-F act-Sheet.pdf

336. "Vancouver medals in condom distribution," CNN, March 1, 2010, http://www.cnn.com/2010/LIVING/03/01/condoms.vancouver.olym pics/index.html

337. "Oppose Federal Funding of Abstinence-Only Education!" ACLU Website, undated, http://www.aclu.org/oppose-federal-funding-abstinence-only-educati on

338. Finer, Lawrence, "Trends in Premarital Sex in the United States, 1954–2003," Public Health Reports, January–February 2007, at 75-76, http://www.guttmacher.org/pubs/journals/2007/01/29/PRH-Vol-122-Finer.pdf

339. Hauser, Debra, "Five Years of Abstinence-Only-Until-Marriage Education: Assessing the Impact," Advocates for Youth, 2008,

http://www.advocatesforyouth.org/index.php?option=com_content&
task=view&id=623&Itemid=177

340. "Premarital Abstinence Pledges Ineffective, Study Finds," The
Washington Post, December 29, 2008,
http://www.washingtonpost.com/wp-dyn/content/article/2008/12/28/
AR2008122801588.html

341. "After long decline, U.S. teen birth rates rise again," McClatchy
Newspapers, January 7, 2009,
http://www.mcclatchydc.com/2009/01/07/59098/after-long-decline-u
s-teen-birth.html

342. "Study finds 'shocking' rate of US teen girls with STDs," New
York Daily News, March 11, 2008,
http://www.nydailynews.com/lifestyle/health/2008/03/11/2008-03-1
1_study_finds_shocking_rate_of_us_teen_gir.html

343. The 2010 Health Care Reform Bill included $50 billion a year
for five years for abstinence only education. "Health bill restores
$250 million in abstinence-education funds," The Washington Post,
March 27, 2010,
http://www.washingtonpost.com/wp-dyn/content/article/2010/03/26/
AR2010032602457.html

344. "If a man is found lying with a woman married to a husband,
then both of them shall die--the man that lay with the woman, and
the woman; so you shall put away the evil from Israel." The Bible,
Deuteronomy 22:22 (King James Version); "If a man lies with a
male as he lies with a woman, both of them have committed an
abomination. They shall surely be put to death. Their blood shall be
upon them." The Bible, Leviticus 20:13 (King James Version).

345. "U.S. divorce rates for various faith groups, age groups, &
geographic areas," Religious Tolerance.org, July 20, 2009,
http://www.religioustolerance.org/chr_dira.htm

346. Jesus allegedly said, "I tell you that anyone who divorces his wife, except for marital unfaithfulness, and marries another woman commits adultery." The Bible, Matthew 19:9.

347. Smith, Tom, "American Sexual Behavior: Trends, Socio-Demographic Differences, and Risk Behavior," GSS Topical Report No. 25, Updated March 2006, at page 54, http://www.norc.org/NR/rdonlyres/2663F09F-2E74-436E-AC81-6F FBF288E183/0/AmericanSexualBehavior2006.pdf

348. "Memorable quotes for Jesus Camp," Internet Movie Database, undated, http://www.imdb.com/title/tt0486358/quotes

349. The Bible, Leviticus 18:22 (King James Version).

350. "Time Names the 25 Most Influential Evangelicals in America," Time, January 30, 2005, http://www.time.com/time/press_releases/article/0,8599,1022576,00. html

351. "Confronting a Scandal," The Colorado Springs Gazette, November 3, 2006, http://www.gazette.com/articles/haggard-10876-church-jones.html

352. "Haggard appeals for financial help," The Colorado Springs Gazette, August 24, 2007, http://www.gazette.com/articles/haggard-26460-church-new.html

353. "Pastor takes leave amid allegations of gay sex," The Denver Post, November 3, 2006, http://www.denverpost.com/ci_4588998

354. Colorado Secretary of State, Amendment 43, February 17, 2006, http://www.elections.colorado.gov/Content/Documents/Initiatives/Ti tle%20Board%20Filings/Final%20Text%2083.pdf

355. "Leader of evangelical group resigns amid allegations," The Colorado Springs Gazette, November 2, 2006, reprinted in ReligionNewsBlog, http://www.religionnewsblog.com/16441/leader-of-evangelical-group-resigns-amid-allegations

356. "Confronting a Scandal," The Colorado Springs Gazette, November 3, 2006, http://www.gazette.com/articles/haggard-10876-church-jones.html

357. For example, the Bible says, "'These are the things you are to do: Speak the truth to each other, and render true and sound judgment in your courts; do not plot evil against your neighbor, and do not love to swear falsely. I hate all this,' declares the LORD." The Bible, Zechariah 8:16-17.

358. "There are no secrets," The Colorado Springs Gazette, January 7, 2007, http://www.gazette.com/articles/haggard-6717-life-church.html

359. "Survey suggests state is warming to gay issues," The Colorado Springs Gazette, December 4, 2008, http://www.gazette.com/articles/gay-44440-marriage-unions.html

360. "Haggard faces 2nd sex claim," The Colorado Springs Gazette, January 24, 2009, http://www.gazette.com/articles/haggard-46797-church-boyd.html

361. "Reopening Old Wounds for New Life," Ministry Today Magazine, undated, http://ministrytodaymag.com/index.php/ministry-news/65-news-main/18250-reopening-old-wounds-for-new-life

362. "Former church member: Haggard performed sex act," The Colorado Springs Gazette, January 27, 2009, http://www.gazette.com/articles/haggard-46951-haas-church.html

363. "More New Life Church Revelations," The Gist:Michelangelo Signorile, February 9, 2009, http://www.signorile.com/2009/02/more-new-life-church-revelations.html

364. "Gayle Haggard: 'I was cut off by my church family at the time I needed them most,'" The Colorado Springs Gazette, January 27, 2010, http://www.gazette.com/articles/haggard-93121-gayle-became.html

365. "Haggard Dismissed," The Colorado Springs Gazette, November 5, 2006, http://www.gazette.com/articles/haggard-10882-church-life.html

366. "Ted Haggard leaves Colorado for Phoenix," 9News.com, undated, http://www.9news.com/news/local/article.aspx?storyid=68347)

367. "Haggard appeals for financial help," The Colorado Springs Gazette, August 24, 2007, http://www.gazette.com/articles/haggard-26460-church-new.html

368. "The resurrection of Pastor Ted," The Colorado Springs Independent, October 1, 2009, http://www.csindy.com/colorado/the-resurrection-of-pastor-ted/Content?oid=1450688

369. "Haggard starting new church at his Springs home," The Colorado Springs Gazette, November 4, 2009, http://www.gazette.com/articles/haggard-65454-ted-church.html

370. "Haggard named overseer at local church, Haggard says," The Pulpit, blog of Mark Barna, Colorado Springs Gazette writer, December 30, 2009, http://thepulpit.freedomblogging.com/2009/12/30/haggard-named-overseer-at-local-church-haggard-says/4255/

371. "Haggards name their in-home church," The Colorado Springs Gazette, May 11, 2010, http://www.gazette.com/articles/church-98503-incorporation-springs.html

372.   The tax exempt status for religion is troubling. By granting religions tax exempt status, the government fosters their strength and growth. The tax exemption is effectively doubled, first, when a parishioner gives money he avoids federal and state taxation on the money. Second, when the religion uses the money, it is additionally exempt from taxation. Religious buildings further benefit from municipal police and fire protection, but pay nothing for it. Taxpayers are forced to pay for municipal services to religious groups.

   Truly charitable acts by any group should be exempt from taxation. Serving food to the homeless or providing medical care to the poor are activities that deserve societal support. But any proselytizing that goes along with these services should be taxed.

   The greatest majority of religious money is spent on propagating and perpetuating the religious myth. This activity is no more deserving of tax exemption than the entertaining myths created by Hollywood.

373. "Haggard makes it official: He's starting a new church," The Kansas City Star, June 2, 2010, http://www.kansascity.com/2010/06/02/1987867/haggard-makes-it-official-hes.html

374. "Ted Haggard Healing Overview," TedHaggard.com, January 21, 2010, http://www.tedhaggard.com/overview.htm

375. "A Skeleton in Barney's Closet," Time, September 25, 1989, http://www.time.com/time/magazine/article/0,9171,958598,00.html

376. "Barney's Great Adventure," The New Yorker, January 12, 2009,

http://www.newyorker.com/reporting/2009/01/12/090112fa_fact_too
bin

377. "Joint Statement from the American Academy of Child and
Adolescent Psychiatry and the American Psychiatric Association for
the Senate Substance Abuse and Mental Health Services
Subcommittee of the Health, Education, Labor and Pensions
Committee Hearing on Suicide Prevention and Youth: Saving
Lives," March 3, 2004, at 4,
http://www.aacap.org/galleries/LegislativeAction/SuicideH.PDF

378. The Bible, Leviticus 20:13 (King James Version).

379. I understand that the currently preferred term is "LGBT," for
lesbians, gays, bisexuals and transgendered people. I prefer to use the
term "gay" for two reasons. First, I do not wish to use too many
acronyms in this book, from my perspective, it makes for difficult
reading. Second, at the start of the gay rights movement, "gay" was
an inclusive term. Perhaps I am being old-fashioned, but I still see it
that way. So if the term "gay" offends you and you prefer "LGBT,"
please think of my use of "gay" as shorthand for "LGBT" wherever
it appears in this book.

380. "Same Sex Marriage, Civil Unions and Domestic Partnerships,"
National Conference of State Legislatures, Updated April 2010,
http://www.ncsl.org/IssuesResearch/HumanServices/SameSexMarria
ge/tabid/16430/Default.aspx

381. "Facts About Homosexuality and Mental Health," U.C. Dàvis,
undated,
http://psychology.ucdavis.edu/rainbow/html/facts_mental_health.ht
ml

382. "History of Sodomy Laws," SodomyLaws.org, updated April
15, 2007, http://www.sodomylaws.org/usa/military/ilnews052.htm

383. *Lawrence v. Kansas*, 539 U.S. 558 (2003) (citations omitted), http://caselaw.lp.findlaw.com/scripts/getcase.pl?court=us&vol=000&invol=02-102

384. "Born to be gay," The Independent, October 15, 2003, http://www.independent.co.uk/news/science/born-to-be-gay-583441.html

385. Regarding the 9/11 attacks, religionist Jerry Falwell said, "I really believe that the pagans, and the abortionists, and the feminists, and the gays and the lesbians who are actively trying to make that an alternative lifestyle, the ACLU, People For the American Way, all of them who have tried to secularize America, I point the finger in their face and say 'You helped this happen.'" "Rev. Jerry Falwell dies at age 73," CNN, May 17, 2007, http://www.cnn.com/2007/US/05/15/jerry.falwell/index.html?iref=alIsearch; Pastor John Hagee said Hurricane Katrina was caused by god because New Orleans was planning a gay parade. "Hagee Says Hurricane Katrina Struck New Orleans Because It Was Planning A Sinful Homosexual Rally," Think Progress, April 23, 2008, http://thinkprogress.org/2008/04/23/hagee-katrina-mccain/

386. "Gay and Lesbian Families in the United States Same-Sex Unmarried Partner Households," Urban Institute, August 22, 2001, at 2, http://www.urban.org/UploadedPDF/1000491_gl_partner_households.pdf

387. Bush said, "A strong America must also value the institution of marriage. I believe we should respect individuals as we take a principled stand for one of the most fundamental, enduring institutions of our civilization. Congress has already taken a stand on this issue by passing the defense of marriage act signed in 1996 by President Clinton. That statute protects marriage under federal law as a union of a man and a woman, and declares that one state may not redefine marriage for other states. Activist judges, however, have

begun redefining marriage by court order without regard for the will of the people, and their elected representatives. On an issue of such great consequence, the people's voice must be heard. If judges insist on forcing their arbitrary will upon the people, the only alternative left to the people would be the constitutional process. Our nation must defend the sanctity of marriage." "Bush Denounces Gay Marriage in State of the Union," Democracy Now, January 21, 2004, http://www.democracynow.org/2004/1/21/bush_denounces_gay_marriage_in_state

388. "Joint Statement from the American Academy of Child and Adolescent Psychiatry and the American Psychiatric Association for the Senate Substance Abuse and Mental Health Services Subcommittee of the Health, Education, Labor and Pensions Committee Hearing on Suicide Prevention and Youth: Saving Lives," March 3, 2004, at 4, http://www.aacap.org/galleries/LegislativeAction/SuicideH.PDF

389. Banks, Christopher, "The Cost of Homophobia: Literature Review on the Human Impact of Homophobia in Canada," National Coalition for LGBT Health, May 2003, http://www.lgbthealth.net/downloads/research/Human_Impact_of_Homophobia.pdf

390. "The Courage Apostolate," Courage International, Inc., undated, http://couragerc.net/TheCourageApostolate.html

391. "Now the Vatican Blames Gays for Catholic Church Sexual Abuse of Children Scandal," The San Francisco Sentinel, April 13, 2010, http://www.sanfranciscosentinel.com/?p=68758

392. "Just the Facts about Sexual Orientation and Youth," American Psychological Association, 2008, reprinted at http://www.naswdc.org/pressroom/media/justthefacts.pdf

393. The Bible, Leviticus 20:13.

394. "If a man commits adultery with another man's wife--with the wife of his neighbor--both the adulterer and the adulteress must be put to death." The Bible, Leviticus 20:10.

395. "If anyone curses his father or mother, he must be put to death. He has cursed his father or his mother, and his blood will be on his own head." The Bible, Leviticus 20:9.

396. "If a man has a stubborn and rebellious son who does not obey his father and mother and will not listen to them when they discipline him, his father and mother shall take hold of him and bring him to the elders at the gate of his town. They shall say to the elders, 'This son of ours is stubborn and rebellious. He will not obey us. He is a profligate and a drunkard.' Then all the men of his town shall stone him to death." The Bible, Deuteronomy 21:18-21.

397. "Observe the Sabbath, because it is holy to you. Anyone who desecrates it must be put to death," The Bible, Exodus 31:14.

398. "'If anyone curses his God, he will be held responsible; anyone who blasphemes the name of the LORD must be put to death. The entire assembly must stone him." The Bible, Leviticus 24:15-16.

399. "Keep my decrees . . . Do not wear clothing woven of two kinds of material." The Bible, Leviticus 19:19.

400. "Do not cut the hair at the sides of your head or clip off the edges of your beard." The Bible, Leviticus 19:27.

401. "Americans' Role Seen in Uganda Anti-Gay Push," The New York Times, January 3, 2010, (subquotes omitted) http://www.nytimes.com/2010/01/04/world/africa/04uganda.html

402. Id.

403. "Pastor Rick Warren Responds to Proposed Antigay Ugandan Legislation," Newsweek, November 29, 2009,

http://blog.newsweek.com/blogs/thehumancondition/archive/2009/1 1/29/pastor-rick-warren-responds-to-proposed-ugandan-legislation.a spx

404. "Islamic view about Homosexuality," Islam Awareness, undated, http://www.islamawareness.net/Homosexuality/homo.html

405. "Religious Groups' Official Positions on Same-Sex Marriage: 2008," Pew Forum on Religion and Public Life, April 1, 2008, http://pewforum.org/Gay-Marriage-and-Homosexuality/Religious-Gr oups-Official-Positions-on-Same-Sex-Marriage-2008.aspx

406. "Argentina Approves Gay Marriage, in a First for Region," New York Times, July 16, 2010, http://www.nytimes.com/2010/07/16/world/americas/16argentina.ht ml

407. "Where Can Gays Legally Marry?" Lesbian Life, About.com, undated, http://lesbianlife.about.com/cs/wedding/a/wheremarriage.htm; "Iceland passes gay marriage law in unanimous vote," Reuters, June 11, 2010, http://www.reuters.com/article/idUSTRE65A3V020100611

408. "Love, Hate and the Law," Amnesty International, 2008, at 47-48, http://www.amnesty.org/en/library/asset/POL30/003/2008/en/e2388a 0c-588b-4238-9939-de6911b4a1c5/pol300032008en.pdf

409. "Public Opinion on Gay Marriage: Opponents Consistently Outnumber Supporters," The Pew Forum on Religion and Public Life, July 9, 2009, http://pewforum.org/docs/?DocID=424

410. *In Re Marriage Cases*, 43 Cal. 4th 757 (2008), http://caselaw.lp.findlaw.com/data2/californiastatecases/s147999.pdf

411. "Opposition to same-sex marriage ban grows," The San Francisco Chronicle, September 18, 2008, http://www.sfgate.com/cgi-bin/article.cgi?f=/c/a/2008/09/18/BATM 12VSRA.DTL&hw=Proposition+field+poll&sn=005&sc=072

412. "Warren waver on Prop 8 stuns leaders," The Washington Times, April 11, 2009, http://www.washingtontimes.com/news/2009/apr/11/warren-waver-s tuns-leaders/?xid=rss-page

413. "Mormons For Proposition 8 Donors," Mormonsfor8.com, undated, http://mormonsfor8.com/

414. "Mormons at the Door," The American Conservative, February 23, 2009, http://www.amconmag.com/article/2009/feb/23/00014/

415. "8: The Mormon Proposition," The Huffington Post, June 2, 2010, http://www.huffingtonpost.com/2010/06/02/8-the-mormon-propositi on_n_597500.html?page=13&show_comment_id=49154413#comm ent_49154413

416. "LDS" is an acronym for "Latter Day Saints," a name preferred by Mormons to describe themselves.

417. "Utah Membership," The Church of Jesus Christ of Latter-day Saints, January 17, 2008, http://www.newsroom.lds.org/ldsnewsroom/eng/news-releases-storie s/utah-membership

418. "Mormons at the Door," The American Conservative, February 23, 2009, http://www.amconmag.com/article/2009/feb/23/00014/

419. Schubert, Frank and Flint, Jeff, "Passing Prop 8: smart timing and messaging convinced California voters to support traditional marriage." Politics Magazine, February 1, 2009,

http://www.accessmylibrary.com/article-1G1-194717807/passing-pr
op-8-smart.html

420. "Same-sex marriage fight roils Maine," The Boston Globe,
October 20, 2009,
http://www.boston.com/news/local/maine/articles/2009/10/20/same_
sex_marriage_fight_roils_maine/

421. The National Organization for Marriage contributed $1.9 to the
gay marriage repeal campaign. "Judge: ID donors to Maine's same-
sex law repeal," The Portland Press Herald, June 7, 2010,
http://www.pressherald.com/news/Judge-ID-donors-to-same-sex-law
-repeal.html. The total spent by gay marriage opponents was about
$3.8 million. "Gay-marriage foes fight state over naming names,"
Morning Sentinel, June 7, 2010,
http://www.onlinesentinel.com/news/gay-marriage-foes-fight-state-o
ver-naming-names_2010-05-13.html

422. "2009 Election Results," The New York Times, November 9,
2009, http://elections.nytimes.com/2009/results/other.html

423. "Same-Gender Attraction," The Church of Jesus Christ of
Latter-day Saints Newsroom, undated,
http://www.lds.org/ldsnewsroom/eng/public-issues/same-gender-attr
action

424. "Official Mormon Church Documents," Mormongate.com,
undated, http://www.mormongate.com/document1.html; "The
Mormons Are Coming!" The Washington Post, May 29, 2009,
http://www.washingtonpost.com/wp-dyn/content/article/2009/05/28/
AR2009052803573.html?hpid=topnews

425. In a leaked memo on Mormon Church letterhead, Mormon
official Loren C. Dunn said, "The coalition is looking for an
articulate, middle-aged mother who is neither Catholic or LDS . . . .
The Coalition's name and mission statement is attached. . . .We hear
from all sources that this issue will recur and will only be put to bed

with a constitutional amendment." (November 21, 1995 Memo of Loren Dunn), http://www.mormongate.com/document2.html. Other letters said, "Regarding the organization of the coalition . . . we have distanced the Church from the coalition itself but still have input where necessary through our local source." (December 20, 1995 letter of Loren Dunn), http://www.mormongate.com/document3.html. "One reason I wanted us organized in Hawaii the way we are is because [Mormon] President Hinckley wanted it that way. A coalition is hard to attack and particularly a young mother who was Chair of the State Board of Education (Chairman), a popular Catholic Priest with a Jewish-Buddhist background who is noted for his work with the socially disadvantaged (Vice-Chairman) and a businessman who is a trustee of the University of Hawaii, a University that is known for its diversity (Vice-Chairman)." (March 6, 1996 letter of Loren Dunn), http://www.mormongate.com/document4.html. "We have shielded previous donors from recognition because of how the funds were used in the preparation of this project. . . . The coalition is in need [of] . . . $50,000 . . . . The coalition continues to raise money locally but as expected, the majority needs to come from us." (March 21, 1996 letter of Loren Dunn), http://www.mormongate.com/document5.html. "[T]he *Wall Street Journal* and the *Salt Lake Tribune* keep wanting to talk . . . about coalition financing . . . We have organized things so the Church contribution was used in the area of coalition activity that does not have to be reported." (June 5, 1996 letter of Loren Dunn), http://www.mormongate.com/document7.html. "I was with Elder Maxwell when President Hinckley told us to go to Hawaii and get the coalition organized and try to head off the legalization of same-gender marriage. . . . With all the talk of same-gender marriage, it has not been legalized in one single state . . . The Lord has blessed the coalition because it has given Hawaiians who oppose HLM [gay marriage] both a voice and focus without the Church being singled out for attack by the opposition. We have been able to make our input into the coalition by having Don Hallstrom poised in such a way that we can get our message through to the leadership without

285

appearing to dominate." (November 19, 1996 letter of Loren Dunn), http://www.mormongate.com/document8.html.

426. "Utah Membership," The Church of Jesus Christ of Latter-day Saints, January 17, 2008, http://www.newsroom.lds.org/ldsnewsroom/eng/news-releases-storie s/utah-membership

427. "Gay Marriage Timeline," Pew Forum on Religion and Public Life, April 1, 2008, http://pewforum.org/docs/?DocID=292

428. "Utah ranks last in attitude to pro-gay policies," Mormon Chronicles, November 12, 2009, http://mormon-chronicles.blogspot.com/2009/11/study-suggests-utah -most-homophobic.html

429. "National Organization for Marriage Donor Names Kept Secret," The Huffington Post, December 21, 2009, http://www.huffingtonpost.com/fred-karger/national-organization-fo r_b_398024.html; "Is the Anti-Gay National Organization for Marriage (NOM) a Secret Mormon Front Group?" Pensito Review, March 24, 2009, http://www.pensitoreview.com/2009/03/24/leaked-docs-mormons-se t-up-anti-gay-front-group/

430. "Religious Right Targets Maine & Marriage Equality with Money, Anti-Gay Swat Teams and Reprise of Prop-8's False Fearmongering Strategies," People for the American Way, Undated, http://www.pfaw.org/rww-in-focus/religious-right-targets-maine-mar riage-equality-with-money-anti-gay-swat-teams-and-reprise-of

431. The National Organization for Marriage contributed $1.9 to the gay marriage repeal campaign. "Judge: ID donors to Maine's same-sex law repeal," The Portland Press Herald, June 7, 2010, http://www.pressherald.com/news/Judge-ID-donors-to-same-sex-law -repeal.html. The total spent by gay marriage opponents was about $3.8 million. "Gay-marriage foes fight state over naming names,"

Morning Sentinel, June 7, 2010,
http://www.onlinesentinel.com/news/gay-marriage-foes-fight-state-o
ver-naming-names_2010-05-13.html; "Setback for Group Fighting
Gay Marriage in Maine," The New York Times, October 29, 2009,
http://www.nytimes.com/2009/10/30/us/30maine.html

432. States mentioned on the National Organization for Marriage
Website, on news Websites and right wing watch include:
California, Iowa, Maine, Massachusetts, Maryland, Minnesota, New
Hampshire, Rhode Island, West Virginia and the District of
Colombia.
http://www.rightwingwatch.org/category/groups/national-organizatio
n-marriage;
http://www.nationformarriage.org/site/c.omL2KeN0LzH/b.3836955/
k.BEC6/Home.htm;
http://www.tcdailyplanet.net/news/2010/05/19/nom-fires-first-salvo-
minnesota-same-sex-marriage-battle

433. Section 15.11, The Ohio Constitution,
http://www.legislature.state.oh.us/constitution.cfm?Part=15&Section
=11

434. "Foes of Cleveland's partner registry are back in court," Gay
People's Chronicle, January 29, 2010,
http://www.gaypeopleschronicle.com/stories10/January/0129101.ht
m

435. "Elections panel drops hidden-donor complaint," Gay People's
Chronicle, March 3, 2006,
http://www.gaypeopleschronicle.com/stories06/march/0303063.htm

436. "Mormons at the Door," The American Conservative, February
23, 2009, http://www.amconmag.com/article/2009/feb/23/00014/

437. Pew 2008 put the Mormon percentage of the U.S. population at
1.7% and the atheist percentage at 1.6%.
http://religions.pewforum.org/affiliations

438. "Same Sex Marriage, Civil Unions and Domestic Partnerships," National Conference of State Legislatures, updated April 2010, http://www.ncsl.org/IssuesResearch/HumanServices/SameSexMarria ge/tabid/16430/Default.aspx

439. I could not find a definitive source for this quote, but it is repeated frequently and from my perspective, justifiably so.

440. Ingersoll, Robert, *The Works of Robert G. Ingersoll*, Volume 7, 2009, at page 466.

441. "Islamic countries push a global 'blasphemy' law," The Christian Science Monitor, October 27, 2009, http://www.csmonitor.com/Commentary/the-monitors-view/2009/10 27/p08s01-comv.html; "Blasphemy law," Wikipedia, undated, http://en.wikipedia.org/wiki/Blasphemy_law

442. "Dutch Filmmaker, an Islam Critic, Is Killed," The New York Times, November 3, 2004, http://www.nytimes.com/2004/11/03/international/europe/03dutch.ht ml?_r=1&scp=5&sq=theo%20van%20gogh%20submission&st=cse

443. The Koran, 4:34 (Shakir).

444. The Koran, 2:222 (Yusuf Ali).

445. The Koran, 24:2 (Shakir).

446. "Dutch Filmmaker, an Islam Critic, Is Killed," The New York Times, November 3, 2004, http://www.nytimes.com/2004/11/03/international/europe/03dutch.ht ml?_r=1&scp=5&sq=theo%20van%20gogh%20submission&st=cse

447. "Clash of Civilizations," Newsweek, November 22, 2004, http://www.newsweek.com/id/55736

448. "English translation--letter left on Theo Van Gogh's body by the militant Islamist killer was 'Jihad Manifesto'--A call to destroy America and all 'unbelievers'" (minor grammatical changes made), Militant Islam Monitor, undated, http://www.militantislammonitor.org/article/id/312

449. "Why I Published Those Cartoons," The Washington Post, February 16, 2006, http://www.washingtonpost.com/wp-dyn/content/article/2006/02/17/AR2006021702499.html

450. "How a meeting of leaders in Mecca set off the cartoon wars around the world," The Independent, February 10, 2006, http://www.independent.co.uk/news/world/middle-east/how-a-meeting-of-leaders-in-mecca-set-off-the-cartoon-wars-around-the-world-466109.html; "70,000 gather for violent Pakistan cartoons protest," The Times of London, February 15, 2006, http://www.timesonline.co.uk/tol/news/world/asia/article731005.ece

451. "Statement by John Donatich," Yale University Press, September 9, 2009, http://yalepress.yale.edu/yupbooks/KlausenStatement.asp;

452. "'South Park' and the Informal Fatwa," The Wall Street Journal, April 27, 2010, http://online.wsj.com/article/SB10001424052748703465204575208163274783300.html

453. Kurt Westergaard, Danish Muhammad Cartoonist, Defiant In Face Of Threats," The Huffington Post, October 28, 2009, http://www.huffingtonpost.com/2009/10/28/kurt-westergaard-danish-m_n_337398.html

454. "Vatican condemns Motoons," Mediawatch.org.uk, February 28, 2008, http://www.mediawatchwatch.org.uk/?s=vatican+condemns

455. "Bounty set over Prophet cartoon," BBC News, September 15, 2007, http://news.bbc.co.uk/2/hi/middle_east/6996553.stm

456. "Seven arrested in Ireland over alleged plot to kill Muhammad cartoonist," The Guardian, March 9, 2010, http://www.guardian.co.uk/world/2010/mar/09/seven-arrested-ireland-muhammad-cartoon

457. "US woman held in Ireland over alleged plot to kill Muhammad artist," The Guardian, March 14, 2010, http://www.guardian.co.uk/world/2010/mar/14/american-woman-ireland-muhammad-artist

458. "Muhammad cartoonist in hiding after arson attack," The Associated Press, May 16, 2010, http://www.google.com/hostednews/ap/article/ALeqM5gfyTngzJoXI5VLnRYFKryLwRumugD9FNT2J00

459. "Road to Radicalism: The Man Behind the 'South Park' Threats," Fox News, April 23, 2010, http://www.foxnews.com/us/2010/04/23/road-radicalism-man-south-park-threats/

460. "'South Park' and the Informal Fatwa," The Wall Street Journal, April 27, 2010, http://online.wsj.com/article/SB10001424052748703465204575208163274783300.html

461. "Threat against 'South Park' creators highlights dilemma for media companies," Los Angeles Times, April 23, 2010, http://articles.latimes.com/2010/apr/23/entertainment/la-et-south-park-20100423

462. "Cartoonist Molly Norris Erases 'Draw Muhammad' Gag," Fox News, April 26, 2010, http://www.myfoxtwincities.com/dpps/news/cartoonist-molly-norris-draw-muhammad-gag-dpgoha-20100426-fc_7252284

463. "Advice for Everyone Draw Muhammad Day," Secular Student Alliance, May 8, 2010, http://www.secularstudents.org/drawingtheprophet

464. "Yale Self-Censors New Book Examining Extreme Muslim Reaction to Danish Cartoons of Prophet Muhammad," CNSNews.com, October 1, 2009, http://www.cnsnews.com/public/content/article.aspx?RsrcID=54844;

465. "Piss Christ," Art Crimes, October 12, 1997, http://www.artcrimes.net/piss-christ

466. "The Holy Virgin Mary," Art Crimes, December 16, 1999, http://www.artcrimes.net/holy-virgin-mary

467. Voltaire, *Questions sur les miracles*, 1765, (condensed translation), http://en.wikiquote.org/wiki/Voltaire

468. The Bible, Genesis 32:30.

469. The Bible, Exodus 33:11.

470. The Bible, Genesis 3:8-13.

471. The Bible, Exodus 33:19-20.

472. The Bible, John 5:37 (King James Version).

473. "They ask thee concerning wine and gambling. Say: 'In them is great sin, and some profit for men; but the sin is greater than the profit.'" The Koran, 2:219 (Yusuf Ali).

474. The Koran, 16.67 (Rodwell)(in Warraq, Ibn, *Why I am not a Muslim*, 2003, at 115).

475. The Bible, Joshua 10:12-14.

476. The Bible, Joshua 10:40.

477. Asimov, Isaac and Asimov, Stanley, *Yours, Isaac Asimov: a lifetime of letters*, 1995, at 316.

478. Altemeyer, Bob and Hunsberger, Bruce, *Amazing Conversions*, 1997, at 111.

479. Hunsberger, Bruce and Altemeyer, Bob, *Atheists*, 2006, at 55.

480. Kasem, Abul, "Who Authored the Qur'an?: An Enquiry," Part 1, November 20, 2005, http://www.islam-watch.org/AbulKasem/WhoAuthoredQuran/who_authored_the_quran.htm

481. Twain, Mark, *Following the Equator*, 1897, from http://atheisme.free.fr/Quotes/Twain.htm

482. "The impact of Bush linking 9/11 and Iraq," The Christian Science Monitor, March 14, 2003, http://www.csmonitor.com/2003/0314/p02s01-woiq.html

483. "Bush: No Iraq link to 9/11 found," The Seattle Post-Intelligencer, September 18, 2003 http://www.seattlepi.com/national/140133_bushiraq18.html

484. "Support for War Modestly Higher Among More Religious Americans," Gallup Polls, February 27, 2003, http://www.gallup.com/poll/7888/Support-War-Modestly-Higher-Among-More-Religious-Americans.aspx; see also: http://www.gallup.com/video/21946/Religion-War.aspx

485. "Protestants and Frequent Churchgoers Most Supportive of Iraq War," Gallup Polls, March 16, 2006, http://www.gallup.com/poll/21937/Protestants-Frequent-Churchgoers-Most-Supportive-Iraq-War.aspx

486. "Palin's Church May Have Shaped Controversial Worldview," The Huffington Post, September 2, 2008, http://www.huffingtonpost.com/2008/09/02/palins-church-may-have -sh_n_123205.html

487. "Sarah Palin's 'Christian Nation' Remarks Spark Debate," ABC News, April 20, 2010, http://abcnews.go.com/Politics/sarah-palin-sparks-church-state-separ ation-debate/story?id=10419289

488. "PolitiFact's Lie of the Year: 'Death panels,'" St. Petersburg Times Politifact.com, December 18, 2009, http://politifact.com/truth-o-meter/article/2009/dec/18/politifact-lie-y ear-death-panels/

489. The bill provided:

> [T]he term 'advance care planning consultation' means a consultation between the individual and a practitioner described in paragraph (2) regarding advance care planning, if, subject to paragraph (3), the individual involved has not had such a consultation within the last 5 years. Such consultation shall include the following:
> (A) An explanation by the practitioner of advance care planning, including key questions and considerations, important steps, and suggested people to talk to.
> (B) An explanation by the practitioner of advance directives, including living wills and durable powers of attorney, and their uses.
> (C) An explanation by the practitioner of the role and responsibilities of a health care proxy.
> (D) The provision by the practitioner of a list of national and State-specific resources to assist consumers and their families with advance care planning . . .
> (E) An explanation by the practitioner of the continuum

of end-of-life services and supports available, including palliative care and hospice, and benefits for such services and supports that are available under this title. (F)(i) Subject to clause (ii), an explanation of orders regarding life sustaining treatment or similar orders…

"False Euthanasia Claims," St. Petersburg Times Politifact.com, July 29, 2009, http://factcheck.org/2009/07/false-euthanasia-claims/. The full text of the bill is available at http://frwebgate.access.gpo.gov/cgi-bin/getdoc.cgi?dbname=111_cong_bills&docid=f:h3200ih.txt.pdf

490. "NBC News Health Care Survey," August 2009, http://msnbcmedia.msn.com/i/MSNBC/Sections/NEWS/NBC-WSJ_Poll.pdf

491. "Health Care Reform Closely Followed, Much Discussed," The Pew Research Center for People and the Press, August 20, 2009, http://people-press.org/report/537/

492. Id.

493. "Palin Wins," The Wall Street Journal, August 14, 2009, http://online.wsj.com/article/SB10001424052970204409904574350400852801602.html

494. "Born in the U.S.A.," Factcheck.org, Annenberg Public Policy Center of the University of Pennsylvania, August 21, 2008, http://www.factcheck.org/elections-2008/born_in_the_usa.html

495. "Birthers are mostly Republican and Southern," Daily Kos, July 31, 2009, http://www.dailykos.com/storyonly/2009/7/31/760087/-Birthers-are-mostly-Republican-and-Southern

496. "Wife says Ted Haggard is completely heterosexual,"

Examiner.com, January 28, 2010,
http://www.examiner.com/examiner/x-8947-LA-Atheism-Examiner
~y2010m1d28-Wife-says-Ted-Haggard-is-completely-heterosexual

497. "Idaho Senator Says He Did Nothing Wrong," The New York Times, August 28, 2007,
http://www.nytimes.com/2007/08/28/washington/28cnd-craig.html

498. Altemeyer, Bob and Hunsberger, Bruce, *Amazing Conversions*, 1997, at 236-7.

499. "Baruch Goldstein," AllExperts Encyclopedia, undated,
http://en.allexperts.com/e/b/ba/baruch_goldstein.htm

500. "Positive Atheism's Big List of Quotations," Positive Atheism, undated, http://www.positiveatheism.org/hist/quotes/quote-p.htm

501. Even those who do not admit law represents a social contract will agree that law provides rules of conduct that, if violated, will be punished.

502. Shahak, Israel and Mezvinsky, Norton, *Jewish Fundamentalism in Israel*, 1999,
http://members.tripod.com/alabasters_archive/goldstein_significance.html

503. Id.

504. "Baruch Goldstein," My Jewish Learning, undated,
http://www.myjewishlearning.com/israel/History/1980-2000/Goldstein_Massacre.shtml

505. "Cave of the Patriarchs/Ibrahimi Mosque," Heritage Key, undated,
http://heritage-key.com/site/cave-patriarchs-ibrahimi-mosque

506. "Israel Panel Says Killer at Hebron Was Acting Alone," The New York Times, June 27, 1994, http://www.nytimes.com/1994/06/27/world/israel-panel-says-killer-at-hebron-was-acting-alone.html?pagewanted=1

507. "Between Hebron and Jerusalem," The Jerusalem Post, March 17, 2008, http://www.jpost.com/Opinion/Op-EdContributors/Article.aspx?id=95272

508. "Bloodlust Memories," The New Republic, March 21, 1994, http://www.tnr.com/articles/world?page=9

509. Shahak, Israel and Mezvinsky, Norton, *Jewish Fundamentalism in Israel*, 1999, http://members.tripod.com/alabasters_archive/goldstein_significance.html

510. "Hebron settlers shed no tears after slaughter: Militant Jews are turning mass killer Baruch Goldstein into a folk hero, writes Sarah Helm from Kiryat Arba," The Independent, February 28, 1994, http://www.independent.co.uk/news/world/hebron-settlers-shed-no-tears-after-slaughter-militant-jews-are-turning-mass-killer-baruch-goldstein-into-a-folk-hero-writes-sarah-helm-from-kiryat-arba-1397002.html

511. "Israel Destroys Shrine to Mosque Gunman," The New York Times, December 30, 1999, http://www.nytimes.com/1999/12/30/world/israel-destroys-shrine-to-mosque-gunman.html

512. "Book Praises Gunman In Mosque Massacre," San Francisco Chronicle, March 15, 1995, http://articles.sfgate.com/1995-03-15/news/17797483_1_jewish-settler-kiryat-arba-palestinians

513. "Sheikh Jarrah Jews sing Purim praises of Baruch Goldstein," The Jerusalem Post, May 3, 2010, http://www.jpost.com/Israel/Article.aspx?id=170298

514. "Army Doctor Held in Ft. Hood Rampage," The New York Times, November 5, 2009, http://www.nytimes.com/2009/11/06/us/06forthood.html?pagewanted=1

515. "Hash Browns, Then 4 Minutes of Chaos," The Wall Street Journal, November 9, 2009, http://online.wsj.com/article/SB125750297355533413.html

516. "Anwar al Awlaki: 'Nidal Hassan Did the Right Thing,'" The NEFA Foundation, November 9, 2009, http://www.nefafoundation.org/miscellaneous/FeaturedDocs/nefaawlakiforthoodshooting.pdf

517. "Transcript of Adam Gadahn's 'A Call to Arms,'" The Long War Journal, March 8, 2010, http://www.longwarjournal.org/threat-matrix/archives/2010/03/transcript_of_adam_gadahns_a_c.php

518. "Pro-Life Turns Deadly," Newsweek, January 26, 1998, http://www.newsweek.com/id/90959

519. "Abortions, Bibles and Bullets, and the Making of a Militant," The New York Times, August 28, 1993, http://www.nytimes.com/1993/08/28/us/abortions-bibles-and-bullets-and-the-making-of-a-militant.html?pagewanted=1

520. "Free speech wasn't meant for this," The Guardian, February 12, 2010, http://www.guardian.co.uk/commentisfree/cifamerica/2010/feb/11/scott-roeder-youtube-free-speech

521. "Abortion doctor killer a soldier in terrorist 'Army of God'?" The Institute for Southern Studies, June 2009, http://www.southernstudies.org/2009/06/abortion-doctor-killer-a-soldier-in-terrorist-army-of-god.html

522. "Backgrounder: Eric Robert Rudolph," The Anti-Defamation League, June 5, 2003, http://www.adl.org/extremism/rudolph_backgrounder.asp

523. "Roeder jury can't consider manslaughter in Tiller killing," McClatchy News Service, January 28, 2010, http://www.mcclatchydc.com/2010/01/28/83274/roeder-admits-he-killed-abortion.html

524. "Militants contact Roeder in jail," The Kansas City Star, August 10, 2009, http://www.kansas.com/2009/08/10/924426/militants-contact-roeder-in-jail.html

525. "Transcript of President Bush's address," CNN, September 21, 2001, http://archives.cnn.com/2001/US/09/20/gen.bush.transcript/

526. "Eid" is a day of thanksgiving celebrated at the end of Ramadan. "Eid-ul Fitr Page," IslamiCity.com, undated, http://www.islamicity.com/ramadan/eid_default.shtml

527. "In his own words; Bush on Islam," Muslim Republicans, July 7, 2007, http://muslimrepublicans.net/Article.asp?ID=164

528. "Bush: All religions pray to 'same God,'" World Net Daily, October 7, 2007, http://www.wnd.com/news/article.asp?ARTICLE_ID=58026

529. "Full text: bin Laden's 'letter to America,'" The Guardian, November 24, 2002, http://www.guardian.co.uk/world/2002/nov/24/theobserver

530. "The Great Divide: How Westerners and Muslims View Each Other," The Pew Global Attitudes Project, June 22, 2006, at 4, http://pewglobal.org/reports/pdf/253.pdf

531. "Bin Laden Admits 9/11 Responsibility, Warns of More Attacks," PBS, October 29, 2004, http://www.pbs.org/newshour/updates/binladen_10-29-04.html

532. "The Great Divide: How Westerners and Muslims View Each Other," The Pew Global Attitudes Project, June 22, 2006, at 4, http://pewglobal.org/reports/pdf/253.pdf

533. "Prominent Arabs blame 9-11 on Jews," WorldNetDaily.com, January 10, 2002, http://www.wnd.com/news/article.asp?ARTICLE_ID=25995

534. "Ahmadinejad: 9/11 Attacks a 'Big Lie,'" The Huffington Post, March 6, 2010, http://www.huffingtonpost.com/2010/03/06/ahmadinejad-911-attacks-a_0_n_488789.html

535. "Mixed Views of Hamas and Hezbollah in Largely Muslim Nations," The Pew Global Attitudes Project, February 4, 2010, at 5, http://pewglobal.org/reports/pdf/268.pdf

536. "Money Woes, Long Silences and a Zeal for Islam," The New York Times, May 5, 2010, http://www.nytimes.com/2010/05/06/nyregion/06profile.html

537. "Chain of Phone Numbers Led Investigators to Bomb Suspect," The New York Times, May 5, 2010, http://www.nytimes.com/2010/05/06/us/06cellphone.html; "Car Bomb a Possible Factor in Broadway Declines," The New York Times, May 3, 2010, http://www.nytimes.com/2010/05/04/theater/04arts-CARBOMBAPOSS_BRF.html?scp=1&sq=car%20bomb%20lion%20king&st=cse

538. The Bible, 2 Chronicles 15:12-13 (emphasis added).

539. The Bible, Deuteronomy 13:12-18 (emphasis added).

Similarly, The Bible, Numbers 25:1-8 provides:

> While Israel was staying in Shittim, the men began to indulge in sexual immorality with Moabite women, who invited them to the sacrifices to their gods. The people ate and bowed down before these gods. So Israel joined in worshiping the Baal of Peor. And the LORD's anger burned against them. The LORD said to Moses, "Take all the leaders of these people, kill them and expose them in broad daylight before the LORD, so that the LORD's fierce anger may turn away from Israel." So Moses said to Israel's judges, "Each of you must put to death those of your men who have joined in worshiping the Baal of Peor." Then an Israelite man brought to his family a Midianite woman right before the eyes of Moses and the whole assembly of Israel while they were weeping at the entrance to the Tent of Meeting. When Phinehas son of Eleazar, the son of Aaron, the priest, saw this, he left the assembly, took a spear in his hand and followed the Israelite into the tent. He drove the spear through both of them--through the Israelite and into the woman's body.

540. The Koran, 33:23-27 (Mohsin Khan).

541. The Koran, 9:111 (Yusuf Ali).

542. The Koran, 9:73 (Yusuf Ali).

543. The Koran, 2:191 (Yusuf Ali).

544. "He who is not with me is against me." The Bible, Matthew 12:30.

545. "Transcript of President Bush's address," CNN, September 21, 2001, http://archives.cnn.com/2001/US/09/20/gen.bush.transcript/

546. "Iraq Deaths," Just Foreign Policy, undated, http://www.justforeignpolicy.org/iraq

547. The Bible, Numbers 19:1-5.

548. As a matter of reverence, some Jews do not spell out god's name in a medium in which it might be erased. "Why Don't You Spell Out G-d's Name?" Chabad.org, undated, http://www.chabad.org/library/article_cdo/aid/166899/jewish/Why-Don't-You-Spell-Out-G-ds-Name.htm

549. "The Red Heifer," The Temple Institute, undated, http://www.templeinstitute.org/red_heifer/introduction.htm

550. Gog and Magog appear in Jewish, Christian and Muslim mythology. They are variably identified as people, supernatural characters, groups of people, or places.

551. "What is the Jewish Belief About Moshiach?" Chabad.org, undated, http://www.chabad.org/library/article_cdo/aid/108400/jewish/The-End-of-Days.htm

552. "Mashiach: The Messiah," Judaism 101, undated, http://www.jewfaq.org/mashiach.htm

553. "Forcing the End," WGBH/PBS, undated, http://www.pbs.org/wgbh/pages/frontline/shows/apocalypse/readings/forcing.html

554. Id.

555. "Millennium Madness," Newsweek, November 15, 1999, http://www.newsweek.com/id/90162

556. "Clash erupts at Temple Mount," The Independent, September 28, 2000, http://www.independent.co.uk/news/world/middle-east/clash-erupts-at-temple-mount-699663.html

557. "Hamas," The Council on Foreign Relations, August 27, 2009, http://www.cfr.org/publication/8968/

558. "American Evangelicals and Israel," The Pew Forum on Religion and Public Life, April 15, 2005, http://pewforum.org/Christian/American-Evangelicals-and-Israel.asp x

559. The Bible, Luke 21:20-33.

560. "The Dead Are Judged . . . I saw the dead, great and small, standing before the throne, and books were opened. Another book was opened, which is the book of life. The dead were judged according to what they had done as recorded in the books. The sea gave up the dead that were in it, and death and Hades gave up the dead that were in them, and each person was judged according to what he had done. Then death and Hades were thrown into the lake of fire. The lake of fire is the second death. If anyone's name was not found written in the book of life, he was thrown into the lake of fire." The Bible, Revelation 16:16-21; "But the cowardly, the unbelieving, the vile, the murderers, the sexually immoral, those who practice magic arts, the idolaters and all liars--their place will be in the fiery lake of burning sulfur. This is the second death." The Bible, Revelation 21:8.

561. "Major Signs before the Day of Judgement," Inter-Islam.org, undated, (minor grammatical corrections made) http://www.inter-islam.org/faith/Majorsigns.html

562. Id.

563. "Dajjal (The Deceiver)," Illaam.net, undated,
http://www.ilaam.net/Articles/Dajjal.html

564. See, for example, "Prophetic Signs that we are in the End
Times," Contender Ministries, undated,
http://contenderministries.org/prophecy/endtimesPF.php

565. Muslim: "O Prophet! strive hard against the Unbelievers and
the Hypocrites, and be firm against them. Their abode is Hell--an
evil refuge indeed," The Koran, 9:73 (Yusuf Ali). Christian: The
Dead Are Judged. . . . I saw the dead, great and small, standing
before the throne, and books were opened. Another book was
opened, which is the book of life. The dead were judged according to
what they had done as recorded in the books. The sea gave up the
dead that were in it, and death and Hades gave up the dead that were
in them, and each person was judged according to what he had done.
Then death and Hades were thrown into the lake of fire. The lake of
fire is the second death. If anyone's name was not found written in
the book of life, he was thrown into the lake of fire." The Bible,
Revelation 16:16-21; "But the cowardly, the unbelieving, the vile,
the murderers, the sexually immoral, those who practice magic arts,
the idolaters and all liars—their place will be in the fiery lake of
burning sulfur. This is the second death." The Bible, Revelation
21:8.

566. The Bible, Revelation 13:11-18.

567. "End Times" Time Magazine, June 23, 2002,
http://www.time.com/time/covers/1101020701/story2.html

568. "The End Times Are Near," ChristiaNet.com, undated,
http://christiannews.christianet.com/1201403987.htm

569. "Congress includes 14 Church members," LDS Church News,
February 28, 2009,

http://www.ldschurchnews.com/articles/56686/Congress-includes-14
-Church-members.html

570. "General Apologizes for Remarks on Islam, Says He's No
'Zealot,'" The Los Angeles Times, October 18, 2003,
http://articles.latimes.com/2003/oct/18/nation/na-general18

571. Stuckert, Brian, "Strategic Implications of American
Millennialism," School of Advanced Military Studies, May 2008,
http://www.dtic.mil/cgi-bin/GetTRDoc?AD=ADA485511&Location
=U2&doc=GetTRDoc.pdf

572. "The Human Beast," Psychology Today, April 7, 2009,
http://www.psychologytoday.com/blog/the-human-beast/200904/ethi
cal-conduct-in-the-moral-right

573. "The Church has always maintained the historic Christian
teaching that deliberate acts of contraception are always gravely
sinful, which means that it is mortally sinful if done with full
knowledge and deliberate consent. This teaching cannot be changed
and has been taught by the Church infallibly." "Birth Control,"
Catholic Answers, August 10, 2004,
http://www.catholic.com/library/Birth_Control.asp; "The teaching of
the Church affirms the existence of hell and its eternity. Immediately
after death the souls of those who die in a state of mortal sin descend
into hell, where they suffer the punishments of hell, 'eternal fire.'"
"The Hell There Is!" Catholic Answers, August 10, 2004,
http://www.catholic.com/library/Hell_There_Is.asp

574. "The Facts Tell the Story: Catholics and Contraception,"
Catholics for Choice, April, 2006,
http://www.catholicsforchoice.org/topics/reform/documents/2006cat
holicsandcontraception.pdf

575. "Trends in Premarital Sex in the United States, 1954–2003,"
Public Health Reports, January–February 2007,

http://www.guttmacher.org/pubs/journals/2007/01/29/PRH-Vol-122-
Finer.pdf

576. Either they do not believe in an eternal paradise, or they do
believe, but think their sinful conduct condemns them to hell. I think
it is the former as opposed to the later since forgiveness for sin is an
essential element of religion. For example, some Christians believe
that criminals as vile as Jeffrey Dahmer can get into heaven simply
by saying some magic words (see Chapter 7). If simply repeating
magic words gets them into heaven, it looks like their vile acts are
not the issue. Rather they have a soft belief in the eternal paradise.

577. "Death Anxiety and Death Acceptance: a Preliminary
Approach," Omega, Vol. 5, No. 4, 1974, at 311-315,
http://jonjayray.tripod.com/death1.html

578. Shuey, John, American Atheist, September/October 2009, at 34.

579. "I Am a Person Who Is Spiritually Committed," Gallup Polls,
May 28, 2002,
http://www.gallup.com/poll/6097/Person-Who-Spiritually-Committe
d.aspx; "Gallup Releases 2003 Spiritual Commitment Data," Gallup
Polls, February 10, 2004,
http://www.gallup.com/poll/10573/Gallup-Releases-2003-Spiritual-
Commitment-Data.aspx (contains this list of factors: 1) I spend time
in worship or prayer every day. 2) My faith is involved in every
aspect of my life. 3) Because of my faith, I have forgiven people who
have hurt me deeply. 4) Because of my faith, I have meaning and
purpose in my life. 5) My faith has called me to develop my given
strengths. 6) I will take unpopular stands to defend my faith. 7) My
faith gives me an inner peace. 8) I speak words of kindness to those
in need of encouragement. 9) I am a person who is spiritually
committed.)

580. Pew 2008,
http://religions.pewforum.org/pdf/comparisons-all_beliefs.pdf

581. "Many Americans Uneasy with Mix of Religion and Politics," The Pew Research Center for the People & the Press, August 24, 2006, http://people-press.org/report/?pageid=1081

582. "How many North Americans attend religious services (and how many lie about going)?" Religious Tolerance.org, August 10, 2007, http://www.religioustolerance.org/rel_rate.htm; "Did You Really Go To Church This Week? Behind the Poll Data," The Christian Century, May 6, 1998, pp. 472-475, http://www.religion-online.org/showarticle.asp?title=237

583. "Just Why Do Americans Attend Church?" Gallup Polls, April 6, 2007, http://www.gallup.com/poll/27124/just-why-americans-attend-churc h.aspx#1

584. "As Attacks' Impact Recedes, a Return to Religion as Usual," The New York Times, November 26, 2001, http://www.nytimes.com/2001/11/26/national/26FAIT.html?ex=100 7442000&en=9b85baa5fd0bbff5&ei=5040&partner=MOREOVER

585. Altemeyer, Bob and Hunsberger, Bruce, *Amazing Conversions*, 1997, at 117.

586. Dennett, Daniel, *Breaking the Spell*, 2006, at 200-246.

587. The Platte: Mile Wide and an Inch Deep," (from "Adams County Crossroads of the West Volume I") undated, http://www.co.adams.co.us/documents/page/history/the_platte.pdf

588. Darwin, Charles, "Certain Beneficial Lines: 1860," The Darwin Correspondence Project, The University of Cambridge, http://www.darwinproject.ac.uk/dramatisation-script#fn90

589. Darwin, Charles, "Letter to E.B. Averling," October 13, 1880, The Darwin Correspondence Project, The University of Cambridge, http://www.darwinproject.ac.uk/entry-12757

590. The Koran, 7:54 (Yusuf Ali).

591. The Koran, 23:12 (Mohsin Khan).

592. The Koran, 7:189 (Mohsin Khan).

593. The Koran, 13:3-4 (Yusuf Ali).

594. The Bible, Genesis 1-2.

595. "On Darwin's Birthday, Only 4 in 10 Believe in Evolution," Gallup Polls, February 11, 2009, http://www.gallup.com/poll/114544/darwin-birthday-believe-evoluti on.aspx

596. "On Darwin's 200th Birthday, Americans Still Divided About Evolution," Pew Research Center, February 5, 2009, http://pewresearch.org/pubs/1107/polling-evolution-creationism

597. *Edwards v. Aguillard*, 482 U.S. 528 (1987), http://supreme.justia.com/us/482/578/case.html

598. "The Darwin Debate," Pew Research Center, June 13, 2007, http://pewresearch.org/pubs/509/darwin-debate

599. "The History of AiG through April 2010," Answers in Genesis, undated, http://www.answersingenesis.org/about/history

600. "Answers in Genesis," Charity Navigator, undated, http://www.charitynavigator.org/index.cfm?bay=search.summary&o rgid=5214

601. "The AiG Statement of Faith," Answers in Genesis, April 29, 2009, http://www.answersingenesis.org/about/faith

602. Andersen, Hans Christian, *The Complete Andersen*, 1949, Translated by Hersholt, Jean,

http://www.andersen.sdu.dk/vaerk/hersholt/TheEmperorsNewClothe
s_e.html?oph=1

603. "Among Wealthy Nations, U.S. Stands Alone in its Embrace of
Religion," The Pew Research Center for the People & the Press,
December 19, 2002,
http://people-press.org/report/167/among-wealthy-nations-.

604. "This Easter, Smaller Percentage of Americans Are Christian,"
Gallup Polls, April 10, 2009,
http://www.gallup.com/poll/117409/easter-smaller-percentage-ameri
cans-christian.aspx

605. Pew 2008, at 5,
http://religions.pewforum.org/pdf/report-religious-landscape-study-f
ull.pdf

606. Pew 2008, at 37,
http://religions.pewforum.org/pdf/report-religious-landscape-study-c
hapter-3.pdf

607. Edgell, Penny, Gerteis, Joseph, and Hartmann, Douglas,
"Atheists As 'Other': Moral Boundaries and Cultural Membership in
American Society," American Sociological Review, 2006, Vol. 71,
at 212, 217,
http://www.soc.umn.edu/~hartmann/files/atheist%20as%20the%20ot
her.pdf

608. "Religious Freedom," Official Web site of The Church of Jesus
Christ of Latter-day Saints, October 13, 2009, (subquotes and italics
omitted) (cached on google)
http://webcache.googleusercontent.com/search?q=cache:Vt78gUDbs
YMJ:newsroom.lds.org/ldsnewsroom/eng/news-releases-stories/relig
ious-freedom+atheism+threat+religion&cd=4&hl=en&ct=clnk&gl=u
s

609. "Public Opinion About Mormons," Pew Research Center, December 6, 2007, http://pewresearch.org/pubs/648/romney-mormon

610. Edgell, Penny, Gerteis, Joseph, and Hartmann, Douglas, "Atheists As 'Other': Moral Boundaries and Cultural Membership in American Society," American Sociological Review, 2006, Vol. 71, at 218, http://www.soc.umn.edu/~hartmann/files/atheist%20as%20the%20ot her.pdf

611. Although I argue that the humanist approach duplicates religion and therefore is undesirable, humanists directly address the concern of religionists that atheists are self-focused and do little to forward the common good. I continue to see answering the "good without god' question an example of letting religionists call the tune, but admittedly humanists can argue that they are addressing the biggest objection religionists have about atheists and therefore are forwarding the atheist movement more than me.

612. Edgell, Penny, Gerteis, Joseph, and Hartmann, Douglas, "Atheists As 'Other': Moral Boundaries and Cultural Membership in American Society," American Sociological Review, 2006, Vol. 71, http://www.soc.umn.edu/~hartmann/files/atheist%20as%20the%20ot her.pdf

613. "Some Americans Reluctant to Vote for Mormon, 72-Year-Old Presidential Candidates," Gallup News Service, February 20, 2007, http://www.gallup.com/poll/26611/some-americans-reluctant-vote-m ormon-72yearold-presidential-candidates.aspx#1

614. See Chapter 26.

615. "Salvation Army to Gays, Atheists, Undocumented Immigrants–'Go to Hell!'" The Politicizer, undated, http://thepoliticizer.com/2009/12/10/baron-salvation-army-to-gays-at heists-undocumented-immigrants-go-to-hell/

616. "Catholic Charities in D.C. adds hiring clause on church tenets," The Washington Post, March 13, 2010, http://www.washingtonpost.com/wp-dyn/content/article/2010/03/12/AR2010031203969.html?hpid=sec-religion

617. "Letter to Director of the U.S. Census Bureau," United Coalition of Reason, May 7, 2010, http://unitedcor.org/census_letter.html

618. *Underhill v. Garcia*, Michigan Court of Appeals (unpublished), December 6, 2005, http://caselaw.lp.findlaw.com/data2/michiganstatecases/appeals/120605/29732.pdf

619. "Discrimination Against Atheists The Facts," Free Inquiry Magazine, February/March 2004, http://www.secularhumanism.org/index.php?section=library&page=downey_24_4

620. "Atheist soldier sues Army for 'unconstitutional' discrimination," CNN, July 9, 2008, http://www.cnn.com/2008/US/07/08/atheist.soldier/index.html; "Army to EO Reps: 'Discrimination Against Atheists OK,'" American Chronicle, April 29, 2007, http://www.americanchronicle.com/articles/view/25659

621. Once again, this is an area where humanists can say they are addressing the problem more directly than me (see note 611). However, in the long run I believe that structuring atheism like religion is a flawed strategy. I believe that seeing atheism as a viewpoint that extends beyond religion will ultimately prove to be more effective.

622. Heinerman, John, and Shupe, Anson, *The Mormon Corporate Empire*, 1985, at 29-32.

623. "Duty to God," Boy Scouts of America, Legal Issues, undated, http://www.bsalegal.org/duty-to-god-cases-224.asp

624. "BSA's Policy on Homosexuals," BSA-discrimination.org, October 28, 2009, http://www.bsa-discrimination.org/html/bsa_gay_policy.html

625. "Some Americans Reluctant to Vote for Mormon, 72-Year-Old Presidential Candidates," Gallup News Service, February 20, 2007, http://www.gallup.com/poll/26611/some-americans-reluctant-vote-mormon-72yearold-presidential-candidates.aspx

626. *Lawrence v. Texas*, 539 U.S. 558 (2003), http://www.law.cornell.edu/supct/html/02-102.ZS.html

627. "Statewide Employment Laws & Policies," Human Rights Campaign, February 17, 2010, http://www.hrc.org/documents/Employment_Laws_and_Policies.pdf

628. "Marriage Equality & Other Relationship Recognition Laws," Human Rights Campaign, April 2, 2010, http://www.hrc.org/documents/Relationship_Recognition_Laws_Map.pdf

629. Id.

630. "Some Americans Reluctant to Vote for Mormon, 72-Year-Old Presidential Candidates," Gallup News Service, February 20, 2007, http://www.gallup.com/poll/26611/some-americans-reluctant-vote-mormon-72yearold-presidential-candidates.aspx

631. "Pride Around The World," Macleans.ca, May 21, 2010, http://www2.macleans.ca/2010/05/21/pride-around-the-world/

632. "San Francisco Pride," Frommers, undated, http://events.frommers.com/sisp/index.htm?fx=event&event_id=51591

633. "Pride-Flyin' Flag," Metro Weekly, October 18, 2007, http://www.metroweekly.com/feature/?ak=3031

634. Shilts, Randy, *The Mayor of Castro Street*, 1982, at 82-84.

635. "Diversity Our Strength," Toronto Long-Term Care Home and Services, December 2008, at 58, http://www.toronto.ca/ltc/pdf/lgbt_toolkit_2008.pdf

636. "Understanding Gay History and Culture," Q2 Ally Network, undated, http://q2.concordia.ca/handbook/section6.shtml

637. "Statewide Employment Laws & Policies," Human Rights Campaign, February 17, 2010, http://www.hrc.org/documents/Employment_Laws_and_Policies.pdf

638. "21st century lands in Riverdale with the arrival of Kevin," The Miami Herald, April 28, 2010, http://www.miamiherald.com/2010/04/28/1601411/21st-century-lan ds-in-riverdale.html

639. *Lawrence v. Texas*, 539 U.S. 558 (2003), http://www.law.cornell.edu/supct/html/02-102.ZS.html

640. "Gay marriage legal in six states," Stateline.org, June 4, 2009, http://www.stateline.org/live/details/story?contentId=347390

641. "Poll: With Higher Visibility, Less Disapproval for Gays," CBS News, June 9, 2010, http://www.cbsnews.com/8301-503544_162-20007144-503544.html

642. "History of National Coming Out Day," Human Rights Campaign, undated, http://www.hrc.org/issues/3338.htm

643. "A Resource Guide to Coming Out," Human Rights Campaign, undated, http://www.hrc.org/documents/resourceguide_co.pdf

644. GLBT is an acronym for "gay, lesbian, bisexual and transgendered."

645. I could not find a quote with this statement, so I am making it myself.

646. "Congress shall make no law respecting an establishment of religion, or prohibiting the free exercise thereof," Amendment I, The United States Constitution, 1789, http://www.archives.gov/exhibits/charters/bill_of_rights_transcript.html

647. "It shall be an unlawful employment practice for an employer... to fail or refuse to hire or to discharge any individual, or otherwise to discriminate against any individual with respect to his compensation, terms, conditions, or privileges of employment, because of such individual's race, color, religion, sex, or national origin." 42 U.S.C. 2000e-2a, http://www.law.cornell.edu/uscode/42/usc_sec_42_00002000---e002-.html

648. *Board of Ed. of Kiryas Joel v. Grumet*, 512 U.S. 687 (1994) (emphasis added), http://caselaw.lp.findlaw.com/scripts/getcase.pl?court=us&vol=000&invol=U10355

649. Specifically adding the term "atheism," would be a prideful and affirmative act. Lawyers who review the policies may be more comfortable with language like, "religion or the absence thereof." Only by trying will we discover which strategy works best.

650. "Polis becomes third openly gay member of Congress," Gay & Lesbian Victory Fund, January 6, 2009, http://www.victoryfund.org/news/view/url:polis_becomes_third_openly_gay_member_of_congress

313

651. "Next President Could Shape U.S. Judiciary More than Predecessors," America.gov, September 11, 2008, http://www.america.gov/st/elections08-english/2008/September/200 80911110810esnamfuak7.642764e-02.html

652. *Newdow v. Rio Lindo USD*, ___ F3rd___, (9th Cir. 2010), http://www.ushistory.org/betsy/images/courtdecision05-17257.pdf

653. *Salazar v. Buono,* 599 U.S. ___ (2010) at 17. http://www.supremecourt.gov/opinions/09pdf/08-472.pdf

654. "On Darwin's Birthday, Only 4 in 10 Believe in Evolution," Gallup Polls, February 11, 2009, http://www.gallup.com/poll/114544/darwin-birthday-believe-evoluti on.aspx

655. "Many Americans Uneasy with Mix of Religion and Politics," The Pew Research Center for the People & the Press, August 24, 2006, http://people-press.org/report/?pageid=1081

656. "Survey: Most Americans Say Founders Intended Christian Nation," The Christian Post, September 13, 2007, http://www.christianpost.com/article/20070913/survey-most-america ns-say-founders-intended-christian-nation/index.html

657. "2009 Year in Review," Freedom From Religion Foundation, undated, http://ffrf.org/about/year-in-review/2009-year-in-review/

658. Id.

659. "The Catholic Church in the United States at a Glance," United States Conference of Catholic Bishops, undated, http://www.nccbuscc.org/comm/catholic-church-statistics.shtml

660. "Whoever mutilates, cuts, defaces, disfigures, or perforates, or unites or cements together, or does any other thing to any bank bill, draft, note, or other evidence of debt issued by any national banking

association, or Federal Reserve bank, or the Federal Reserve System, with intent to render such bank bill, draft, note, or other evidence of debt unfit to be reissued, shall be fined under this title or imprisoned not more than six months, or both" 18 U.S.C. 333, http://codes.lp.findlaw.com/uscode/18/I/17/333

661. "Holiday Messages," HobbyLobby.com, undated, http://www.hobbylobby.com/holiday_messages/holiday_messages.cf m

662. www.atheistnexus.org.

663. "MySpace: No place for Atheists?" Secular Student Alliance, undated, http://www.secularstudents.org/node/1933

664. I am particularly subject to this criticism as I have written my book with a distinctively American slant. However, America is where I live and the place I know best. But excuses aside, I recognize that creating an international movement will help our people in the most oppressed countries and allow us to learn from those in the most progressive.

665. In their survey of psychological and sociological literature, Hunsberger and Altemeyer found virtually no systematic, objective studies of atheists. Hunsberger, Bruce and Altemeyer, Bob, *Atheists*, 2006, at 19.

666. Altemeyer, Bob and Hunsberger, Bruce, *Amazing Conversions*, 1997, at 110-111. Now, did you look to see if I put a special comment in footnote 666? Well, just for you, here is a joke. Question: What is 666F? Answer: The proper temperature for cooking roast beast.

667. Hunsberger, Bruce and Altemeyer, Bob, *Atheists*, 2006, at 55.

668. Lincoln, Abraham, *Abraham Lincoln: Speeches and Writings 1832-1858*, 1989, http://www.goodreads.com/quotes/show/90552

669. The book is *The Intimate World of Abraham Lincoln,* by C.A. Tripp, 2005. "Was Lincoln Gay?" The New York Times, January 9, 2005, http://query.nytimes.com/gst/fullpage.html?res=9f05e5d61439f93aa35752c0a9639c8b63

670. An alternate date could be the same day as the "National Day of Prayer," May 6. That date would allow us to educate about the separation of church and state and the concerns of atheist and nonreligious citizens. A shortcoming is that the "National Day of Prayer" is limited to the U.S. It would be great to have an international atheist day–and a day like Darwin's birthday is more international in scope.

671. Hunsberger, Bruce and Altemeyer, Bob, *Atheists*, 2006, at 71-2.

672. (Ayatollah) Ruhollah Khomeini, in Warraq, Ibn, *Why I Am Not a Muslim*, 1995, at 9-10.